D1515982

ONLY IN
BOSTON

Duncan J. D. Smith

ONLY IN
BOSTON

A Guide to Unique Locations,
Hidden Corners and Unusual Objects

Photographs by
Duncan J. D. Smith
except where stated otherwise

**The
Urban
Explorer**

For Roswitha,
who first alerted me to the joys of Boston,
and for all the friendly Bostonians I met along the way

Above: Mount Auburn Cemetery, Cambridge (see no. 106)

Page 2: Bunker Hill Monument and Colonel William Prescott, Charlestown (see no. 4)

Contents

DOWNTOWN (inc. Boston Common, Downtown Crossing, Financial District, Government Center, Theater District, Waterfront) & CHINATOWN–LEATHER DISTRICT

SOUTH BOSTON & SOUTH END

BACK BAY (inc. Bay Village) & FENWAY-KENMORE

Introduction

> "Boston … is often called the 'hub of the world', since it has been the source and fountain of the ideas that have reared and made America."
>
> Rev. F. Barham Zincke, *Last Winter in the United States*, 1868

Boston, state capital of Massachusetts, is America's oldest major city. It was founded in 1630, where the Charles River meets the Atlantic, by Puritan colonists from England. Visitors today are fascinated by the city's modest Colonial-era remains, which coexist harmoniously alongside its towering modern skyscrapers.

That is only a part of the Boston story though. Inevitably the colonists morphed into patriots keen to sever ties with their mercantile-minded British overseers. Accordingly Boston played a crucial part in the American Revolutionary War (1775–1783), the ousting of the Redcoats in 1776 enabling the country to begin its journey to independence.

Since then Boston's fortunes have waxed and waned. Seafaring brought boom times, recession prompted home-grown manufacturing, and by 1820 the presence of Harvard University saw Boston at the forefront of American intellectual life. As the 'Athens of America', the city spawned Transcendentalism and the abolitionist movement.

The Great Fire of 1872 necessitated the redevelopment of the city's commercial heart reaffirming Boston's allure for waves of immigrants: Irish, Jews, Italians, and Chinese. Together with African-Americans, they've added distinction and diversity to Boston's 23 neighbourhoods. More recently, massive civic projects such as the Big Dig, Waterfront renewal, and the facelift of world-class cultural institutions have resulted in a city trading as much on present-day energy as historic charm.

This book is for both the carefree stroller and the determined city explorer. Armed with a decent street map readers can quickly get off the beaten track and under the city's skin. This is the Boston of Colonial-era relics and heritage trails, industrial remains and ethnic enclaves, hallowed universities and contemporary art spaces. The locations described represent the author's own odysseys – from Charlestown down to South Boston and from Cambridge across to East Boston.

The story begins on the north bank of the Charles River in Charlestown, which was only annexed by Boston in 1874. Remains of the first settlers, together with the once-mighty shipyard that followed in their wake, are highlights here. Locations in neighbouring but little-visited East Boston include memorials recalling the September 11 Attacks.

Across the water is the North End, at the tip of the original Shawmut Peninsula and once cut off from the rest of Boston by a tidal creek.

Land reclamation for wharves has long ago subsumed the original shoreline but the old streets (and the city's oldest church) remain, now bustling with Italian shops and cafés.

Much of the neighbouring West End was razed in the 1960s. Fortunately its colourful memories are preserved in an eponymous museum, with new attractions dedicated to science and sport. By contrast Beacon Hill remains intact, its gas lit streets lined with red brick Federal-style townhouses built in the early 19th century for the Boston Brahmins, the city's Protestant merchant elite.

Below is Boston Common, the nation's oldest public park and starting point of the well-trodden Freedom Trail. This runs through Downtown taking in such sites as the Old State House, which today share the tangled Colonial-era street plan with tower blocks. Also here are Chinatown (the last in New England), and the Leather and Theater Districts.

The residential South End stretches south-west along Tremont and Washington Streets. Blessed with a remarkable concentration of Victorian architecture, it subsequently attracted Irish Catholics, African-Americans, and Puerto Ricans. Such diversity has drawn the artistic community, too. The Irish and artistic presence continues across the Fort Point Channel in South Boston (known affectionately as Southie). Annexed by Boston in 1804, the area's industrial and maritime heritage is now finding new uses. The vast 'Streetcar Suburbs' of Dorchester, Roxbury and Jamaica Plain sprawl southwards from here.

Flanking the South End is Back Bay, another example of the ambitious land-from-water reclamation that has so extensively reshaped post-Colonial Boston. A grid-iron of streets here is lined with Victorian brownstone row houses and mansions, interspersed with several impressive churches. Fenway–Kenmore Square beyond boasts the venerable stadium of the Boston Red Sox, as well as Back Bay Fens Park, a link in Frederick Law Olmsted's Emerald Necklace.

A final selection of locations covers Cambridge, a separate city on the north bank of the Charles River. Old Cambridge is dominated by Harvard University, a byword for academic excellence. By contrast the Massachusetts Institute of Technology (MIT) is renowned for its modern art and architecture, in an area once famous for candy factories.

Whilst walking is the best way to explore central Boston, the suburbs are quickly accessed using the extensive MBTA subway and bus system, known locally as the T (www.mbta.com). Whether exploring America's oldest subway in Downtown, drinking Guinness in Southie, visiting mansions in Back Bay, or spending a night in a Cambridge monastery, it is hoped that *Only in Boston* will encourage readers to set out on their own urban expedition. Happy Exploring!

1 The Founding of Charlestown

MA 02129 (Charlestown), a stroll through Charlestown beginning at City Square Park
T Green or Orange Line to North Station then cross Charlestown Bridge and follow the Freedom Trail to City Square Park, or MBTA F4 Ferry from Long Wharf to Charlestown Navy Yard (Pier 4) then follow the Freedom Trail, or Bus 93 from Haymarket to City Square Park

Despite being geographically removed from Boston proper and not annexed until 1874, Charlestown on the north bank of the Charles River is really where Boston's story begins. Most visitors follow the Freedom Trail here to see the USS *Constitution* and the Bunker Hill Monument – but there is much more besides.

This walk begins in City Square Park near to where the first ferry crossing was established in the 1630s. Back then the area was a peninsula bounded by the Charles and Mystic Rivers, connected to what is now East Cambridge (itself an island at high tide) by a narrow isthmus. Subsequent land reclamation has entirely reshaped it.

Embedded in the grass are the foundations of Charlestown's first public building, the Great House. English settlers first arrived on the peninsula in 1624 from the failed colony of Weymouth and were soon joined by members of the Massachusetts Bay Colony. In 1628 they founded Charlestown together naming it after their king, and a year later built the Great House.

For several months in 1630 the Great House was occupied by John

The Warren Tavern and Bunker Hill Monument beyond

Winthrop (1587–1649), Governor of the Massachusetts Bay Colony. When he decreed that the area lacked suitable water, however, the colonists moved across the Charles to the Shawmut Peninsula and founded Boston instead (see nos. 8, 38, 45). From then on Charlestown developed slowly, with the Great House converted into the Three Cranes tavern. In 1775 it was destroyed along with the rest of Charlestown by the British during the Battle of Bunker Hill (see no. 4).

Now follow the Freedom Trail along Main Street to 55, which is an example of the sort of clapboard house built after the destruction. This was the home of Deacon John Larkin (1735–1807), who provided Paul Revere with a horse for his famous midnight ride to Lexington (see no. 16). Another example is the Warren Tavern farther along on Pleasant Street (see no. 33).

Beyond in Thompson Square is a building from Charlestown's more recent past. The Charlestown Five Cents Savings Bank closed in the 1970s but still retains its external vault alarm (the upper floors were once home to the King Solomon Masonic Lodge). Continue to the junction with Phipps Street to reach the Phipps Street Burying Ground of 1630, which contains numerous Revolutionary War-era graves.

Walk southwards across West School and Austin Streets to reach the Emmons Horrigan O'Neill Memorial Rink, which features in Ben Affleck's film *The Town*. Also featured is the shingle-clad former Old Sully's 'dive bar' at the bottom end of Union Street. In the film it is the haunt of a gang of bank robbers, a nod to the 1960s, when Charlestown was known for its Irish Mob presence.

By the late 1980s Charlestown was being gentrified, its clapboard triple-deckers and red-brick row houses attracting middle class professionals to the once predominantly Irish-American neighbourhood. Their prim homes can be seen by walking along Washington Street, turning left onto Old Rutherford Avenue and Devens Street, then continuing across Main Street into the maze of streets centred on Monument Avenue. At the top on Winthrop Street rejoin the Freedom Trail and head back to City Square Park passing Winthrop Square, a former Colonial-era training field containing memorials to those who died on Bunker Hill.

What *won't* be found on this walk is evidence of the area's original Native American population, the Massachusett, after whom the state of Massachusetts is named. They called the Charlestown area *Mishawum* (meaning 'great spring'), presumably because they found the local water more potable than the Puritan settlers.

Other locations nearby: 2, 3, 4, 5

2   A Once Mighty Shipyard

MA 02129 (Charlestown), a stroll around the Charlestown
Navy Yard
MBTA F4 Ferry from Long Wharf to Charlestown Navy Yard
(Pier 4), or T Green or Orange Line to North Station then walk
east along Causeway Street, cross Charlestown Bridge, and
follow the Freedom Trail to Charlestown Navy Yard, or Bus 93
from Haymarket to Charlestown Navy Yard (note: ID is required
to board the USS *Constitution*)

An abandoned crane in the Charlestown Navy Yard

There are numerous ways to approach the historic Charlestown Navy Yard but the best is by water. An MBTA ferry makes the 10-minute journey from Boston's Long Wharf several times an hour. It affords visitors an overview of one of the country's first and once busiest naval shipyards.

The ferry drops its passengers at Pier 4 from where they should turn left to reach the Main Gate, where visitors arriving by bus or by foot arrive. The long, red-brick former warehouse here contains the Charlestown Navy Yard Visitor Centre, which provides a potted history of the Yard and its importance to Boston. Using historical artefacts and photographs it explains how the Yard opened in 1800, one of six deep-water ports created to support the fledgling United States Navy. For the next 174 years it not only kept existing vessels seaworthy but also built replacements for them as shipbuilding technology improved. Many personnel lived here too, as witnessed by the red-brick Officers'

Quarters opposite the Visitors' Centre, and the elegant bow-fronted Commandant's House beyond.

Moored on Pier 1 on the other side of the Visitor Centre is the USS *Constitution* (see no. 3). This undefeated frigate launched in 1797 is the world's oldest commissioned naval vessel afloat. Although built in a North End shipyard, she represents the sort of wooden vessels built when the Charlestown Navy Yard first opened.

Although some 25 vessels (mostly sloops of war) were built here during the 19th century, the Yard acted primarily as a repair and storage facility. This is represented by Dry Dock 1 on the opposite side of Pier 1. Inaugurated in 1833 in the presence of the country's Vice President, it was the first naval dry dock in New England. Ironically the first vessel to use it was the USS *Constitution* and it still operates today.

Only in the 1890s did the Yard start to build steel ships for America's 'New Navy'. An illustration of the transition from timber and sail to steel and steam is provided by the USS *Cassin Young*, a California-built Second World War Fletcher-class destroyer also moored at Pier 1 (remarkably it was twice hit by Japanese *kamikaze* pilots during the Second World War). The workforce changed, too, with carpenters and riggers gradually replaced by riveters and welders.

Piers 2 and 3 reflect these changes through their ensemble of historic service structures, including cranes and paint shops, a pitch store later used to charge submarine batteries (and now the café), and the remains of a marine railway (the former dry dock pump house today contains the USS *Constitution* Museum). Beyond Pier 3 is a second dry dock (Dry Dock 2) added in the early 20th century. Here during the Second World War damaged vessels were repaired and over 80 frigates and destroyer escorts were built for the US Navy, as well as the Royal Navy. Notably the workforce at this time included over 8,000 women. After the war, vessels were modified at Charlestown for Cold War service. This continued until 1974, when the Yard eventually closed and the area became part of the Boston National Historical Park.

Before leaving, be sure to explore the criss-crossing streets behind Dry Dock 2. The Boston Marine Society at 100 1st Avenue is the world's oldest and has supported mariners and their families since 1742 (their small museum is open by appointment). The tower on 5th Street is the former Muster House, where civilian workers reported for work during the 19th century, and in the quarter-mile-long granite building beyond, all the Yard's rope was made from 1837 until 1955.

Other locations nearby: 1, 3, 4, 5

3 All Aboard Old Ironsides!

MA 02129 (Charlestown), the USS *Constitution* at Pier 1 in the Charlestown Navy Yard
MBTA F4 Ferry from Long Wharf to Charlestown Navy Yard (Pier 4), or T Green or Orange Line to North Station then walk east along Causeway Street, cross Charlestown Bridge, and follow the Freedom Trail to Charlestown Navy Yard, or Bus 93 from Haymarket to Charlestown Navy Yard (note: ID is required to board the USS *Constitution*)

The reason most visitors cross Boston Harbor to Charlestown is to visit the USS *Constitution*. Launched in the late 18th century and never defeated, she is the world's oldest commissioned naval vessel afloat.

The USS *Constitution* is berthed at Pier 1 at the historic Charlestown Navy Yard (see no. 2). Before boarding though visit the USS *Constitution* Museum in the former dry dock pump house between Piers 2 and 3. Here the story is told of how the wooden-hulled, three-masted frigate was one of six commissioned by the first President of the United States, George Washington (1732–1799). Approved under the Naval Act of 1794, they were better constructed and more heavily armed than any other ships of the day.

The USS *Constitution* was not, however, built in the Charlestown Navy Yard. She was built in the North End shipyard of Edward Hartt (1744–1824) near Battery Wharf, where she was launched in 1797 to safeguard American merchant vessels from Barbary pirates. With a length of 304 feet from bowsprit to stern, and masts towering as high as a 20-storey building, she would have been an impressive sight.

The USS *Constitution* is moored in the Charlestown Navy Yard

To understand how impressive, show your ID and board her. On the main deck two things impress: her incredibly sturdy construction and her elaborate rigging capable of supporting dozens of sails totalling an acre of cloth. Her strength was best demonstrated during the War of 1812, when Britain imposed a naval blockade on the United States. She vanquished four British frigates, including the *Guerriere*, during which cannonballs were seen to bounce off her tough evergreen oak hull (an oak ship's timber is preserved in the tiny Maritime Museum in the Battery Wharf Hotel). The nickname Old Ironsides was born out of this event.

It is also possible to tour the vessel below deck but only as part of a guided tour. Here can be seen replicas of the ship's 54 cannon and the hammocks used by the 450-strong crew, who subsisted on ship's biscuits and suffered many discomforts.

The USS *Constitution* won 33 battles and commandeered many enemy vessels before being retired from active service in the 1830s. She then made a round-the-world cruise under John "Mad Jack" Percival (1779–1862), acted as flagship in the Mediterranean and African fleets, served as a training ship during the American Civil War (1861–1865), and carried freight to the Paris Exposition of 1878. She was eventually decommissioned in 1881 and used as a barracks ship at Portsmouth Navy Yard. By 1896 her condition had deteriorated but thanks to Massachusetts congressman, John F. Fitzgerald (1863–1950), interest in her history and plight was piqued and she was towed back to Boston for preservation.

Funds for the restoration, however, were hard to find and it was not until 1940 that President Franklin D. Roosevelt (1882–1945) placed the vessel on permanent commission. Initially used as a brig for officers awaiting court-martial, she was now safe from further deterioration. Full restoration followed in the 1970s as part of the country's Bicentennial celebrations, a reminder that the vessel is named after the United States Constitution drafted in 1776.

Subsequent restoration means that today little of the USS *Constitution* is original. The up side of this is that she can still sail under her own power albeit only for a short harbour cruise each Independence Day (Fourth of July). With a crew of 60 these days, she has been designated America's Ship of State.

To take to the water yourself, take a cruise between June and September on a replica tall ship from Central Wharf (www.libertyfleet.com).

Other locations nearby: 1, 2, 4, 5

4 The Truth about Bunker Hill

MA 02129 (Charlestown), the Bunker Hill Monument & Museum in Monument Square
T Green or Orange Line to North Station then cross Charlestown Bridge and follow the Freedom Trail to Monument Square; or MBTA F4 Ferry from Long Wharf to Charlestown Navy Yard (Pier 4) then follow the Freedom Trail; or Bus 93 from Haymarket to Bunker Hill Monument

Boston's Freedom Trail finds its northern terminus in Charlestown at the Bunker Hill Monument. Built to commemorate the first major battle of the American Revolutionary War (1775–1783), this sturdy Quincy granite obelisk accompanied by a statue of American commander Colonel William Prescott (1726–1795) is understandably a place of pilgrimage. It is also a place where fact sometimes merges into folklore.

Boston in the 1770s has been called the Cradle of Liberty but recently some historians have challenged this long-held patriotic epithet. They suggest that separatist groups such as the Sons of Liberty were not necessarily seeking full-blown American independence but rather a more conservative return to their pre-1760s status, before the British Crown began imposing punitive taxes.

The situation became more complex once blood was shed during the Boston Massacre (1770) (see no. 32). Tensions inevitably rose and in 1775 the skirmishes at Lexington and Concord left the British Redcoats holed up in Boston, with American militiamen occupying the surrounding countryside (see no. 16). A two-month standoff ended during the night of June 16th, when a thousand citizen-soldiers from various colonial militia were ordered to march from Cambridge to fortify Bunker Hill.

A musketeer re-enacts the Battle of Bunker Hill

Bunker Hill is a 110 foot-high mound on Bunker Hill Street, which in the 1770s jutted into Boston Harbor. The Americans, however, by-passed it and instead began fortifying Breed's Hill, a smaller mound closer to Boston – and to the British. Why they did this is unclear but it was probably deliberate. The Americans' inexperience with cannon perhaps meant they could do more damage from Breed's Hill; additionally their closeness may have been designed to goad the British into attacking before they were fully prepared. Either way, Breed's Hill has been synonymous with Bunker Hill ever since.

On the morning of June 17th the British under General Thomas Gage (1718–1787) began their bombardment from Copp's Hill (see no. 12). The well-trained Redcoats quickly torched Charlestown and began ascending Breed's Hill. There, however, they faced an obstacle course of long grass, boulders, and pitfalls, and were successfully driven back. The claim that Colonel Prescott told his soldiers not to fire on the British "until you see the whites of their eyes" is probably hearsay but if true may have referred to their white breeches.

Remarkably the British were rebuffed twice and only at a third attempt were they able to snuff out the Americans "like an old candle". Despite their defeat, however, the outnumbered and outgunned Americans felt emboldened by their performance. The bloodied British realised they were no longer punishing a mob but waging a war (see no. 60).

Not everything is all it seems with the Bunker Hill Monument either (see frontispiece). Although the cornerstone was laid in 1825, the 221-foot tall obelisk was not completed until 1843. Its construction necessitated the building of America's first commercial railroad, which bankrupted the project early on. It was only completed when further funds were raised by magazine editor and author of the nursery rhyme *Mary Had a Little Lamb*, Sarah Josepha Hale (1788–1879) (see no. 18).

Inside the obelisk are 294 steps leading up to a viewing platform. From here it can be appreciated just how compact the battlefield must have been and why the British losses were so high. The bloody scene is recreated in the Bunker Hill Museum at the bottom of the hill. Also also visible from the viewing platform is the real Bunker Hill over on Bunker Hill Street, crowned today by the St. Francis de Sales Church.

Since 1786 the battle has been celebrated with a lively street parade on the Sunday nearest June 17th.

Other locations nearby: 1, 2, 3, 5

5 Bridging the Charles River

MA 02129 (Charlestown), a tour of Charles River bridges beginning on Charlestown Bridge
T Green Line C, E or Orange Line to North Station, then walk along Causeway Street to Keany Square and turn left onto the Charlestown Bridge

The Charles River rises at Echo Lake near Hopkinton, Massachusetts then zigzags 80 miles to reach the Atlantic at Boston. Along the way it is fed by 80 streams and drains 33 lakes; it also passes through 23 cities and towns, and is crossed by a hundred bridges. Despite such statistics, however, the river only measures 26 miles as the crow flies from source to sea. At the narrow point where it disgorges into Boston Harbor lies the border between Boston, Charlestown, and Cambridge. Here can be found a fascinating nexus of historic river, road and rail crossings.

This tour begins on the Charlestown Bridge, which is best accessed from Keany Square at the edge of Boston's North End (follow the red line of the Freedom Trail). Here in the 1630s the first official ferry crossing of the Charles was located and the revenue granted to the fledgling Harvard College. The first bridge on the site, the Charles River Bridge, was completed in 1786. The current bridge was completed in 1900, its six lanes designed to accommo-

The Leonard B. Zakim Bunker Hill Memorial Bridge

date not only automobiles but also the Charlestown Elevated railway, which ran down the middle. A century of wear and tear will soon see it replaced.

At the end of the bridge, drop down into Paul Revere Park. At the water's edge stands the Charles River Dam, a flood control facility opened in 1978 to prevent salt water from entering the Charles River Basin (it occupies the site of the earlier Warren Bridge, which opened in 1828). A walkway across the three locks is part of the Boston Harborwalk and includes *Charlestown Bells*, a chiming art installation created by Paul Matisse (b. 1933), grandson of the famous French artist.

Now cross the park and pass directly beneath the Leonard B. Zakim Bunker Hill Memorial Bridge, named after a Boston civil rights activist and the famous Charlestown battle. Constructed as part of the Big Dig and opened in 2003, this 10-lane bridge solved the traffic bottleneck caused by its predecessor, the Charlestown High Bridge. The new bridge employs cable-stayed technology, whereby cables are strung directly between pylons and deck, like the strings on a harp. The construction of the bridge irrevocably changed the shoreline of the Charles, which is memorialised by the art installation *Five Beacons for the Lost Half Mile*.

The footpath continues onwards beneath another road bridge and then over the rail tracks leading into the North Station before touching down in North Point Park in Cambridge. From here can be accessed two further river crossings, the Lechmere Viaduct of 1912 carrying the MBTA's Green Line, and the Charles River Dam Bridge. The latter was constructed in 1910 to transform the lower Charles River tidal estuary into the freshwater Charles River Basin, which separates Back Bay and Cambridge. With this function now fulfilled by the Charles River Dam, the bridge serves mainly as a road crossing, and since 1951 as the location of the Museum of Science (see no. 21).

From here the Charles River Basin stretches away westwards, with its abundant opportunities for water sports, including the country's oldest public sailing centre, Community Boating Boston, at 21 David G. Mugar Way. Each October the Head of the Charles Regatta, the world's largest two-day rowing race, is staged here. Along the Back Bay side of the basin runs the Charles River Esplanade designed in Venetian style by landscape architect Arthur Asahel Shurcliff (1870–1957). An interesting feature on the Cambridge side is the Lechmere Canal Park, a former industrial waterway once used to deliver raw materials to long vanished factories.

Other locations nearby: 1, 2, 3, 5

6 A Walk through Eastie

MA 02128 (East Boston), a walk through East Boston commencing in Maverick Square
T Blue Line to Maverick

As with South Boston and Southie, so East Boston is known affectionately as Eastie. The two neighbourhoods share things in common, including historical waterfronts on reclaimed land, with wharves in the throes of redevelopment, and hinterlands subject to varying degrees of gentrification. Whilst new-look Southie is attracting many visitors, Eastie has so far seen fewer, which is a pity since a walk here reveals some interesting history.

A good walk begins in Maverick Square, named after English colonist Samuel Maverick (c.1602–c.1670), who settled on Noddle's Island in the 1630s (it's difficult today to imagine that East Boston originally comprised five islands only joined together in the early 1900s). As a staunch Anglican, Maverick would not have been tolerated by the Puritans across the water in Boston. After farming for a while, he became one of the first slave owners in Massachusetts.

Boston annexed the islands in 1836, after which the waterfront became a busy shipping and commercial area. In the 1840s the first

Abandoned piers in East Boston, with Downtown beyond

transatlantic ships began arriving with immigrants – first Irish, then Jews, and Italians – and a large hotel, Maverick House, was built in Maverick Square to accommodate them. By the early 1900s, East Boston rivalled Ellis Island as a point of entry for immigrants. The hotel remained in business until 1924, when it was demolished to make way for the subway station. Looking at the restaurants in the square today shows the most recent arrivals into Eastie are Latinos.

The waterfront is accessed by walking east along Maverick Street and then south down Bremen Street. The serpentine green space here is part of the East Boston Greenway, a linear park opened in 2007. The abandoned railcar at the end of the street is a reminder that a railway once ran along here connecting the waterfront with the national rail network. Joshua Slocum (1844–1909), the first man to sail alone around the world, departed from here in 1895.

The waterfront stretches along nearby Marginal Street and today consists of abandoned piers, a working shipyard and marina, and Piers Park. Opened in 1995 on a former pier, the park features salt-tolerant plants and pavilions. Moored in the still-bustling marina beyond is the historic red-hulled lightship *Nantucket*, which can be visited.

After leaving the marina walk up the nearby steps to reach Webster and Sumner Streets, both lined with typical clapboard and red-brick row houses, turning left to regain Bremen Street. From here the Greenway continues northwards. If hunger beckons, make a detour to Santarpio's Pizza at 111 Chelsea Street, a throwback to Eastie's Italian-American past. Otherwise continue beneath the overpass into Bremen Street Park. Points of interest here include the East Boston YMCA, housed in a former railway shed, an over-sized bust of shipbuilder Donald McKay (1810–1880), who built some of the finest clipper ships in his East Boston shipyard, and the East Boston Public Library. Opened in 1869, this was the first municipally-supported branch library in the United States (the present building opened in 2013 is fronted by one of East Boston's many community gardens).

From here it's not far to the Wood Island T station. Those wishing to extend the walk can head north up Prescott Street, which leads eventually via Trenton and White Streets to East Boston High School, backdrop for the television series *Boston Public*. The Greek Revival house at 78–80 belonged to shipbuilder McKay.

Alternatively continue eastwards from the library to take in Massachusetts' oldest Jewish cemetery at 147 Wordsworth Street, and eventually the towering Don Orione Madonna on Orient Heights, another of East Boston's original five islands, where Boston's first Italian immigrants arrived in the 1860s.

7 Remembering 9/11

MA 02128 (East Boston), the 9/11 Memorial on Logan Memorial
Way at Logan International Airport
T Silver Line 1 to Terminal A or Blue Line to Airport and Bus 22
to Terminal A, then cross the sky bridge to a parking garage and
descend to ground level and walk to the memorial

Readers of a certain age will remember where they were on the day Brookline-born John F. Kennedy was assassinated. Many more will recall their whereabouts on September 11th, 2001, when terrorists flew civilian aircraft into the World Trade Center. With the media focussed squarely on New York City, it is easy to forget that the aircraft flew from Boston's Logan International Airport, where several memorials recall the fateful day.

There are actually five 9/11 memorials at Logan. Three are American flags flying over the gates where the two flights pushed back ready for departure. The flag over gate B-32 honours the crew and passengers of American Airlines Flight 11, which hit the North Tower of the World Trade Center at 8.46am. The flag over neighbouring gate C-19 is for those who died on United Airlines Flight 175,

The 9/11 Memorial at Logan International Airport

which hit the South Tower 17 minutes later. Within two hours both towers had collapsed resulting in the deaths of 2,753 people.

The flags were erected by the airlines in the weeks after the attacks as a sign of respect. Few passengers notice them, however, and there is nothing to say why they are there. In 2014, when United Airlines moved to gate B-27, they erected a new flag. JetBlue, which took over gate C-19, has retained United's existing flag, which means there are now three flags flying.

The fourth memorial to the events of 9/11 is one the flying public never sees. It is a daily security meeting attended by representatives from the airport, airlines, security and police. The meeting was inaugurated on the morning following the attack and has continued ever since. Staff at Logan are determined that nothing similar will ever befall the airport again.

The fifth memorial is Logan's official public memorial to the victims and stands on Logan Memorial Way in front of the Hilton hotel. Designed by Boston-based Moskow Linn Architects and unveiled in 2009, it consists of a modest square glass cube representing the twin towers, inscribed with the departure times of both aircraft. The two winding paths leading up to it recall the flight paths taken by the hijacked aircraft. Placing the cube on a hill encourages people to look upwards and beyond the tragedy that happened here. Likewise the trees planted around the memorial impart something living and optimistic.

Like most commercial airports, Logan has seen its fair share of conventional accidents. The earliest occurred on July 24th 1923, when Lieutenant Kitchell Snow (1899–1923) of the 101st Observation Squadron of the Massachusetts National Guard died after nosediving into nearby mudflats. In a twist of fate, Snow, whose grave at Forest Hills Cemetery (Jamaica Plain) is marked by a bronze eagle, had been the first pilot to land at the airport when it opened a month earlier.

A fine view of Logan can be gained from Orient Heights to the north. Near the summit at 111 Orient Avenue is a 40-foot-high statue of the Madonna. Erected in 1954, it forms part of the US headquarters of the Catholic Don Orione order (see no. 6). Also visible from Orient Heights are the sludge digesters of the Deer Island Waste Water Treatment Plant. To find out how Boston formerly dealt with its sewage visit the Metropolitan Waterworks Museum at 2450 Beacon Street (Brookline).

A memorial labyrinth unveiled on September 11th 2003 at Boston College in Chestnut Hill recalls 22 alumni lost in the 9/11 tragedy. A memorial unveiled in Boston's Public Garden a year later commemorates the 206 people from Massachusetts killed during the attacks.

8 Reshaping the Shawmut Peninsula

MA 02113 (North End), Boston's landfill projects including a short walk from the junction of North and Fleet Streets down to Creek Square
T C/E/Orange Line to Haymarket

It is staggering to think that almost three quarters of central Boston is built on land reclaimed from water. Back in 1630, when settlers of the Massachusetts Bay Colony first arrived, the place was virtually an island connected to the mainland only by a narrow isthmus called Boston Neck. Named *Shawmut* by the Native Americans, this ragged-edged peninsula suited the settlers, who were looking for a well-watered and easy-to-defend location to practice their Puritan faith. By the late 18th century, however, after Puritanism had waned, Boston faced the problem of accommodating a burgeoning population and a thriving maritime industry on an island bound by tidal mudflats. The answer was to create more land.

Only by looking at old maps can one really appreciate how much Boston's shoreline has been altered. There are signs in the landscape, too, that speak of how the shoreline once looked. Take, for example, North Street in the North End. The reason it curves away southwards from the watery-named Fleet Street is because it sits

Fleet Street reflects Boston's watery origins

on the original eastern shoreline of the area, which during the 17th century was a bulbous promontory separated from the rest of the Shawmut by a narrow tidal creek used to power flour mills (the western shoreline ran along North Margin Street). The location of the creek itself is recalled by Creek Square in Downtown, one of a cluster of remarkably intact Colonial-era streets that make up the so-called Blackstone Block (Marsh Lane and Salt Lane add to the area's liquid legacy).

The meaning of *Shawmut* is uncertain. Possibly it relates to the fresh water spring that lured the colonists from their original place of arrival in Charlestown (see no. 1). The so-called Great Spring was located south of the creek, where it is remembered by a plaque on the aptly-named Spring Lane. It was hereabouts, between Washington and Tremont Streets, that the colonists built their settlement (see no. 38).

From the early 1800s onwards, eight major landfill projects aimed at increasing the Shawmut's original landmass of 478 acres were undertaken, detailed here in chronological order:

1) In 1803 work began on filling the West Cove, part of a large area of tidal flats in the mouth of the Charles River located approximately where the Massachusetts General Hospital stands today. The project added just over 200 acres of new land along Charles Street on the western side of what is now the West End.

2) Around the same time, the land that in 1837 became the Public Garden was created (see no. 69). Boston Common was part of the original Shawmut and since 1794 its western edge had been used as a ropewalk. As a condition of its use, the ropemakers were required to build a seawall along Charles Street and to reclaim the mudflats beyond. They used fill excavated from nearby Mount Vernon, the westernmost of three hills that prompted the first settlers to call the area Trimountain, from which 'Tremont Street' is derived (property developers later razed what remained of Mount Vernon to create Louisburg Square; Beacon Hill was levelled to build the Massachusetts State House, and Pemberton Hill was removed and replaced by Pemberton Square).

3) Also during the early 1800s, the Mill Pond was filled. This 50-acre area of mudflats located between the promontory of the North End and another forming the West End had been dammed across its mouth in the 1640s (using an existing Native American raised causeway) and the tide used to turn several mills. In 1807 permission was given to infill the area using material from another of the Shawmut's hills, Copp's Hill in the North End (see no. 12). American architect Charles Bulfinch (1763–1844) then drew up a street plan resulting in the Bulfinch Triangle bounded by Merrimac, Market, Washington and Causeway Streets, completed in the early 1820s (see no. 20).

4) The next landfill project commenced in 1806 on the east side of the Shawmut. The South Cove was an area of tidal flats that narrowed the Shawmut dramatically to a point where today the aptly-named Beach Street meets Washington Street. On the 186 acres of new land created, Boston's Chinatown and Leather District were built, as well as in 1899 the South Station (see nos. 48, 50).

5) A similar project on the opposite side of the Shawmut saw the creation between 1814 and the 1820s of Bay Village (see no. 66). Bounded by Stuart, South Charles, Tremont, and Berkeley Streets, the subsequent filling of Back Bay means this former shoreline community is now landlocked.

6) Starting in the early 1820s, another 112 acres were added to the Shawmut by filling the Great (or East) Cove. This lay between the

North End promontory and a bluff called Fort Hill, at the junction of today's Oliver and High Streets (Downtown). As already demonstrated by North Street, the shoreline was pushed far beyond that of the original, using material excavated from Fort Hill. Other graphic examples of the shift include the now land-locked Union Oyster House, Custom House and Faneuil Hall, all of which once stood at the water's edge (see nos. 33, 34, 36). Existing wharves, such as Long Wharf and Union Wharf, the latter with its Greek Revival warehouse of 1846, became shorter as a result and were later serviced by Atlantic Avenue, which was built using rubble from the Great Boston Fire (1872).

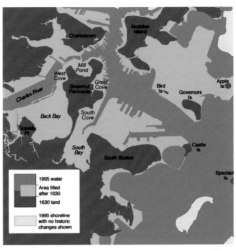

A map showing how Boston's shoreline has changed since 1630

7) The penultimate project on the Shawmut commenced in the 1830s with the filling of the South Bay to create the South End. This lay directly south of South Cove on the east side of Boston Neck, which tapered to its narrowest point where Washington Street (once the only route out of Boston) crosses what is now East Berkeley Street. The work, in conjunction with the simultaneous reclamation of the South Boston Waterfront around Dorchester Neck, created today's Fort Point Channel (see nos. 57, 60).

8) The last great Shawmut reclamation project commenced in 1857 with the filling of much of the Charles River tidal basin. In 1814, the Mill Dam had been constructed here, which doubled as a toll road connecting Boston to Watertown bypassing Boston Neck. When the project failed, architect Arthur Gilman (1821–1882) advocated infilling the space between the dam, the original shore and Arlington Street, and building houses (see no. 71). For over 30 years trains laden with gravel arrived from Needham Heights and by 1882 the Back Bay neighbourhood had been created. Subsequent filling reached Kenmore Square in 1890 and eventually the Fens in 1900. By then the project had added as many new acres as had comprised the original Shawmut Peninsula!

Other locations nearby: 9, 15, 16, 17

9   An Outdoor Shrine to the Saints

MA 02109 (North End), All Saints Way in an alley between
4 and 8 Battery Street
T Green/Orange Line to North Station or Haymarket

There is no street in Boston called All Saints Way. Instead the name is applied unofficially to a narrow alley between 4 and 8 Battery Street (North End). Lined with images of Roman Catholic saints, it is an idiosyncratic tribute to the Italian faith.

All Saints Way is testimony to one man's devotion to Catholicism, collecting, and community. Peter Baldassari is a dyed-in-the-wool Northender and proud of it. As a child he attended the St. Agrippina Society (Sant Agrippina di Mineo Sicilia), a religious and cultural organisation around the corner at 459 Hanover Street. Unimpressed with the way some of the children spoke to him there, and realising that his community's old fashioned values might be under threat, he decided to one day do something about it.

Baldassari had always collected effigies and mementoes of the saints. As an adult he believed it would be in his community's interest if he were to put these on year-round public display. Seeing such images he hoped would inspire piety in passers-by, in much the same way that wayside statues of the saints did during the Baroque period.

As a boy Baldassari delivered newspapers to homes along Battery Street, including those in the brick-built alley between numbers 4 and 8. People there remembered him fondly and when the time came for him to make public his collection they granted him permission to use the alley in exchange for keeping the place tidy. Beginning where the alley joins the street, he began erecting statues and nailing images to the walls – and he's continued doing so ever since.

All Saints Way, as Baldassari's open-air shrine has become known, remains on private property. Fortunately a good part of the collection is visible from the street, which is useful when the alley gate is locked. At other times Baldessari is on the premises and is usually happy to give a guided tour of his remarkable collection, including images of the latest saints to be canonised. He will often ask a visitor for their birth date and then proudly locate the relevant saint on the wall. Some visitors even make their own contribution to his ever-growing collection.

Despite dwindling to barely a quarter of its peak in 1930, Italian-Americans still comprise around 40% of the North End's resident population (see no. 17). Their religious street Feasts *(Festas)*, staged

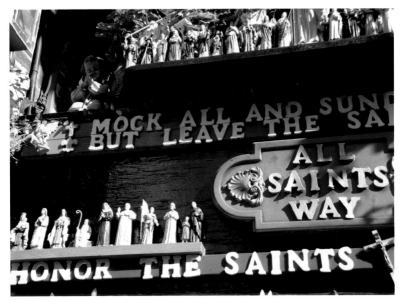

A small part of the All Saints Way shrine

throughout July and August, draw enthusiastic crowds of locals and outsiders, who come to enjoy the Italian food, music and parades. During the parades, the faithful pin dollar bills to statues of patron saints, which are held aloft and carried through the streets.

The Feasts are organised by the North End's charitable societies, which still reflect the culture and traditions of distinct regions of Italy, whence the first immigrants came. A dozen out of an original 50 still exist, including Peter Baldassari's St. Agrippina Society on Hanover Street founded in 1914. A little farther along at 467 is another, the St. Joseph Society (Societa di San Giuseppe) founded in 1925.

Yet another is the San Antonio Di Padova Da Montefalcione society at 201–203 Endicott Street. Founded in 1919 by immigrants from Montefalcione in Campania, their St. Anthony's Feast is the largest in New England. During the festivities, members parade a statue of St. Anthony for ten hours through the streets of the North End, accompanied by food carts, street decorations, and religious services. It is a vibrant and colourful sight to behold.

Other locations nearby: 12, 13, 14, 15

10 The Great Boston Molasses Flood

MA 02109 (North End), the site of the Great Boston Molasses Flood on Commercial Street at the foot of Copps Hill Terrace
T Green/Orange Line to North Station or Haymarket

Boston is famous for its wall plaques. Hundreds of them record the city's history, and they're especially useful where the physical landscape of a particular event has changed. A case in point is a plaque on Commercial Street at the foot of Copps Hill Terrace (North End). It marks the site of the city's most unusual disaster: the Great Boston Molasses Flood.

The old wharves lining Commercial Street were the place where immigrants once arrived, bales of cotton were landed, and penny ferries docked from East Boston. They were also where cargoes of molasses and sugar were unloaded for use in making candy, alcoholic drinks and even gunpowder. One of the companies benefitting from this was the Purity Distilling Company, which fermented molasses at their plant in Cambridge to produce rum.

Before transporting the molasses to Cambridge, the company stored it in a huge 2.3 million gallon cylindrical steel tank. Standing 50 feet tall and measuring 90 feet across, it stood in what is now Langone Park. Surrounding it at the time was a Purity Distilling Company warehouse and office, as well as a firehouse and police station, the North End Paving Company, and a Boston Gas Light building. Facing the tank on the opposite side of Commercial Street were domestic residences.

Disaster struck at 12.30 on the afternoon of January 15th 1919. Without warning and with "a thunderclap-like bang", the tank burst. A syrupy wave of molasses 25 feet high rushed out onto Commercial Street at an estimated 35 mph. As it did most of the surrounding buildings were engulfed, the elevated railway along Commercial Street buckled, and the domestic residences across the road flattened.

In the immediate aftermath, the streets were waist-deep in sticky molasses. First on the scene to help were cadets from the training ship *USS Nantucket*, which was conveniently moored alongside what is now the Puopolo Athletic Field. They began plucking survivors from the sticky chaos until the Boston Fire Department arrived. The search for survivors went on for four days by which time 21 people were reported dead, either crushed or asphyxiated, and another 150 injured.

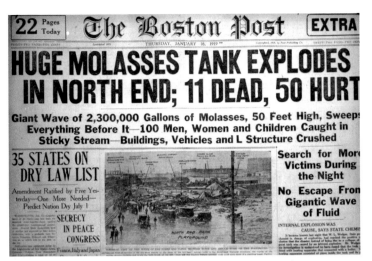

The Great Boston Molasses Flood was headline news

In the aftermath, over 300 people were involved in the cleanup, with salt water from a fireboat used to wash the worst of the molasses away. Those families affected brought one of the first class-action lawsuits in Massachusetts against the United States Industrial Alcohol Company (USIA), which had bought Purity Distilling in 1917. In spite of the company's attempts to claim the tank had been blown up by anarchists or Italian fascists, the court found them guilty. As a result, the relatives of those who died were paid $7,000 per victim.

Structural defects in the tank combined with climatic conditions were the reasons cited for the disaster. The steel used in the tank's construction was found to be too thin and lacking in manganese, which made it brittle. A fatigue crack at the base of the tank was probably the trigger, exploited when pressure in the tank increased due to an unseasonably rapid rise in air temperature.

In a twist to the story, it was later claimed that the USIA had filled the tank to the maximum to outrun prohibition, which was ratified by means of the Eighteenth Amendment just one day after the disaster.

One of those who perished in the disaster was wagon-driver Ralph Martin. A concrete model of his home forms part of an unusual model village created in 2006 at Forest Hills Cemetery (Jamaica Plain) (see no. 91). The owner of each model house is buried in the cemetery.

Other locations nearby: 11, 12, 13, 14

11   A Memorial to Radio Operators

MA 02109 (North End), the Merchant Marine Memorial
in Langone Park on Commercial Street
T Green/Orange Line to North Station or Haymarket

Six miles out in Boston Harbor is Gallops Island. Here during the Second World War several thousand volunteer civilians trained as United States Merchant Marine radio operators. Although the island is off limits to the public, their bravery and dedication is recorded in a modest memorial in Langone Park on Commercial Street (North End).

Gallops Island is named after John Gallop, a Puritan settler and one of the first Boston Harbor pilots, who lived there in the 17th century. Like other islands in Boston Harbor, Gallops was subsequently used for defensive purposes. During the American Civil War (1861–1865), for example, it housed a military camp for 3,000 Union soldiers. Thereafter it served as a temporary quarantine station for immigrants to reduce the risk of disease entering Boston.

By the time of the Second World War, and with fighting now occurring overseas, Gallops took on a different role. In 1940 the United States Maritime Service opened the Gallops Island Radio Training Station, which by 1941 was graduating as many as 50 expertly-trained radio operators a week. Armed with their radio telegraph licences, which were granted at Boston's Custom House after 20 weeks' training, the graduates were quickly posted to active sea duty. There they helped safeguard vessels of the United States Merchant Marine, which were carrying food, clothing and munitions to troops around the world.

Of those radio operators that went to sea, 170 brave souls went down with their ships. They are remembered in the easy-to-miss memorial in Langone Park. Presented to the people of Boston by the United States Maritime Service, it consists of a grey granite pillar topped with the sculpture of a ship's stern in the process of sinking. Morse code is inscribed around the pillar, a reminder that graduates were required to copy incoming code at a rate of 24 or more words a minute. The sides of the pillar are carved with various names, and at the top are the phrases "Message Sent", "Country Served" and "Duty Done". One side is reserved for the seal of the United States Maritime Service and the words "By Their Deeds, Measure Yours".

Gallops Island is unlikely to welcome sightseers any time soon. In

1949 a stranded fisherman lit a fire to catch people's attention and managed to destroy part of the abandoned Training Station. Although visits were made to the island subsequently, these were banned in 2000, when asbestos was found in the debris.

Fortunately Gallops is only one of the 34 islands that make up the Boston Harbor Islands National Recreation Area inaugurated in 1996. Of these, half a dozen can be reached easily and quickly by ferry from Long Wharf (Downtown), namely Spectacle, Georges, Lovells, Peddocks, Bumpkin, and Grape. Spectacle is interesting because it was used to deposit 3.7 million cu-

The easy-to-miss Merchant Marine Memorial in Langone Park

bic yards of earth excavated during the Big Dig (see no. 40). Georges is interesting for the 19th century remains of Fort Warren, which was used to imprison captured Confederate soldiers. Farther out to sea, and reached by ferry from Fan Pier (South Boston), is Little Brewster Island, which is home to the Boston Light, the country's oldest lighthouse (1783).

A plaque at 325 Harvard Street (Brookline) marks the former site of another Second World War training school. Here the Army Intelligence Espionage and Training Services Counter Intelligence Corps trained 150 Harvard and MIT men for spying missions not only in North Africa, the Pacific and post-war Germany but also at home to observe domestic subversives.

Other locations nearby: 10, 12, 13, 14

12 Copp's Hill Burying Ground

MA 02113 (North End), the Copp's Hill Burying Ground
at 21 Hull Street
T Green/Orange Line to North Station or Haymarket
(note: to find individual graves of interest it is advisable
to consult the map at the entrance to the cemetery)

When colonists first arrived on the Shawmut Peninsula they found a landscape very different to the one seen today. The northern end of the peninsula was separated from the rest by a tidal creek and dominated by a low hill. Long before the land reclamation that eventually shaped the area into the North End, the colonists used this hill for the nation's first windmill, and later to bury their dead.

The colonists' first burying ground was opened in 1630 at the King's Chapel on Tremont Street (Downtown) (see no. 38). Thirty years later, when it had reached capacity, the Old Granary Burying Ground was opened across the road (see no. 32). This was then supplemented by a third burying ground farther north, where the windmill stood. Opened in 1659 as the North Burying Ground, it was later renamed for William Copp, the land's original settler.

The story of Copp's Hill Burying Ground is a colourful one. At the start of the American Revolutionary War (1775–1783), British troops installed batteries on what is now Copp's Hill Terrace from where they bombarded Charlestown during the Battle of Bunker Hill (see no. 4). They also used the burying ground's headstones for target practice, which explains why some of them carry musketball scars. Several pockmark the headstone of one Captain Daniel Malcolm, whose epitaph describes him as "a true son of liberty".

In 1806 part of Copp's Hill was removed to provide material to fill the nearby Mill Pond, one of the first of several ambitious projects to increase Boston's landmass (see no. 8). To avoid disturbing the burying ground, retaining walls were built around the perimeter.

Today Copp's Hill Burying Ground contains some 1,200 grave markers, many of which sport macabre winged skulls. Not all those buried, however, have remained where they were laid. Some were disinterred in 1831 and taken to the new and more fashionable Mount Auburn Cemetery (Cambridge) (see no. 106). Others were removed to make way for new burials, and it is even said that a few were exhumed by grave robbers and sold for dissection at the Harvard Medical School. By the mid-19th century, when the burying ground had fallen into disuse, headstones were even being removed to patch roofs and floors in neighbouring buildings!

The most famous grave is that of the Mather family just inside the gate on Charter Street. Increase Mather (1639–1723) and his son Cotton (1663–1778) were both influential Puritan ministers during Boston's Colonial period (see no. 31).

Along the Snow Hill Street perimeter a thousand men from the New Guinea Community, a local Colonial-era enclave of free blacks, are buried. One of them was Prince Hall (1735–1807), an African-American community leader, who campaigned for the abolition of slavery and founded the world's first African Masonic Lodge. His simple headstone is accompanied by a granite column.

An old headstone in Copp's Hill Burying Ground

Nearby is the grave of Robert Newman (1752–1804), sexton at the Old North Church. He famously hung lanterns in the steeple as a signal from Paul Revere that British forces were advancing towards Lexington (see no. 14). Also here is the grave of Edward Hartt (1744–1824) in whose North End shipyard the USS *Constitution*, the world's oldest floating commissioned naval vessel, was built (see no. 2).

Mention should also be made of the grave of Shem Drowne (1683–1774), the first American weathervane maker, who designed the grasshopper atop Faneuil Hall, and the triple grave of George Worthylake (1673–1718), first keeper of the Boston Light, who drowned with his family whilst rowing to East Boston.

Other locations nearby: 10, 11, 13, 14

13   Why the Skinny House?

MA 02113 (North End), the Skinny House at 44 Hull Street
T Green/Orange Line to North Station or Haymarket
(note: the building is a private residence)

According to the Boston Landmarks Commission, the city's historic preservation agency, Boston's narrowest house can be found at 44 Hull Street (North End). Despite being several storeys high it measures little more than ten feet at its widest point. Known locally as the Skinny House, the clapboard property flanked by red-brick houses has long caught the eye of photographers and passers-by.

The Commission goes on to state that "in a city where there are many narrow lots, this far exceeds the norm". This inevitably begs the question as to why the Skinny House is so narrow? The reason given is that it was built as a so-called Spite House to deliberately punish a neighbour.

According to local legend, the land occupied by the Skinny House was once part of a much larger plot inherited by two brothers from their deceased father. When one of the brothers returned from serving in the American Civil War (1861–1865), he discovered that the other had built a home on more than his fair share of the land. Understandably grieved, he built the Skinny House in the 1870s on the remaining sliver of land to spite his brother. Filling what remained of the plot and soaring up four storeys, the building not only blocked sunlight from reaching his brother's house but also restricted his views of the Charles River. Whilst no further details are available to corroborate the story, the chronology is supported by the Hopkins Atlas of 1874 at the Boston City Archives (West Roxbury), which clearly shows the footprint of 44 Hull Street.

The precise dimensions of the Skinny House are worth repeating here. The façade facing onto Hull Street is 10.4 feet wide, the building's widest point. There is no entrance here, which instead is located down the narrow side alley. This side of the building measures 30 feet in length and tapers to the rear of the building, which is 9.25 feet wide. These present-day dimensions prove that at some point the building was extended from its original footprint of 274 square feet.

Inside the building, the outer walls are as little as 8.4 feet apart. The narrowest point is just 6.2 feet across, which means that an adult can touch opposing walls simultaneously. The living room and bathroom are located on the second floor, and are among the few spaces separated by a door. Apparently when anyone wants to visit the bathroom, all other occupants of the living room must stand up! In an article in *The Boston Globe*, the occupants of the Skinny House were described as leading "a vertical life".

The Skinny House is not, however, Boston's only example of a Spite House. Another, the O'Reilly Spite House, can be found at 260 Concord Avenue (Cambridge). It was built in 1908 by one Francis O'Reilly, who wanted to sell a thin unwanted strip of land to his neighbour. When the neighbor refused what O'Reilly considered a fair price, he built a house measuring eight feet wide and 37 feet long on the plot to annoy the neighbor. The building serves today as an unusual office space.

The Skinny House on Hull Street is a so-called Spite House

There are numerous other Spite Houses recorded across the United States. Examples in New England include the Newburyport Pink House, the Marblehead Old Spite House, and the Phippsburg McCobb Spite House.

Spite Houses are now a thing of the past. Modern building code standards and zoning restrictions make it very difficult to punish neighbours through spiteful construction.

Other locations nearby: 10, 11, 12, 14

14 One if by Land, and Two if by Sea

MA 02113 (North End), the Old North Church at
193 Salem Street
T Green/Orange Line to North Station or Haymarket (note: the
steeple and crypt can only be visited as part of a guided tour)

It is no surprise that the Old North Church at 193 Salem Street (North End) – officially Christ Church in Boston – attracts half a million visitors annually. After all it is Boston's oldest surviving church and it played an emblematic part in the American Revolutionary War (1775–1783).

Every element of the Old North Church – from spire to crypt – is of interest. The weathervane for instance, which crowns the 174-foot steeple, is the original, installed when the church was completed for a predominantly pro-British congregation in 1723. The steeple itself, however, is later having been rebuilt twice after being lost to storms in 1804 and 1954.

It is the story of the first steeple that draws the crowds. On the evening of April 18th 1775, church sexton Robert Newman (1752–1804) and his vestryman Captain John Pulling (1737–1787) climbed it and held two lanterns aloft. This was a signal from Paul Revere (1734–1818) to his fellow Patriots in Charlestown that British forces were moving across the Charles River on their way to Lexington to seize Patriot munitions. Revere was making his famous midnight ride to Lexington at the time and knew he might not get through. The pre-arranged lantern signal ensured his warning did, heralding the start of the Revolutionary War (see no. 16). The poet Longfellow memorialised the lantern signal with the immortal words: "One if by land, and two if by sea".

Several years before the lantern episode, the steeple was the scene of a less well-known event. In 1757 to the cheers of onlookers below, John Childs descended from it on a wire, as recorded in a plaque by the main entrance. The loss of business as workers gawped in amazement resulted in a ban on any similar antics in the future!

The brick body of the steeple contains the bell ringing chamber. The set of eight bells cast in England in 1744 were the first to be brought to America. Having tolled the passing of every US president, they can be heard each Sunday after the 11 am service. An old document lists a 15-year-old Paul Revere as a volunteer bell ringer.

The interior of the church is simple, with Palladian windows illuminating the white walls. Curiosities include the four cherubim beneath the organ, looted in 1746 from a French vessel, a clock made in 1726 that is the oldest in any American public building, and original high box pews (number 62 belonged to General Thomas Gage (1718–1787), commander of the British Army in North America). Bricks in the vestibule come from a prison cell in Boston, England, where a group of early Pilgrims were incarcerated for their beliefs.

Beneath the wooden floor is a crypt. Eleven hundred souls were laid to rest here between 1732 and 1860, including Anglicans, who were tolerated by the congregation but not allowed their own graveyard. Also British soldiers such as Major John Pitcairn (1722–1775) killed at the Battle of Bunker Hill, and smallpox victims from 1813.

Patriot Paul Revere with the Old North Church behind him

The grounds of the church contain further attractions. The Clough House built in 1713 is one of Boston's oldest brick residences and today houses Captain Jackson's Historic Chocolate Shop and the Printing Office of Edes & Gill, which both offer visitors a sense of Colonial-era life. Even the gift shop is historic, occupying a former chapel built in 1918 for Italian immigrants. A handful of gardens complete the scene, including the Washington Memorial Garden commemorating past churchgoers and a Memorial Garden to American lives lost in Iraq and Afghanistan.

Other locations nearby: 9, 10, 12, 13

15 Ghosts of the Kennedys

MA 02113 (North End), a selection of Kennedy family sites including the birthplace of Rose Kennedy at 4 Garden Court
T Green Line C, E or Orange Line to Haymarket

In Boston there are many ghosts of the Kennedys. This is where the ancestors of America's most famous 'First Family' settled upon arrival from Ireland, and it's where their most famous son, John F. Kennedy, cut his political teeth. From back streets to public buildings, the family's spirit lives on here.

The first Kennedy to reside in the United States was Patrick Kennedy (1823–1858). As the third son of an Irish farmer, he had little chance of running the family business, so instead in 1849 he sailed to East Boston to work as a cooper. He settled there and married fellow Irish immigrant Bridget Murphy (1824–1888), who bore him five children.

The year 1858 was a pivotal year for the burgeoning clan. On January 14th their youngest child, Patrick Joseph "P.J." Kennedy (1858–1929), was born in the family's modest home on Meridian Street (East Boston). As a teenager he worked as a stevedore on the docks, then opened a successful bar in East Boston's Maverick House hotel and acquired a whisky importing business (see no. 6). His success enabled him to become a major figure in the Democratic Party and thereby help his fellow Irish Catholics gain representation in Boston's Protestant-dominated political system. This kickstarted the Kennedy family's long involvement in American politics. On November 22nd of the same year, however, P.J. succumbed to cholera aged just 35. Exactly 105 years later his great grandson John would be assassinated prompting claims that the famous Kennedy Curse started here.

Before his premature death, P.J. and his wife added four children to the Kennedy clan. Of these the oldest, Joseph Patrick "Joe" Kennedy Sr. (1888–1969), studied at Harvard and eventually amassed a fortune from banking and investments. In 1914 he married Rose Elizabeth Fitzgerald (1890–1995), the eldest daughter of John Francis "Honey Fitz" Fitzgerald (1863–1950), who in 1906 had become the country's first American-born Irish mayor (see no. 59). Rose was born at 4 Garden Court Street (North End) in a now-demolished property marked by a plaque. She was christened like her father at St. Stephen's Church on Hanover Street (see nos. 17, 18).

"Joe" and Rose had nine children, including John Fitzgerald "Jack"

Kennedy (1917–1963) (known as JFK), who was born in a clapboard detached house – now the John Fitzgerald Kennedy National Historic Site – at 83 Beals Street (Brookline). Like other Kennedys, he studied at Harvard, where as an upperclassman he occupied Room F-14 of Winthrop House, now adorned with Kennedy memorabilia. After retiring from military service in 1945 he announced his candidacy for Congress at the Omni Parker House hotel on School Street (Downtown), where in 1953 he also held his bachelor party (see no. 23). As a congressman he enjoyed mussel stew at Boston's Union Oyster House, and in 1960 gave his final campaign speech at Faneuil Hall before becoming America's 35th (and first Roman Catholic) President (see no. 33).

This door marks where President Kennedy's mother was born

There are numerous memorials to JFK in Boston, including a statue outside the Massachusetts State House and a park on Memorial Drive (Cambridge). It was his dream to have his presidential library here overlooking the Charles River but it was eventually built at Columbia Point in Dorchester. Housed in an eyecatching I.M. Pei-designed building, the John F. Kennedy Presidential Library and Museum encapsulates JFK's life, loves, and legacy.

Across from the Library is the Edward M. Kennedy Institute for the U.S. Senate, with its replica of the Senate Chamber. Nearby is the Massachusetts Archives and Commonwealth Museum containing the 1780 *Constitution of the Commonwealth of Massachusetts*, the world's oldest written document still used for governance.

Other locations nearby: 8, 9, 16, 17

16 Home of the Midnight Rider

MA 02113 (North End), the Paul Revere House
at 19 North Square
T Green Line C, E or Orange Line to Haymarket

Paul Revere (1734–1818) is remembered today as the legendary messenger, who on the evening of April 18th 1775 set out on horseback for Lexington and Concord to warn his fellow Patriots Samuel Adams (1722–1803) and John Hancock (1737–1793) that British Redcoats were crossing the Charles River to seize rebel munitions. Yet when Revere died his obituaries made little of this, and instead emphasised his achievements as a metalworker. His legendary status only came about much later, when poet Henry Longfellow (1807–1882) memorialised his exploits in *Paul Revere's Ride* (1860). The poem's stirring opening lines have ensured the legend's survival: "Listen, my children, and you will hear/Of the midnight ride of Paul Revere".

This duality in the historical record actually makes Boston-born Revere a more rounded character. That he figures so large in the city's landscape is also because his home at 19 North Square (North End) is still standing. One of the country's first historic house museums, the clapboard building with its overhanging upper storey was built in 1680 making it the city's oldest extant residential address.

Revere occupied the house between 1770 and 1800. For the first three years he was accompanied by his first wife, Sarah, who died shortly after giving birth to their eighth child. Revere's second wife, Rachel, bore him another eight children, and it was she who kept the family together when Revere was captured by the British during his ride and imprisoned (fortunately the message he was carrying had already been conveyed to Charlestown and beyond by means of lanterns shone from the steeple of the Old North Church) (see no. 14). Revere returned to North Square in March 1776 following the British evacuation of Boston, and his wife's support was honoured in 1946 with the creation of the Rachel Revere Park opposite their house.

Shoehorned into the yard alongside the house is a visitor centre highlighting not only Revere's ride but also his early work as a dentist, silversmith and engraver (he famously engraved the Boston Massacre), as well as his industrial work after the Revolution. His French Huguenot father Apollos Rivoire (later anglicised to Revere) had arrived in Boston aged 13 and trained as a silversmith. Revere followed in his footsteps and after the war moved successfully into ironworking, bell-founding, and copper rolling. He made the first bell in Boston (one of his bells is on display) and provided the sheet copper for the dome of the Massachusetts State House (see no. 28). Along the way he also improved labour practices, standardised production, and became a Masonic Grand Master. Little wonder therefore that when Revere died at his final home on Charter Street his midnight ride was considered the lesser of his achievements. Although that building no longer stands, he is commemorated by the nearby Paul Revere Mall, which features an equestrian statue of him unveiled in 1940.

The Paul Revere House is not the only

The Paul Revere House is Boston's oldest residential address

historic building on this gaslit, sett-laid street. Next door is the Pierce/ Hichborn House, Boston's oldest brick residence, built in 1711 by glazier Moses Pierce and owned later by Revere's shipbuilding cousin, Nathaniel Hichborn. Note the narrow Baker's Alley running between the buildings, a reminder of how the area would have appeared in Colonial times.

The Boston home of William Dawes (1745–1799), who accompanied Revere on his ride, is marked by a plaque at the corner of Union and North Streets (Downtown). A third rider, Samuel Prescott (1751–1777), was the only one of the three to get safely all the way to Concord, where his home is also marked by a plaque.

Other locations nearby: 8, 15, 17, 18

17 North End Caffè and Cannoli

MA 02113 (North End), some traditional Italian stores including
Polcari's Coffee at 105 Salem Street
T Green Line C, E or Orange Line to Haymarket

Three waves of European immigrants washed over Boston's North End during the 19th century: Irish, Jewish, and Italian. By the turn of the century the Irish had begun moving away, and by the 1920s the Jews had followed suit. This left the Italians holding sway, with their influence only lessening slightly towards the end of the century.

The first Italians to arrive were Genoese in the 1860s. They settled alongside a Jewish slaughterhouse on Fulton Street and made a living selling fruit and vegetables. They were followed by Campanians (including Neapolitans and Avellinese), Sicilians, and Abruzzesians. The Sicilians worked in the fishing fleets, whilst others entered the construction industry. Each group created its own enclave and together they changed the North End.

The Irish had already converted several Protestant churches to Catholicism: the Seamen's Bethel at 12 North Square, for example, became the Sacred Heart Church, and the New North Congregational Society designed by Charles Bulfinch (1763–1844) at 401 Hanover Square became St. Stephen's. These were joined in 1873 by St. Leonard's at 320 Hanover Street, New England's first Italian church, its ornate interior in stark contrast to Boston's Protestant churches. The social infrastructure changed, too, with the North End Union settlement house and North Bennet Street Industrial School providing educational facilities for immigrants (see no. 18). Despite only inhabiting a square mile of territory, there were 44,000 North End Italians by 1930.

Although the Italian-American population today is barely a quarter of that, there is still a distinctly mediterannean vibe about the North End, especially between Cross and Prince Streets. Italian can still be heard here (including Italian-language Mass at St. Leonard's), and the religious street Feasts *(Festas)* staged in July and August draw enthusiastic crowds (see no. 9). Some of the traditional family stores survive, too, including Polcari's Coffee at 105 Salem Street. Opened in 1932 by immigrant Anthony Polcari, its wooden shelves groan not only with coffee, spices, oils, and nuts but also antique shop paraphernalia and family photos. In the summer months refreshing lemon slush is dispensed from a barrel.

Of the area's dozen original bakeries, only Bova's at 134 remains.

Also founded in 1932, it sells the best Sicilian *cannoli* and Campanian *sfogliatelle*. Strung out between Polcari's and Bova's are newer *salumerias* trading Italian cheese, salami, oil, and pasta, and an increasing number of restaurants.

By turning left along Prince Street (where Prince Pasta originated and mobster Jerry Angiulo once operated), Pizzeria Regina can be reached at 11½ Thacher Street. Opened in 1926, it serves brick oven pizzas in cosy 1940s-era wooden booths. By turning right along Prince Street, Hanover Street is reached, once home to fraudster Charles Ponzi, and where at 290 stands the venerable Caffé Vittoria. Opened in 1929, it is Boston's oldest

Weighing coffee at Polcari's on Salem Street

Italian café, with vintage marble-top tables and a jukebox playing Italian favourites (the Stanza dei Sigari cigar bar occupies the basement). Around the corner at 173 North Street is wine and spirit merchants V. Cirace & Sons. Established as a grocery in 1906 by immigrants from Salerno, the store gained the city's first licquor license after prohibition.

Like the Irish before them, the Italians attracted discrimination. A wall plaque at 256 Hanover Street recalls Sacco and Vanzetti, two immigrants executed for murder in 1927 without sufficient evidence. Their wake held at the Langone Funeral Home on the same street was attended by thousands. Immigrant undertaker Fred Langone and his descendants would later help gain political power for Boston's Italians, culminating in 1993 with the election of Thomas M. Menino (1942–2014), the city's first Italian-American mayor.

Other locations nearby: 8, 15, 16, 18

18 Remember the Ladies!

MA 02109 (North End), the North End Boston Women's
Heritage Trail beginning with the Rose Fitzgerald Kennedy
Greenway at the junction of Hanover Street and Cross Street
T Green C/E/Orange Line to Haymarket

"Remember the Ladies," wrote Massachusetts-born Abigail Adams (1744–1814) to her husband John Adams (1735–1826) referring to the women who had helped shape the New Republic. The second President of the United States did not heed his wife though, not even in Boston, the self-appointed Cradle of Liberty.

Only in 1989 was Abigail Adams's plea finally answered with the founding of the Boston Women's Heritage Trail. Taking the well-trodden Freedom Trail as a template, a group of likeminded teachers and librarians mapped out a city-wide network of self-guided women's history walks. Each chronicles the valuable contributions made by women to the development of Boston. What follows is their recommended walk through the North End.

The walk begins with the Rose Fitzgerald Kennedy Greenway at the junction of Hanover Street and Cross Street. Named in honour of the Boston-born matriarch of the Kennedy Family, it encompasses 300 acres of landscaped gardens (see no. 40). Next head up Salem Street remembering Sophie Tucker (c.1884–1966), a Russian Jewish émigre, who grew up here before becoming a vaudeville singing sensation with songs like *My Yiddishe Momme*. Turn onto Parmenter Street, where in 1886 at the North End Union a group of philanthropic women created Boston's first public playground, opposite today's North End Public Library.

Cross Hanover Street and walk along Richmond Street to North Street. Here on the right is the North Bennet Street Industrial School founded in 1881 by Pauline Agassiz Shaw (1841–1917) to train newly arrived Italian and Jewish immigrants. America's first trade school, it relocated here from North Bennet Street in 2013.

North Square to the left boasts three locations on the trail. The brick-built house at number 33 was once home to Clementine Poto Langone (1898–1964), who as wife of Massachusetts senator Joseph Langone Jr. helped many Italian immigrants obtain U.S. citizenship. Beyond at number 19 is the former home of Paul Revere and his wife Rachel, who bore eight of the Patriot's children (see no. 16). The Mariners House at number 11 is a former seamen's mission founded by magazine editor Sarah Josepha Hale (1788–1879), who campaigned for the creation of the Thanksgiving holiday, wrote *Mary Had a Little Lamb*, and raised funds to complete the Bunker Hill Monument (see no. 4).

Continue north along Garden Court Street to find the birthplace of Rose Kennedy (1890–1995) at number 4 (see no. 15). Thereafter rejoin Hanover Street, where a large brick building at 332 occupies the site of Boston's first Universalist church, where progressive ideas on gender equality were preached as early as 1800. Farther along at 401 is St. Stephen's Church, where Rose Kennedy was christened. On the left-hand wall of Paul Revere Mall opposite are plaques to further important North End women, including self-taught doctor Harriot Keziah Hunt (1805–1875) and successful actress Charlotte Cushman (1816–1876).

The Rose Fitzgerald Kennedy Greenway

Farther west at 18 Hull Street is the former home of the Paul Revere Pottery founded in 1909 to provide work for Jewish and Italian women. From there head south down Salem Street to Baldwin Place, where a faded Star of David recalls the Hebrew Industrial School for Girls established in 1899 by Jewish philanthropist, Lina Hecht (1848–1920).

The walk finishes back on Hanover Street at St. Leonard's Church, restored in 1988 thanks to a fundraising project in which local women were prominent (see no. 17).

> The Boston Women's Heritage Trail website (www.bwht.org) details walks in a dozen other neighbourhoods. One of them includes the Boston Women's Memorial (2003) on Commonwealth Mall (Back Bay), which features Abigail Adams, suffragist Lucy Stone (1818–1893), and the first published African-American woman, Phillis Wheatley (see no. 48).

Other locations nearby: 15, 16, 17, 33

19 A Temple for New England Sports

MA 02114 (West End), the Sports Museum of New England
at 100 Legends Way
T Green Line C, E to North Station

Boston is fanatical about sport. Not only is it home to national baseball, basketball, and ice hockey teams but the geography of the place also encourages walking, running, cycling, roller skating, ice skating, and watersports. All get a mention at the Sports Museum of New England in the TD Garden, a multipurpose arena above Boston's North Station (West End).

Founded in 1977 in Cambridge, the Sports Museum relocated to 'The Garden' after it opened in 1995 (the current structure replaced an earlier incarnation called the Boston Garden opened by boxing promoter Tex Rickard (1870–1929) in 1928). Like the Boston Garden before it, the TD Garden is home to basketball's Boston Celtics and ice hockey's Boston Bruins. It is the Bruins, however, who own the Boston Garden and in 1979 the Celtics threatened to leave the then-crumbling building unless the Bruins lowered the rent. In response the Bruins threatened to leave New England completely prompting the decision to demolish the Boston Garden and replace it with the TD Garden, a solution amenable to both teams. The name reflects the building's current sponsor, the New Jersey-based TD Bank.

Bruin Bobby Orr
with the TD Garden
behind him

It's no surprise that the Sports Museum pays homage to both Bruins and Celtics. Founded in 1924, the Bruins are America's oldest ice hockey team and the third oldest in the National Hockey League. Their name, an old English word for brown bears, was chosen because it suggested ferocity and alliterated with 'Boston'; their black and gold colours mirrored those of founder Charles Adam's chain of grocery stores.

The first facility to host the Bruins was the Boston Arena built in 1910 on St. Botolph Street (Fenway–Kenmore). They remained there until 1928, when they relocated to the Boston Garden (the Boston Arena, the world's oldest functioning indoor ice hockey venue, was eventually taken over by Northeastern University and renamed Matthews Arena). A Sports Museum highlight is some original wooden seating from the Boston Garden. The Bruins' most famous player is undoubtedly Canadian defenceman Bobby Orr (b. 1948), whose 1970 goal in overtime helped the team win the Stanley Cup. A bronze statue outside the TD Garden depicts the memorable event.

The Celtics were founded in 1946 as a charter member of the Basketball Association of America, which in 1949 became part of the National Basketball Association. Their 17 championship wins make them the most successful of any NBA team, helped along by star players such as forward Larry Bird (b. 1956), whose locker is displayed in the museum alongside life-sized wooden sculptures of both Bird and Orr.

The Sports Museum also encompasses baseball's Boston Red Sox, who are based at Fenway Park, a prize exhibit being the 2004 banner from when the Red Sox beat rivals the New York Yankees after an 86-year wait (see no. 90)! Mention is also made of annual college sports such as the rivalrous Harvard-Yale football game and the Beanpot hockey match, the Boston Marathon, and football's New England Patriots and soccer's New England Revolution, who play their home matches at the Gillette Stadium in Foxborough (see no. 78).

Whilst guided tours of the Sports Museum are available on the hour, 'Behind the Scenes' tours taking in the TD Garden's locker room and parquet playing field are only available from the end of Playoffs until the weekend of Labor Day (the first Monday in September).

Candlepin Bowling, a Massachusetts' variant on tenpin bowling using a smaller ball and pins, should also be mentioned here. Despite being on the decline, it can still be played at South Boston Candlepin at 543 East Broadway.

Other locations nearby: 20

20   In Memory of the West End

MA 02114 (West End), the West End Museum at
150 Staniford Street (Suite 7)
T Green Line C, E to North Station or Blue Line to Bowdoin

Half way along Lomasney Way in Boston's West End is a tiny traffic island. On it stands an abandoned sliver of a red-brick building clad with billboards. Now hemmed in by busy roads and tower blocks, it is a poignant reminder of how the West End used to look, before much of the neighbourhood was razed in the name of urban renewal.

The West End is bounded by Cambridge Street, New Chardon Street, and Washington Street. Once an area of tidal mudflats, the land was reclaimed in the early 1800s, beginning with what is now Charles Street and continuing, in a separate project, with the infilling of the so-called Mill Pond to create the Bulfinch Triangle bounded by Merrimac, Market, Washington and Causeway Streets (see no. 8).

From 1850 onwards, West Boston (as the West End was originally known) was the main port of entry for immigrants. Waves of Irish, Jews and Italians arrived here, including maritime traders and transient sailors, whose presence added a colourful, rough-and-tumble element. By the mid-20th century the neighbourhood was home to around 7,500 blue collar residents living in modest red-brick tenements.

Despite long being a cherished neighbourhood and one with a distinctive communal identity, 46 acres of the West End were indiscriminately swept away between 1958 and 1960 displacing some 2,700 families in the process. In their place came oversized government and public buildings, including the Government Service Center on Staniford Street, the O'Neill Federal Building on Causeway Street, and the sprawling Massachusetts General Hospital centred on Fruit Street. Like the contemporary I. M. Pei-designed City Hall Plaza and Government Center nearby, they have Brutalist (and for some, inhumane) overtones. Admittedly by the 1960s the city was in need of new infrastructure but in order to achieve this 'New Boston' much of the West End's original character was effaced.

Fortunately echoes of the old West End remain. They include the pavement plaques along Martha Road giving the name and position of long lost streets, and there are surviving historic buildings such as the Harrison Gray Otis House on Cambridge Street, the former Liberty jail on Charles Street, and St. Joseph's Catholic Church on William Cardinal O'Connell Way (see nos. 23, 24). The old narrow streets of the Bulfinch Triangle remain, too – notably Portland, Friend, and Canal Streets – where today old warehouses rub shoulders with friendly neighbourhood shops and bars.

The greatest repository of memories though is to be found in the West End Museum at 150 Staniford Street. The origin of the museum dates back to 1991 and the formation of the Old West End Housing Corporation (OWEHC) to create affordable housing for displaced former residents. The result was West End Place at 150 Staniford Street, where in 2002 the OWEHC was awarded space for its offices and a museum.

The museum may only be small but it's big on nostalgia. Wonderful photos and historic arte-

An old West End building now dwarfed by a modern skyscraper

facts are used to bring the old West End back to life. At its heart is a permanent exhibit called *The Last Tenement*, donated in 2003 by the Bostonian Society. It tugs at the heartstrings to consider all that's been lost. Additionally the museum hosts temporary exhibitions using material drawn from its extensive archives (typical is the story of the Boston Canal that once ran along Canal Street connecting Boston with the Merrimac River). The volunteer-run museum's ongoing mission is to preserve the legacy of the old West End not only for former residents but also for outsiders wishing to learn more about what has been called "The Greatest Neighborhood this Side of Heaven".

Other locations nearby: 19, 24

21 An Electrifyingly Good Museum

MA 02114 (West End), the Museum of Science at 1 Science Park
T Green Line E to Science Park/West End

For a place that celebrates technology and innovation, Boston's Museum of Science is well situated. Since 1951 its modernist galleries have sat on the Charles River Dam Bridge, an impressive piece of early 20th century engineering that transformed the tidal Charles River into the freshwater Charles River Basin (prior to that its collections occupied another state-of-the-art structure in Back Bay) (see nos. 5, 73).

The Museum of Science is the country's first museum to unite all the sciences under one roof, from natural history and geology to computing and astronomy. With its hundreds of interactive exhibits, engaging public events, and enthusiastic outreach programme, it's not surprising that the museum draws around 1.4 million visitors annually.

The museum has been in a permanent state of improvement since its relocation. In 1956 it was given its own T station bringing visitors almost to the front door. Two years later the Charles Hayden Planetarium was installed, which today is New England's most advanced digital theatre. It is complimented by the Gilliland Observatory on top of the museum's multi-storey car park (see no. 89).

The early 70s saw the completion of the museum's West Wing, which contains the hugely atmospheric Elihu Thomson Theater of Electricity. Taking centre stage here is the world's largest air insulated Van de Graaf generator built in 1933 by Dr. Robert J. Van de Graaf (1901–1967). He used it to research high-energy X-rays and atom smashing at the Massachusetts Institute of Technology. It consists of two columns each topped with a 15 foot-wide hollow aluminium sphere. Originally the spheres were oppositely charged creating lightning-like discharges of 5 million volts. Today, the spheres are joined together and discharge 2.5 million volts down to objects below.

Just as popular is the Mugar Omni Theater, which opened in 1987. The latest film technology is used here to project science and nature documentaries onto a five storey-high, domed, wraparound IMAX screen giving viewers a dizzyingly immersive experience. More recent additions include the Hall of Human Life, which uses current life science discoveries to engage visitors with their own biology, the Science behind Pixar exhibit exploring the technology underpinning Pixar Ani-

The Van der Graaf generator at the Museum of Science

mation Studios' award-winning films, and the Yawkey Gallery on the Charles River examining the museum's watery location.

Perhaps the museum's most important innovations though have been social. In 2001 it opened the Gordon Current Science & Technology Center, where important scientific news stories are broken to the public by museum staff – and sometimes even the scientists involved. In 2004 the National Center for Technological Literacy was created, with the aim of making everyone in America technologically literate. It is the country's only museum facility working to overhaul 21st-century school curricula to include the human-made world, and has so far reached over eight million students.

The future certainly looks bright for the museum. In 2015 it successfully completed the largest fundraising effort in its 185-year history, raising almost $300 million. With these funds in place the museum aims "to become the leading science centre worldwide, expanding the public's access to, understanding of, and critical thinking around engineering, technology, and the sciences".

An unexpected exhibit in the museum is the reconstructed gun and trophy room of Colonel Frances Colby (1882–1953), a well-to-do hunter and soldier, and the museum's most generous early benefactor. Visitors interested in science and books might also consider attending the museum's Book Club for the Curious held each second Thursday of the month at 5.30pm in the Cambridge Innovation Center at One Broadway (Cambridge).

22 Beneath the Ether Dome

MA 02114 (West End), the Ether Dome in the Bulfinch Building
at 55 Fruit Street (4th Floor) at the Massachusetts General
Hospital
T Blue Line to Bowdoin, or Red Line to Charles/MGH, or Green
Line E to Science Park/West End

At the end of Marlborough Street, just inside the Public Garden, is a memorial depicting a doctor holding a cloth and the limp body of a patient. An inscription explains that it commemorates the first public use of ether as an anesthetic, which occurred in 1846 at Boston's Massachusetts General Hospital (Mass General).

The sprawling hospital, the country's third oldest, is a 15-minute walk north of the Ether Monument. The original building, which opened in 1821, is still standing and was designed by America's first professional architect, Charles Bulfinch (1763–1844) (see no. 27). Rendered in the Greek Revival-style, it is built from white Chelmsford granite hewn by inmates from the Charlestown prison.

Known as the Bulfinch Building, it was a carefully considered structure, with novel features including a central heating system and flushing water closets. A key element was the operating theatre. During the 19th century it was important to admit as much light and fresh air to such theatres so Bulfinch placed it at the top of his building. There it was illuminated from above by windows in a copper dome, which also admitted breezes blowing in off the Charles River. The seats for onlookers were ranged precipitously along the south wall, affording the best view of the operations below.

Another reason for placing the theatre at the top of the building was to muffle patients' screams! This was certainly true in the early years, when surgery was performed without anesthetic. That changed on 16th October 1846, however, when three men made medical history here. Dentist Dr. William T. G. Morton (1819–1868) was invited to perform a public demonstration of the use of ether to render a patient insensible to pain. The patient was Edward Gilbert Abbott, a local man with a tumour on his jaw. With the ether administered, Harvard Medical School surgeon Dr. John Collins Warren (1778–1856) removed the tumour without causing Abbott any significant discomfort. Afterwards the usually sceptical Warren quipped, "Gentlemen, this is no humbug", a reference to the unsuccessful demonstration of nitrous oxide anesthesia in the same theatre a year earlier. That had ended with

The Ether Dome at Massachusetts General Hospital

cries of "Humbug!" after the patient audibly groaned with pain! News of Morton's successful 'anesthesia', a term coined by Boston poet and physician Oliver Wendell Holmes Sr. (1809–1894), circulated quickly around the world changing medical practice forever.

The Ether Dome, as the theatre is known today, can be found on the 4th floor of the Bulfinch Building at 55 Fruit Street (West End). Now used for lectures and meetings, this architectural gem has been declared a National Historic Landmark and is open to the public. Visitors will see where more than 8,000 operations were carried out between 1821 and 1868, and can sit where onlookers witnessed them. The names of important figures in the discovery of ether are inscribed on brass plaques on the seats.

Not surprisingly the Ether Dome contains a teaching skeleton and a collection of early surgical implements. The painting on the wall depicts a re-enactment of the 1846 event with hospital staff in period dress. More surprising is the Egyptian mummy and marble statue of *Apollo*, both of which were given to the hospital as gifts.

Of related interest is the Paul S. Russell, MD Museum of Medical History and Innovation. Located nearby at 2 North Grove Street, it includes a glass inhaler of the type pioneered by Dr. Morton for the administration of ether. The rooftop garden affords sweeping views of Beacon Hill and the State House dome.

Other locations nearby: 20, 23, 24

23 Hotels with History

MA 02114 (West End), a selection of historic hotels including
The Liberty Hotel at 215 Charles Street
T Red Line to Charles/MGH

Boston's hotels come in all shapes and sizes. The Lenox, for example, built in 1900 at 61 Exeter Street (Back Bay) offers high-end luxury and vintage features, including working fireplaces and an operational *Cutler* mail chute. Equally grand is the Fairmont Copley Plaza built a little later at nearby 138 St. James Avenue, with its colourful lobby (dubbed Peacock Alley) and wood-panelled Oak Room restaurant.

Modest by comparison are two hotels built originally as premises for the Boston branch of the YWCA, the country's oldest, founded in 1866. The 40 Berkeley at 40 Berkeley Street (South End) dates from 1884 and is now a budget traveller's hostel; the Hotel 140 at 140 Clarendon Street (Back Bay) was built in 1929 and is today an affordable boutique hotel. Another boutique hotel is the John Jeffries House at 14 David G. Mugar Way (Beacon Hill), which opened in 1909 as a hostel for nurses working at the nearby Massachusetts Eye and Ear Infirmary. Of related interest is the College Club of Boston at 44 Commonwealth Avenue (Back Bay), opened in 1890 for college-educated women and now the country's oldest women's club.

Boston also lays claim to the longest continuously-operating hotel in the United States. The Omni Parker House at 60 School Street (Downtown) opened in 1855 and was for several years home to the Saturday Club, a series of literary gatherings led by transcendentalist Ralph Waldo Emerson (1803–1882), which spawned *The Atlantic Monthly*. Charles Dickens gave a recitation of *A Christmas Carol* to the Club whilst staying at the hotel in 1867. The present building dates from 1927 and includes a bar named for Edwin O'Connor's novel *The Last Hurrah* based on the life of James Michael Curley (1874–1958), Boston's colourful Irish-American mayor. The hotel also claims to be the birthplace of Massachusetts' state dessert, Boston Cream Pie.

Several Boston hotels are the result of adaptive reuse, occupying buildings that previously served very different purposes. The Harborside Inn at 185 State Street (Downtown) and the Marriott Residence Inn at 370 Congress Street (South Boston) both occupy early 20th century warehouses (see no. 51). The Langham at 250 Franklin Street (Downtown), Loews Boston Hotel at 350 Stuart Street (Back Bay), and the Kendall Hotel at 350 Main Street (Cambridge), occupy a former bank

(1922), police headquarters (1920s), and fire station (1894) respectively. And the Ames Hotel at 1 Court Street and the Marriott Custom House at 3 McKinley Square (Downtown) were both once office blocks, completed in 1893 and 1915 (see nos. 36, 79).

A singular example of adaptive reuse is The Liberty Hotel at 215 Charles Street (West End), which occupies the former Suffolk County Jail. Completed in 1851 to a design by Boston architect Gridley J.F. Bryant (1816–1899), it is made of Quincy granite and comprises four wings extending from a central, octagonal atrium. Notably Bryant collaborated on the plans with the pioneering prison reformer Louis Dwight

The former Suffolk County Jail is now the Liberty Hotel

(1793–1854), whose humanitarian approach called for individual cells and larger rooms for communal work and exercise. Additionally the riverside location ensured fresh air and ample natural light.

Before its closure in 1990, when the jail relocated to new premises on Nashua Street, several famous inmates were incarcerated here. They included Mayor Curley, Malcolm X, the Italian anarchists Sacco and Vanetti, and the captured crews of two German Second World War U-Boats. Thereafter the empty jail was cleverly converted into the 300-room Liberty Hotel, which opened in 2007. Original cell doors can still be found in the foyer and the bar!

Other locations nearby: 22, 25, 26

24 Three Homes for Mr. Otis

MA 02114 (West End), the Harrison Gray Otis House at
141 Cambridge Street
T Blue Line to Bowdoin or Red Line to Charles/MGH (note:
the Harrison Gray Otis House can only be visited as part of
a guided tour)

There's not much left of Boston's old West End. The main port of entry for immigrants in post-Colonial times, the once-lively neighbourhood was largely razed in the 1960s in the name of urban renewal (see no. 20). This makes the late 18th century Harrison Gray Otis House at 141 Cambridge Street a cherished survivor.

The house was completed in 1796 for Boston-born congressman and real estate entrepreneur, Harrison Gray Otis (1765–1848). State attorney for Massachusetts, a leading light in the country's first political party, the Federalists, and eventually the city's Mayor, Otis was one of Boston's wealthiest men. It is therefore no surprise that he commissioned America's foremost architect, Charles Bulfinch (1763–1844), to design his home. Bulfinch was a pioneer of Federal-style architecture, a practical red-brick idiom with neo-Classical flourishes that reflected the values of the newly-founded United States between the 1780s and 1830s (see no. 27).

Inspired by a house Bulfinch had seen in Philadelphia, which in turn was inspired by one in London, the Harrison Gray Otis House is notable as one of Boston's earliest three-storey brick houses, which came to epitomise the Federal style. Five bays wide, with an elegant doorway added a little later, the symmetrical façade features a fine Palladian window at first floor level, and a lunette window above. Such refined elements are clearly influenced by the work of British neo-Classical architect, Robert Adam (1728–1792), who had published his designs in 1792. Adam's influence can also be detected in the interiors, which consist of pairs of rooms placed either side of the central hallway. It was here that Otis and his wife entertained lavishly.

The subsequent history of the Harrison Gray Otis House is an eventful one. In the 1830s it served as a medical facility offering 'Champoo Baths', an old fashioned aromatherapy treatment, and later became a genteel boarding house. In 1916 it was acquired by the Society for the Preservation of New England Antiquities (now Historic New England) for use as its headquarters. In 1925 under their watchful eye the entire building was rolled back 40 feet after it was threatened by road widening. Since careful restoration in 1960, the house has been open to visitors, who are often taken aback by the surprisingly loud colour schemes of the Federal-style interiors.

The Harrison Gray Otis House on Cambridge Street

Today the Otis Gray Harrison House sits incongruously against a backdrop of modern office buildings. From one angle though there is the Old West Church, a monumentally-scaled example of ecclesiastical Federal-style architecture, whose 1806 design was widely copied throughout New England. Together they offer a glimpse of the lost West End.

The house on Cambridge Street is but one of three grand Federal-style homes commissioned by Otis from Bulfinch over a ten-year period. The second, located at 85 Mount Vernon Street (Beacon Hill), was completed in 1802. Again three storeys and retaining part of its original cobblestoned drive, it is a remnant of the original vision for the development of Beacon Hill as an area of well-to-do stand-alone houses rather than the more economical row houses that soon followed. Note the recessed brick arches with fretwork balconies, the Corinthian pilasters, and the octagonal rooftop cupola. Otis lived in this house until 1806, when his third home at 45 Beacon Street (Beacon Hill) was completed. The largest of the three houses, this one boasts four storeys and would have been freestanding when built. It is here that Otis lived until his death in 1848. A century later the American Meteorological Society took up residence in the building and they've been there ever since.

Other locations nearby: 22, 25, 26

25 Hidden Gardens of Beacon Hill

MA 02114 (Beacon Hill), the Peter Faneuil House Garden at 30 South Russell Street
T Blue Line to Bowdoin or Red Line to Charles/MGH

For almost 90 years members of the Beacon Hill Garden Club (BHGC) have opened their normally hidden gardens on a Thursday in May. Not only is this an opportunity for the public to see some of Boston's loveliest private gardens but it is also a chance for the club to honour the city's long tradition of urban gardening.

The Club was founded in 1928, at a time when Beacon Hill was being rediscovered after decades of decline. Neglected properties were being restored and green-fingered residents were turning their attention to the walled yards that lay behind them. Once used for laundry lines, wood storage and waste, these unloved pockets of land were now converted into charming small gardens.

The original members met at 130 Mount Vernon Street, the home of watercolourist Gertrude Beals Bourne (1868-1962), which can be easily identified by the sunflower relief adorning its gable. Their number included renowned landscaper Arthur Asahel Shurcliff (1870–1915) and architect Eleanor Raymond (1887–1989), who is credited with designing the world's first solar-powered home. In 1929 the members embarked on two projects that have since become annual club traditions: in March they contributed an exhibit to the Massachusetts Horticultural Society's New England Spring Flower Show, and for a day in May they opened their gardens to the public. Participants paid $1 to visit 11 gardens and the proceeds were used for charitable donations and civic planting projects.

Although support for the open day waned during the Great Depression, it rallied during the Second World War, when proceeds were used to support the British War Relief Society. It has been well supported ever since and these days around 2,500 people take a self-guided tour around a dozen lovely gardens on the third Thursday in May (tickets available at www.beaconhillgardenclub.org). The gardens are open from 9am to 5pm and maps are available from club members at information tables on the day.

The BHGC also manages two gardens that are open all year round. One of them, the Peter Faneuil House Garden at 30 South Russell

Street, was created for the occupants of Faneuil House, an affordable housing project inside the former Peter Faneuil School. The other is the meditative Washington Memorial Garden at the Old North Church in the North End (see no. 14).

Boston's other hidden gardens come in all shapes and sizes. In the West End on the eighth floor of the Massachusetts General Hospital's Yawkey Center for Outpatient Care there is the Howard Ulfelder Healing Garden for patients and their families. Hidden in the same neighbourhood in the lobby of an office building at 101 Merrimac Street is a different sort of garden: an incredible six-storey-high *trompe l'oeil* painting of a plant-filled con-

A delightful private garden hidden on Beacon Hill

servatory by New York muralist Richard Haas (b. 1936). In the North End, the Lewis Wharf Hidden Garden off Commercial Street was created by architect Carl Koch (1912–1998) in memory of his wife and echoes 18th century garden design. Different again is the Cambridge Center Roof Garden on top of a multi-storey car park at 90 Broadway (Cambridge). Concealed from the streets below, it offers trees, winding paths and splendid views. Another hidden garden, also in Cambridge, is the Sunken Garden in Radcliffe Yard on Appian Way, where Harvard students study *al fresco* in the summer months.

Founded in 1829, the Massachusetts Horticultural Society is the oldest horticultural organisation in the United States. It helped create the first garden cemetery at Mount Auburn Cemetery in 1831, introduced the Concord grape in 1853, and promoted the concept of wartime victory gardens in the 1940s (see nos. 91, 106).

Other locations nearby: 23, 24, 26

26   Boston's Jewish Diaspora

MA 02114 (Beacon Hill), a tour of Jewish synagogues including the Vilna Shul at 18 Phillips Street
T Blue Line to Bowdoin or Red Line to Charles/MGH

Walking around Central Boston today it is remarkable to think that 54 synagogues once existed here. Established by European immigrants during the 19th and early 20th centuries, most of their worshippers have since moved out to the suburbs and beyond. Traces of their presence, however, still remain.

Massachusetts' first permanent Jewish congregation was established in 1843 by Germans. Known as Ohabei Shalom, their story is a tale typical of the Jewish diaspora. In 1844 they established the state's first Jewish cemetery at 147 Wordsworth Street (East Boston), which can still be visited (www.ohabei.org). Then in 1852 they consecrated the first synagogue, with 400 seats, on Warrenton Street (Downtown). An influx of Polish Jews, however, caused a rift in the congregation and in 1854 the Germans seceded to form Congregation Israel. In 1885 they built Boston's first monumental synagogue at 600 Columbus Avenue (South End) (today an African Methodist Episcopal Church) and in 1906 built another in the style of the Temple of Solomon at 602 Commonwealth Avenue (now Boston University's Morse Auditorium). The Poles meanwhile continued as Ohabei Shalom and in 1921 they purchased land at 1187 Beacon Street (Brookline), where they built their own magnificent Byzantine-Romanesque synagogue. Modelled on Hagia Sophia in Istanbul, it has room for 1,800 worshippers and is still used today.

In 1858, Jews from East Prussia also broke away from Ohabei Shalom to form Mishkan Tefila. In an illustration of Boston's ever-shifting demographics, when in the late 1950s they left their synagogue at 2016 Seaver Street (Roxbury), it became a school, where civil rights leader Elma Lewis (1921–2004) taught arts and dance to the young Afro-Caribbeans now moving into the neighbourhood.

Another distinct congregation was Anshei Vilner (The People of Vilnius), comprising Lithuanians, who arrived in Boston in the 1890s. They worshipped in makeshift synagogues until 1919, when they consecrated the Vilna Shul at 18 Phillips Street on the north side of Beacon Hill, which like the West End was popular with newly-arrived immigrants. Abandoned in 1985, when the congregation had dropped to just three worshippers, it is Boston's last immigrant-era

The Vilna Shul is unique among Boston's old synagogues

synagogue and now functions as a combined museum and Jewish cultural centre.

A fusion of East European synagogue and New England meeting house, the Vilna Shul's second-floor sanctuary is L-shaped to segregate the sexes. Large skylights illuminate the space, which contains high-backed wooden pews, stained glass windows, folk art murals peeping out from beneath layers of later paint, and a Holy Ark bearing the priestly hand blessing *(birkat kohanim)* (*Star Trek* fans will note it resembles Mr. Spock's "Live long and prosper" gesture, indeed actor Leonard Nimoy (1931–2015) grew up not far from here). A *Kabbalat Shabbat* (Reception of the Sabbath) service is held at the Vilna Shul once a month.

Of the Jews that once made up a third of Boston's North End population, nothing significant remains. From the 1870s onwards they lived on Salem Street (nicknamed 'Shalom Street'), where they opened clothing stores, synagogues, and schools, and financed construction. But by the 1920s, as the Italians took sway, they moved on. Some bolstered the Jewish community in the neighbouring West End, where more synagogues came and went. They are represented there today by the Boston Synagogue at 55 Martha Road (West End), which opened in 1970 after much of the West End had been razed in the name of urban renewal (see no. 20).

The New England Holocaust Memorial in Union Street Park (Downtown) comprises six glass towers representing the six million Jews exterminated over six years in six death camps. They also represent the six branches of the *menorah* candelabra.

Other locations nearby: 23, 24, 25

27 America's First Professional Architect

MA 02108 (Beacon Hill), a tour of Beacon Hill homes
beginning in Louisberg Square
T Red Line to Charles/MGH

Few architects have left their mark on Boston like Charles Bulfinch (1763–1844). A pioneer of the first distinctly American architecture – the Federal Style – his work helped define the fledgling nation after the American Revolutionary War (1775–1783). For this he is regarded as America's first professional architect.

Born on Bowdoin Square, his father a physician, Bulfinch graduated Harvard in 1784 and made the Grand Tour of Europe, where he observed contemporary English and Italian architecture. Once back in Boston he set himself up as a gentleman architect, taking as inspiration the neo-Classical stylings of British architect Robert Adam (1728–1792), with its pillars and pediments. This Bulfinch fused with practical New England red-brick and clapboard, applying it to everything from homes to public buildings (see nos. 17, 20, 22, 28, 34, 96). In his larger projects, he used the Federal Style to consciously connect the newly-founded United States with ancient Greek democracy and the republican values of ancient Rome.

Unfortunately Bulfinch's greatest contribution is long gone. In 1858 his Tontine Crescent on Franklin Street (Downtown) was demolished to make way for commercial structures. Completed in 1795, this 480-foot long arc of townhouses was Boston's first row house complex and one of America's earliest urban housing schemes. Its failure forced Bulfinch into becoming a jobbing professional architect.

Much of Bulfinch's time was now taken up designing private homes on the south side of Beacon Hill. This well-to-do area of gaslit streets and brick sidewalks was created from the 1780s onwards by a development syndicate called the Mount Vernon Proprietors. The three hills that originally defined the area were levelled allowing Bulfinch to impose a grid of streets along which homes were built for the city's Protestant merchant elite, the Boston Brahmins.

This walk starts in Louisberg Square. The smart, bow-fronted homes here dating from the 1830s and 40s overlook America's first resident-owned park. Among the well-heeled inhabitants was Louisa May Alcott (1832–1888) of *Little Women* fame. By contrast drop down nearby Willow Street onto cobblestoned Acorn Street, where a series of diminutive homes were occupied by coachmen and servants.

Back up on Mount Vernon Street at 87 is a classic Bulfinch residence built in 1805 for a merchant and shipmaster. It displays a Federal-style portico and neo-Classical flourishes to the first floor windows. Even grander is 85, one of three homes designed by Bulfinch for wealthy Bostonian Harrison Gray Otis (1765–1848) (see no. 24). It is a reminder that the Mount Vernon Proprietors originally envisaged standalone houses and not the more economical row houses that followed.

Architect Charles Bulfinch designed Louisberg Square

To see inside a Bulfinch house continue along Mount Vernon Street (passing the single-storey former stables between 50 and 60) to reach the Nichols House Museum at 55. Built in 1804, this four-storey townhouse offers a taste of upper class life in Beacon Hill during the 19th century.

After glimpsing the extension to Bulfinch's masterwork, the Massachusetts State House, at the end of the street, walk down onto Chestnut Street to see his semi-detached house at 6–8, and his Swan Houses at 13, 15 and 17 designed for the daughters of heiress Hepzibah Swan. The house at 29A, whilst not a Bulfinch house, is notable as being the first of the properties erected by the Mount Vernon Proprietors. It features London-made purple glass window panes (in reality a manufacturing fault) that bizarrely became a fashion!

The tour concludes down on Beacon Street, where at 45 there is another Bulfinch home for Harrison Gray Otis. The bow-fronted William Hickling Prescott House nearby at 55 was designed by Bulfinch understudy Benjamin Asher (1773–1845) and is also open to the public.

Other locations nearby: 25, 26, 28

28 Freedom Writ Large

MA 02113 (Beacon Hill), the Massachusetts State
House at the corner of Park and Beacon Streets
(General Hooker entrance)
T Red/Green B/C/D/E Line to Park Street
(note: a security check is conducted on entry)

If one building expresses the ebullient mood in Boston following the Declaration of Independence (1776) it is the Massachusetts State House. Crouching sphinx-like at the corner of Park and Beacon Streets, it was built to last, and as the seat of government for the Commonwealth of Massachusetts still impresses today. The building's strident design is freedom writ large.

Back in the 18th century this part of Beacon Hill was used by Massachusetts' first elected governor and first signee of the Declaration of Independence, John Hancock (1737–1793), to graze his cattle. The seat of Boston's Colonial-era government prior to 1776 was the Old State House on State Street (see no. 38). This same building served thereafter as the seat of the Massachusetts' state government but it was clear that a more representative structure was needed.

The commission to design the new building was given to Boston architect Charles Bulfinch (1763–1844) (see no. 27). Regarded as the first professional American architect, he used his brand of neo-Classical Federal-style architecture to consciously associate the fledgling nation with ancient Greek democracy and the republican values of ancient Rome. These themes are represented by the new building's temple-like colonnade and Pantheon-esque dome respectively.

When the Massachusetts State House was completed in 1798 it had a wooden dome, something Bulfinch would later deploy at the Capitol in Washington. In 1802 this was sheathed in copper by the foundry of Paul Revere (1734–1818), which pioneered the commercial rolling of copper (only in 1874 was it gilded). The pine cone at the top is a reminder that the wood for the dome came from Maine, which until 1820 was a part of the Commonwealth of Massachusetts.

A large extension to Bulfinch's red-brick building was completed in 1895, and in 1917 the two side wings were added. It is through the right-hand wing that visitors enter the building today. Once inside and through security proceed to the second floor and enter the Doric Hall. The large doors in this reception room, which open onto the building's external staircase, are only used to admit a visiting presi-

A golden dome crowns the Massachusetts State House

dent, to allow a governor to leave office, and to deliver the annual Christmas tree!

The Nurses Hall beyond lies within the building's 1895 extension and is named for its statue of a Civil War-era nurse. Murals here depict important Revolutionary episodes, including lawyer James Otis Jr. (1725–1783) speaking out against unfair British taxation. Beyond is the circular Memorial Hall (or Hall of Flags), where Massachusetts' regimental colours have been returned after every conflict since the Civil War. A stained glass skylight incorporates the Massachusetts' state seal, with earlier seals depicted in the window of the Grand Staircase beyond.

Up on the third floor of the extension is the oval House of Representatives, which relocated here from the Bulfinch building in 1865. Here more murals depict *Milestones on the Road to Freedom*. Hanging over the public gallery is the famous Sacred Cod, a wooden effigy symbolising the importance of fishing in the early Massachusetts economy.

Finally back in the Bulfinch building, the original House of Representatives (located directly beneath the dome) today contains the Senate Chamber, which itself relocated from what is now the Senate Reception Room, where much of Bulfinch's original interior is preserved (it is closed for restoration until 2019).

Ashburton Park behind the East Wing features the country's first monument to the Revolution. A copy of Bulfinch's original, it stands near the site of the original warning beacon after which Beacon Hill was named, albeit 60 feet lower owing to the hill's excavation for landfill projects (see no. 8).

Other locations nearby: 29, 30, 31, 32

29 In the Foosteps of African-Americans

MA 02108 (Beacon Hill), the Black Heritage Trail beginning with the 54th Massachusetts Regiment Memorial at the corner of Beacon and Park Streets
T Red/Green B/C/D/E Line to Park Street (note: downloadable maps, audio tours, and guided tour details at www.maah.org)

That Boston played a pivotal role in America's fight to abolish slavery will always be something to celebrate. Today the locations associated with it form the 1.6 mile-long Black Heritage Trail, established in the 1960s and hailed by President Jimmy Carter as preserving "a vital, but long neglected, part of American heritage".

Boston's first Africans arrived in 1638, as slaves with the early colonists. Over the next century their children were increasingly born free to white mothers, whilst some slaveholders began freeing their slaves legally through manumission. Northern cities such as Boston offered better opportunities to free blacks, so it is no surprise that after the American Revolutionary War (1775–1783) – in which many free blacks volunteered – Massachusetts became the first state to declare slavery unconstitutional.

Prior to the American Civil War (1861–1865) most of Boston's African-Americans lived on the north slope of Beacon Hill, beyond Pinckney Street and out of sight of the homes of wealthy whites. Although by the early 20th century they had moved away, their former homes, schools and churches survive (see no. 62).

The Black Heritage Trail begins at the corner of Beacon and Park Streets, where a memorial commemorates the 54th Massachusetts Volunteer Infantry Regiment, the first black fighting unit raised in the North. Their leader, Colonel Robert Gould Shaw (1837–1863), son of a well-to-do Boston abolitionist, died alongside them during a failed attempt to take a fort from the Confederates during the Civil War.

From here cross onto Joy Street and turn left onto Pinckney Street. Here at 5–7 is the George Middleton House of 1797, the first African-American-built home. Middleton led the all-black Bucks of America militia during the Revolutionary War, helped found the African Benevolent Society, and belonged to Prince Hall's African Masonic Lodge.

Beyond, at the junction with Anderson Street, is the Phillips School,

Boston's first integrated school resulting from a state law of 1855 requiring desegregation. The John J. Smith House nearby at 86 was home to a free black abolitionist, who helped fugitive slaves to freedom as part of a system of safe houses known as the Underground Railroad.

Turn left onto Charles Street to find at 70 the former Charles Street Meeting House. Completed in 1807 for the Baptists, its strictly segregated seating spawned the founding in 1836 of the First Free Baptist Church, the country's first integrated church, which built the Tremont Temple at 88 Tremont Street (Downtown).

Return to Pinckney Street and walk north along West Cedar Street to reach the Lewis and Harriet Hayden House at 66 Phillips Street. The owner here

The 54th Massachusetts Regiment Memorial on Beacon Street

was an escaped slave, who also sheltered fugitive slaves on the Underground Railroad. Similar activities occurred at the John Coburn House at number 2.

Now turn right up Irving Street to Myrtle Street, and head east to rejoin Joy Street. Here at 46 is the Abiel Smith School built in 1834 as the first publicly-funded school for black children. Today it is part of Boston's Museum of African American History, which also includes the African Meeting House next door at 8 Smith Court. Opened in 1806, this is America's oldest black Baptist church and the place where from 1832 onwards the first calls for the abolition of slavery were voiced by both black and white activists, including William Lloyd Garrison (1805–1879) and Frederick Douglass (1818–1895). Also here are homes typical for Beacon Hill's black community in the 1800s, including number 3 where William Cooper Nell (1816–1874), one of the country's first black historians, lived.

From 1898 onwards, Boston's African-Americans relocated to the South End and then Roxbury, where black history walking tours today take in Malcolm X, Donna Summer, Louis Farrakhan, and black senator Edward W. Brooke (www.discoverroxbury.org).

Other locations nearby: 28, 30, 31, 32, 42

30 A Library Built by Brahmins

MA 02108 (Beacon Hill), the Boston Athenæum
at 10½ Beacon Street
T Red/Green B/C/D/E Line to Park Street (note: visitors
must leave their bags in lockers at the entrance)

The Boston Athenæum at 10½ Beacon Street (Beacon Hill) is one of the oldest independent libraries in the United States. Built by the Boston Brahmins, the city's Protestant merchant elite, it still retains the air of a private members' club. With subscriptions dwindling recently, the trustees have now opened parts of the first floor to the paying public. The rest of the building is accessible several times a week by appointment as part of a guided tour.

Athenæums were once quite common in the United States but now there are less than a dozen. Named after Athena, the Greek goddess of wisdom, they were established for members to conduct research, read newspapers, and promote learning. The Boston Athenæum was founded in 1807 by members of the Anthology Club, a literary society led by the father of Ralph Waldo Emerson (1803–1882). Their mission was to accumulate great works of literature and science, and to house them in a landmark building adorned with art.

The Boston Athenæum grew rapidly through purchases and donations. In doing so it outgrew several locations before settling in 1849 on Beacon Street. Remarkably the new building was not designed by a renowned architect. Instead the members chose Edward Clarke Cabot (1818–1901), who was an artist as much as an architect. They were impressed by his ingenious use of an arch to span graves in the Old Granary Burying Ground, which lies immediately behind the site (see no. 32). This allowed for floor space above without disturbing the dead below.

Cabot's design was influenced by Italianate designs being deployed in London by English architect Charles Barry (1795–1860). Accordingly the façade, which uniquely for Boston is built of Patterson Sandstone, is neo-Palladian in style. When it opened, the building was three storeys tall. When two further storeys were added in 1913–1915 they were set back so as not to detract from Cabot's original façade.

For nearly 50 years, the Athenæum was the centre of intellectual life in Boston and one of the five largest libraries in America. Today its collections comprise over 600,000 volumes, with around 3,000 new titles added annually. Highlights include the original library of

Inside the Boston Athenæum on Beacon Street

King's Chapel and books from President George Washington's personal library. A fraction of the collection can be found on the first floor in the galleried Henry Long Room, the adjacent Bow Room for new books, and Children's Library. They are shelved alongside significant works of art by the likes of portraitists John Singer Sargent (1856–1925) and Gilbert Stuart (1755–1828), and sculptor Daniel Chester French (1850–1931). More art is displayed in the Norma Jean Calderwood Gallery.

To see the rest of the building visitors should sign up for an Art and Architecture Tour led by an Athenæum expert. The tour includes the basement conservation laboratory, where rare books, maps, and manuscripts are conserved, and the first floor Albert Gordon Newspaper Reading Room. The second floor contains the Reference Department and the Vershbow Special Collections Reading Room (including a first edition of Audubon's *Birds of America* and the memoirs of highwayman James Allen bound in his own skin). Best of all is the magnificent fifth floor Reading Room, with its barrel-vaulted roof and alcoves for silent study.

The term 'Brahmin' was originally coined to describe the highest ranking caste in India. In the United States in the 19th century it was applied to wealthy refined New England families of British Protestant origin, who were influential in the development of American institutions and culture. The self-appointed term underscored their conviction that they were a people apart.

Other locations nearby: 28, 29, 31, 32

31 Relics of the Puritans

MA 02108 (Beacon Hill), Congregational Library & Archives
at 14 Beacon Street
T Red/Green B/C/D/E Line to Park Street (note: the Reading
Room and Pratt Room are open to the public; the Archives
can be visited by appointment only)

Boston's beginnings go back to 1628, when English Puritans settled Charlestown, and then in 1630 moved over to the Shawmut Peninsula. They held sway over the colony for almost a century and are remembered for their asceticism, intolerance of other faiths, and refusal to celebrate Christmas.

By their very nature, the Puritans left few monuments beyond their no-nonsense meeting house, town hall, and burying ground (see no. 38). Anyone wishing to delve deeper should head to the Congregational Library & Archives at 14 Beacon Street (Beacon Hill). Here can be found more intimate relics of the Puritans preserved by their present-day representatives, the Congregationalists, which round out their starchy reputation more equitably.

The Congregational tradition dates back to the 16th century English Reformation, when Protestant reformers sought to create independent local churches free from liturgical ceremony and the hierarchical control of the Church of England. Persecuted for their actions, these 'Puritans' emigrated to New England in the mid-1600s to establish what they called a "godly commonwealth" of locally-governed churches, with dramaticly simple forms of worship. A denomination founded on strong community bonds, Congregationalism continued to influence American notions of social reform long after Puritan hegemony in Boston had waned.

Since 1898, Congregational House has provided a headquarters for the denomination and their various benevolent, missionary, and educational organisations, as well a space for their library and archives. The four marble bas reliefs on the façade illustrate the "lasting ideals" of Congregationalism: *Religious Faith* (the Pilgrim Fathers, the first permanent settlers in New England, observing the Sabbath in 1620), *Law* (the Pilgrims signing the Mayflower Compact, the first governing document of Plymouth, the first colony), *Education* (the founding of Harvard College in 1636), and *Philanthropy* (Puritan missionary John Eliot preaching to Native Americans in Nonantum, now Newton, Massachusetts, in 1642).

Inside Congregational House, on the second floor, is the Congregational Library & Archives (CLA) containing some 225,000 items pertaining to Congregational history. They include rare Puritan works, including a copy of the *Cambridge Platform*, a doctrinal statement for Puritan Congregational churches in Colonial-era New England published in 1649. There are also Colonial-era

Puritan missionary John Eliot preaching at Congregational House

church records, including those of the congregation of the Old South Meeting House gathered in 1669, early sermons, and a missionary Bible written in the Algonquin language.

The Reading Room is superbly appointed, with a high Tiffany-style ceiling, Persian carpet, and large windows overlooking the Old Granary Burying Ground (see no. 32). Above the fireplace hangs a portrait of Cotton Mather (1663–1728), the Puritan minister and pamphleteer, whose *Memorable Providences, Relating to Witchcraft and Possessions* helped foment the infamous Salem Witch trials. His death in 1728 brought an end to Puritan authority in Boston, which had begun under his grandfather, Richard Mather (1596–1669), and been extended under his father, Increase Mather (1639–1723).

The adjoining Pratt Room was once called the Biblearium since it contained a renowned collection of old bibles. Some are still displayed, including several in Native American translations, alongside Puritan relics such as a piece of Plymouth Rock, where the first Pilgrims disembarked the *Mayflower* in 1620, the writing desk used by their leader, William Brewster (1568–1644) in Scrooby, England, and various Biblical relics and missionary souvenirs.

When the majority of Congregational churches merged to form the United Church of Christ in 1957, most of the original occupants of Congregational House moved to new headquarters in New York City and later Cleveland. Since then the CLA has sought to preserve these historic relics of the Puritans and to promote their "lasting ideals" to a modern audience.

Other locations nearby: 28, 29, 30, 32

32 Old Stones and Bones

MA 02108 (Beacon Hill), the Old Granary Burying Ground
on Tremont Street
T Red/Green B/C/D/E Line to Park Street

Boston's three 17th century burying grounds provide a measure of tranquillity for those walking the busy Freedom Trail. The first of them, the King's Chapel Burying Ground, was opened in 1630 on Tremont Street (see no. 38). This was supplemented in 1659 by the Copp's Hill Burying Ground, and a year later by the Old Granary Burying Ground (see no. 12). Also located on Tremont Street, the Old Granary Burying Ground is chock-full of old stones and bones.

Originally a part of Boston Common, the Old Granary Burying Ground was first known as the South Burying Ground (likewise Copp's Hill was initially called the North Burying Ground). Only in 1753 was it renamed after the granary that stood where in 1809 the Park Street Church was built. During a makeover in 1830, trees were planted around the cemetery to soften its appearance, and a decade later an Egyptian Revival gateway was added on Tremont Street (around the same time the gateway's architect, Isaiah Rogers (1800–1869), gave the inside of the Old State House a Greek Revival makeover, including its distinctive spiral staircase).

Today the Old Granary Burying Ground has 2,345 grave markers, although historians estimate that as many as 5,000 people have been buried here. This might explain the mysterious absence of grave markers dating from the first seven years of the cemetery's existence (the oldest, for one John Wakefield, is only dated 1667). It should also be noted that many of the markers have subsequently been rearranged to conform to 19th century notions of order, and to facilitate use of the newly-invented lawnmower. This means that some markers may no longer lie over the remains for which they were intended.

It is no surprise that the Old Burying Ground is the last resting place of many freedom-loving Bostonians. Amongst them are the five people shot by British soldiers in 1770 during the Boston Massacre. Hailed as the first victims of the American Revolution, their grave additionally includes the remains of Christopher Snider, a young boy killed several days earlier during a protest in the North End against British taxation. Also here are notable Patriots from the time of the American Revolutionary War (1775–1783), including Paul Revere (1735–1818) and the lawyer James Otis (1725–1783) (see no. 16). Three of the signees of

the Declaration of Independence in 1776 are buried here, too, namely Samuel Adams (1722–1803), John Hancock (1737–1793), and Robert Treat Paine (1731–1814).

A prominent feature is the granite obelisk honouring the parents of Boston-born polymath and Founding Father, Benjamin Franklin (1706–1790). Erected in 1827, it replaced their original grave markers, which by this time had deteriorated. Franklin himself was born at 1 Milk Street (Downtown), where his bust on a later building marks the spot. He was baptised around the corner in the Old South Meeting House, although his grave is in Philadelphia.

Other notable burials include long-serving Massachusetts Bay Colony Governor John Endecott (c. 1588–1665), the benefactor of Faneuil Hall Peter Faneuil (1700–1743), the first published African-American woman Phillis Wheatley (1753–1784), the first mayor of Boston John Phillips (1770–1823), and the abolitionist Wendell Phillips (1811–1884).

The quirkiest grave is that of Mary Goose (d. 1690), who some claim to have been the Mother Goose of nursery rhyme fame. The Charlestown-born Elizabeth Foster Goose (1665–1758) has been similarly credited although in reality the Mother Goose legend is much older than both of them.

Other locations nearby: 28, 29, 30, 31

33 The Oldest Food and Drink

MA 02108 (Downtown/Financial District), the Union Oyster House at 41 Union Street
T Blue/Orange Line to State or Blue/Green C/D/E Line to Government Center or Green C/E/Orange Line to Haymarket

As America's oldest major city, it's no surprise that Boston is home to some of the country's oldest taverns and restaurants. A venerable example is the Union Oyster House at 41 Union Street. This fine Georgian brick building dates back to 1717 and is one of a clutch of Colonial-era buildings that make up the so-called Blackstone Block (see no. 38). America's oldest continuously-operating restaurant, it has been serving food since 1826, when the craze for oysters hit the country.

Before becoming a restaurant, the building was already renowned. In 1742, when Boston's waterfront lapped at the back door, it was a silk and dress store. In 1771 the country's oldest newspaper, the pro-Patriot *Massachusetts Spy*, was published here, and during the American Revolutionary War (1775–1783) members of the Continental Army were paid here. Later in 1796, the exiled future French King Louis Philippe I (1773–1850) lived upstairs eking out a living teaching French to Boston's fashionable young ladies.

The restaurant's menu today includes lobster, clam chowder, and other New England seafood standards, including whitefish scrod. The semi-circular Oyster Bar installed by the restaurant's first owners is still used and it was here that Massachusetts Senator and Secretary of State, Daniel Webster (1782–1852), daily washed down 36 oysters with a tumbler of brandy. Other celebrity patrons have included John F. Kennedy, who as a congressman dined on mussel stew in an upstairs booth, and Barack Obama, who stopped by for chowder.

It is said that the country's first toothpick was used here. Certainly the first commercially-produced ones were, manufactured by Charles Forster of Maine, who promoted them by hiring Harvard boys to dine at the restaurant and request them. However, it should be said that archaeologists in Florida have discovered 7500-year-old molars of Native Americans that clearly show grooves made using far older toothpicks!

Next door at number 45–55 is the Bell in Hand, Boston's oldest continuously-operating tavern. Opened in 1795 by the city's last town crier (hence the name), its famous ale attracted journalists, politicians, printers, and sailors. A reminder of the area's market heritage, which stretches back to 1743, when produce was sold at Faneuil Hall, is pro-

Shucker Dan Col at the Union Oyster House

vided by the open-air Haymarket active since the 1830s (and open Fridays and Saturdays) at the corner of Blackstone and Hanover Streets, with bronze sculptures of ancient market "garbidge" embedded in the pavement. This was supplemented in 2015 by Boston Public Market at 100 Hanover Street, the country's first market with a local food-only requirement.

Another long-established restaurant is Durgin-Park not far away at 340 North Market Street. In business since 1827, it originally fed sailors and workers at Quincy Market, which was built around the same time (see no. 34). In keeping with its old fashioned status, diners sit at long communal tables and are served by staff trained in a faux surly manner. The menu is famous for its hearty portions of New England fare, including broiled lamb chops, corned beef with cabbage, chicken pot pie, and baked Indian Pudding.

Only a little younger is Jacob Wirth at 31–37 Stuart Street (Chinatown – Leather District), established in 1868 by a German immigrant and still serving hearty European fare in the area's only surviving bowfront Greek Revival row house.

Across the water in Charlestown there is another historic watering hole. The clapboard Warren Tavern at 2 Pleasant Street opened in 1780, five years after the British torched Charlestown during the Battle of Bunker Hill (1775). It is named for Dr. Joseph Warren (1741–1775), who having sent Paul Revere (1734–1818) on his famous midnight ride to Lexington was killed during the fighting (see no. 16). Both Revere and George Washington (1732–1799) drank here in what is today the oldest standing structure in Charlestown.

Other locations nearby: 18, 34, 37, 38

34 The Cradle of Liberty Revealed

MA 02109 (Downtown/Financial District), Faneuil Hall and Faneuil Hall Marketplace on Congress Street
T Blue/Orange Line to State

Although Faneuil Hall Marketplace is the most-visited tourist destination in New England, the area still retains some mystery. How, for example, is the name 'Faneuil' pronounced? When did Faneuil Hall become the 'Cradle of Liberty'? What is hidden in its attic? And why are marine motifs etched on the pavement outside?

The idea of a centralised public market building was first mooted in the early 18th century. Despite Boston being a growing town, however, it was a contentious idea: opponents feared it would mean higher prices and a lack of healthy competition. Thus, when in 1740 merchant Peter Faneuil (1700–1743) offered to finance the construction, the plan was only narrowly appproved.

The son of French Huguenots, who had emigrated to New York to escape persecution, Peter Faneuil relocated to Boston to be with a well-to-do uncle, whose death in 1738 made him one of the town's wealthiest men. It is often forgotten that his business interests included not only fish, molasses, and timber, but also slaves. Bostonians pronounce his French surname either 'Fannel', 'Fanyel' or even 'Fanuel', although in Colonial times it was probably pronounced 'Funnel'.

The building was completed in 1742 to an English market hall design by artist John Smibert (1688–1751), with an open ground floor, where merchants sold their wares, a covered assembly room above, and a grasshopper weathervane on the roof symbolising good fortune. At the time it sat at the water's edge on land created by in-filling the 17th century Town Dock. Although the waterfront has since been moved several roads farther east, the original shoreline is etched on the pavement of Congress Street along with fish, crabs and seaweed.

Faneuil Hall's assembly room quickly became an important part of Boston's civic and social life. Town meetings and public ceremonies were held here, and votes were cast annually for the Massachusetts' legislature, although admission was restricted to property-owning males aged 21 and over. They had no voice in the British Parliament though, so when Faneuil Hall was rebuilt in 1763 following a fire, lawyer James Otis Jr. (1725–1783) dedicated it to the cause of liberty, giving rise to the sobriquet 'Cradle of Liberty'.

Otis spoke again at Faneuil Hall two years later, this time against British taxes, his catch-phrase "Taxation without representation is tyranny" becoming a Patriotic slogan. As tensions increased following the Boston Massacre (1770), access to Faneuil Hall was granted to any man wishing to help in the struggle for independence. By the time of the Boston Tea Party (1773), so many attended meetings that the Old South Meeting House was used instead (see no. 38).

After the Revolutionary War, Faneuil Hall continued in its various role, and in 1806 was expanded by renowned architect Charles Bulfinch (1763–1844), who added a third floor and neo-Classical pilasters to the facade. Boston's continued growth, however, meant that by the 1820s the town meeting and voter system was becoming unwieldy and eventually a separate City Hall was constructed.

Ever-popular Faneuil Hall still holds a few secrets

Faneuil Hall's role as a market was largely replaced in 1826 by the Greek Revival Quincy Market built on land reclaimed from the harbour. As Boston's 'Cradle of Liberty', however, Faneuil Hall continued as a civic space. Its meeting hall has subsequently been used by abolitionists, suffragists, and politicians from Kennedy to Obama, and even today it stirs deep-seated emotions. Every American war from 1812 to Iraq, for example, has been debated here.

Before leaving, don't forget to visit the building's attic, which contains the museum of the Ancient and Honorable Artillery Company of Massachusetts, the oldest military company in the western hemisphere, formed in 1638 to protect the colony against Indian attack.

Other locations nearby: 33, 36, 37, 38

35 Aquaria Old and New

MA 02110 (Downtown/Waterfront), the New England
Aquarium at 1 Central Wharf
Blue Line to Aquarium

The New England Aquarium on Boston's Downtown Waterfront attracts well over a million visitors a year. With a backdrop formed by
Boston Harbor, it enables people to get up close to marine life without
getting their feet wet. With so much to catch their attention, however,
from playful penguins to giant turtles and sharks, it is little wonder
that few visitors realise the aquarium has three forgotten predecessors.

America's first aquarial display opened in 1856, as part of showman
Phineas T. Barnum's American Museum in New York. Barnum had seen
the stir caused by such displays in England and endeavoured to repeat it
in America. Although bankruptcy temporarily halted his ambitions, one
of his partners, Englishman Henry D. Butler (1820–1880), developed
the idea. Author of the country's first book on aquaria, he joined forces
with Boston-based inventor James Ambrose Cutting (1814–1867), and
in 1859 they opened the Boston Aquarial Gardens.

Located at 21 Bromfield Street (Downtown Crossing), the Boston
Aquarial Gardens aimed to educate and entertain the public. According
to *The Boston Post* the small glass aquaria were "filled with rare marine
animals imported and collected exclusively for this establishment…a
perfect and striking illustration of life beneath the waters." In reality
there was nothing more exciting here than a sea anemone but still the
attraction caused a sensation primarily because it was the country's
first freestanding public aquarium.

In 1860 the renamed and expanded Boston Aquarial and Zoological
Gardens relocated to Central Court off Washington Street (today the
site of Macy's). Here a 25 foot-wide tank was constructed and filled
with salt water pumped by steam engine from the harbour. It contained
a 12-foot long Beluga whale caught in the St. Lawrence River, which
was the first cetacean in the world to be held in captivity. Around the
tank were ranged 56 smaller tanks containing eels, trout, haddock, and
shrimp. A zoology department was housed in the basement, where a
grizzly bear, assorted monkeys, and two lions were displayed. An al-
ligator shared a cage with a snapping turtle, and the so-called 'Den of
Serpents' contained pythons and an anaconda. Additionally there was
Barnum-inspired circus fare, including performing animals, "live Africans from their native shores", and fortune tellers.

Sea life at the New England Aquarium

In 1862 a financially-revived Barnum acquired the attraction and renamed it Barnum's Aquarial Gardens. Despite the name, this incarnation relied increasingly on circus entertainment for its success. A Great National Dog Show was staged, for example, and a Baby Show featuring "fine and fancy specimens of infantile humanity". There were also visits by Barnum's American Museum performers, including General Tom Thumb and Commodore Nutt ("two rival pigmies"), the snake-wrestling Madame Lanista, the double-voiced Dora Dawron, and Miss Leone "attired as Venus, in her nautilus shell boat".

Despite such diversification by 1863 visitor numbers had declined. 'Aquarium Mania' was over and there were new attractions in Boston, notably the Public Garden. Barnum closed and removed most of the exhibits to his American Museum in New York, where they were later destroyed in a fire. Another casualty was James Ambrose Cutting, who Barnum had retained to look after the Beluga. Distraught that the Gardens would be converted into an amusement hall, Cutting suffered a breakdown and died in an asylum.

It would be a century before plans were drawn up for the New England Aquarium, which opened on Central Wharf in 1969. Highlights today include the enormous Giant Ocean Tank containing a shark-filled coral reef, the ever-popular penguin and jellyfish exhibits, and a display of playful Harbor Seals on the Front Plaza.

Other locations nearby: 36

36 Once Boston's Tallest

MA 02109 (Downtown/Financial District), the Custom House
Tower at 3 McKinley Square off State Street
T Blue/Orange Line to State

One of Boston's great visual pleasures is its skyline. The city's sky-scrapers, especially when viewed from the water at night, appear every bit as exciting as those of New York and Hong Kong. In amongst all the sleek steel and glass, however, there is a building that really stands out. The Custom House Tower at 3 McKinley Square off State Street (Downtown) is built of carved stone, and for half a century it was the tallest building in Boston.

During Boston's early years, its tallest structures were church stee-ples. The Colonial-era Old North Church, for example, towered over the Old State House (see no. 14). Not until 1893 was the city's first sky-scraper, the 13-storey Ames Building, an office block on Court Street (Downtown), completed for rail tycoon Frederick Ames (1835–1893). At 187 feet high, however, it fell far short of the 236-foot-high spire of the Church of the Covenant built in the 1860s on Newbury Street (Back Bay) (see no. 70). Only in 1915 did the accolade of tallest building pass from a church to the 496-foot-high Custom House Tower.

The story of the tower begins back in 1835, when President An-drew Jackson (1829–1837) authorised construction of a new custom house in Boston, as a symbol of the city's growing maritime prosper-ity. The site chosen was land reclaimed from the harbour in the 1820s for the construction of Quincy Market. The architect was Ammi Burn-ham Young (1798–1874), who as Supervising Architect of the United States Treasury Department was responsible for designing federal gov-ernment buildings. His penchant for Greek Revival and neo-Classical styles lent such buildings grandeur and a sense of permanence.

Completed in 1849, Young's Custom House took the form of a four-sided Greek temple, each side terminated with a Doric portico formed by columns of Quincy granite, and the whole topped with a Roman dome. The entire structure was supported on 3,000 wooden pilings driven down through the reclaimed land to bedrock.

It's worth noting that when it first opened, the Custom House stood where the Long and Central Wharves made landfall allowing custom officials to easily inspect newly-arrived ships and collect maritime du-ties. The waterfront has subsequently been moved eastwards.

By the early years of the 20th century it was clear that increased shipping warranted an expansion of the Custom House. With space at a premium, local architects Peabody & Stearns were commissioned to build upwards and in a style that complemented the original building. The result was the now-famous Custom House Tower, which they designed in a matching Greek Revival style, topped out with a clock and viewing balcony. Although at the time Boston had a height restriction of 125 feet, the Custom House was deemed exempt because it was federally owned. Not until 1964 was it exceeded in height by the 749-foot-high Prudential Tower (see no. 79). Since then it has slipped to 18th place.

The Custom House Tower is now a hotel

In 1986 custom officials relocated to the O'Neill Federal Building in the West End and the Custom House became redundant. It has subsequently been converted into a Marriott hotel, with each floor re-designed to contain up to five suites. Guests and visitors alike can enjoy the splendid rotunda in the original building and the observation deck on the 26th floor, which is open Monday to Thursday at 2pm.

Also on State Street and recalling Boston's maritime importance is the Cunard Building at 126 (its decorative anchors are a reminder that Boston was the North American terminus of the first transatlantic steamship mail service). The Richards Building next door is a former clipper ship company's office.

Other locations nearby: 34, 35, 37

37 A Grand Old Staircase Reused

**MA 02109 (Downtown/Financial District), Exchange Place
at the corner of Congress Street and State Street
T Blue/Orange Line to State**

Prosthetic Architecture is an innovative form of architectural preservation, whereby important elements of an old building are preserved by incorporating them into a new structure built on the same site. A superb example is Exchange Place, a towering 1980s skyscraper at the corner of Congress Street and State Street (Downtown). Incorporated into its contemporary blue glass structure are intriguing fragments of Boston's 19th century Stock Exchange.

The Boston Stock Exchange was built between 1889 and 1891 to a design by local architectural firm Peabody & Stearns (their most famous work is the Custom House Tower in nearby McKinley Square). Rendered in a fusion of Romanesque Revival and Italianate Palazzo style, it was eleven storeys high, stretched 170 feet along State Street, and was faced with pink granite. One of the largest business premises in America at the time, it offered traders and brokers (as well as tenant office workers on the upper floors) all mod cons, including steam heating, electric lighting, and high speed elevators.

None of this deterred developers a century later from demolishing much of the old Exchange and replacing it with a 510-foot-high tower containing a million square feet of lucrative new office space. Boston's preservationists were up in arms and fought valiantly to stave off the wrecker's ball. Although they were unable to preserve the entire building they did manage to save the original façade on State Street.

The result is a brilliant piece of Prosthetic Architecture. From a distance the modern tower dominates the scene but walk along State Street and the 19th century façade remains unaltered. The former main entrance at number 53 remains just as it was, flanked by a pair of ornate lanterns, with the new 40-storey tower set back far enough so as not to detract from it.

The entrance would originally have given access to an impressive foyer, which in 1891 was described as "the tallest and largest" in New England. Today it opens instead onto a five-storey atrium that effectively unifies the old and the new structures, known collectively as Exchange Place.

Here can be found a second example of Prosthetic Architecture and another triumph for the preservationists. Best seen through the

This staircase at Exchange Place has a story to tell

glitzy new glass entrance on Congress Street is a grand white marble staircase. As part of the Exchange it would have given access to brokers' offices on the second floor, and to a gallery overlooking the vast 115-foot-long trading room, with its Corinthian columns supporting a 35-foot-high coffered ceiling. According to a Boston guidebook written at the time, the trading room "affords very exciting scenes when the stock market is agitated".

In 1984, when this part of the Exchange was demolished to make way for the tower, the staircase was taken apart and stored. It was then rebuilt in the new atrium in exactly the same position it had occupied in 1891. The only difference is that today it leads to the offices of the *Boston Globe* newspaper, which relocated here in 2017. It is an intriguing piece of architecture, especially at night when the atrium is lit, causing passers-by to stop and wonder how such an old fashioned staircase ended up in such a sleek and modern tower block.

Before the Stock Exchange was built, 53 State Street was the site of the Bunch of Grapes Tavern. Founded in 1713, it was a popular meeting place in the years prior to the American Revolution for the anti-British Sons of Liberty, and in 1733 housed the country's first Masonic Lodge (see no. 44).

Other locations nearby: 33, 34, 36, 38

38 Crooked Streets and Skyscrapers

MA 02109 (Downtown/Financial District), a tour
of Colonial-era sites including the Old State House
at 206 Washington Street
T Blue/Orange Line to State

Boston's Downtown embraces both the city's modern and historic hearts. It comprises tower blocks and 18th century buildings, built on a tangle of crooked Colonial-era streets and cowpaths. The result is a modern metropolis on a human scale.

It's an oft-told tale how England's Puritans sought religious freedom in the New World. In the case of Boston, many hailed from a town in Lincolnshire of the same name (most likely a contraction of 'St. Botolph's Town'). Encouraged by their vicar, John Cotton (1585–1652), they crossed the Atlantic to New England to help found the Massachusetts Bay Colony.

The colonists arrived in Charlestown in the 1620s but frustrated by a lack of drinking water relocated in 1630 to the Shawmut Peninsula (see nos. 1, 8, 45). They landed on what is now Commercial Street in the North End, then headed south across a tidal creek (today's Creek Square) to reach the main body of the peninsula. Here they found a defensible spot – the peninsula was at the time separated from the mainland by Boston Neck – with a dependable source of drinking water recalled by Spring Lane. On September 7th they named their new settlement 'Boston'.

For the next century the Puritans held sway in Boston, enjoying considerable autonomy from England, whilst developing a major maritime centre (see no. 31). Their original village, with its church, market, prison, burying ground and governor's house, occupied roughly the area enclosed by Tremont, School, Washington, and Court Streets.

This tour of Colonial-era remains begins with the King's Chapel Burying Ground at 58 Tremont Street. Boston's first cemetery, it opened in 1630. Governor of the Massachusetts Bay Colony, John Winthrop (1587–1649), is buried here, as is Mary Chilton (1607–1679), the first European woman to step ashore in 1620. King's Chapel at the corner with School Street was completed in 1754, the pillared portico added in 1789, when the building became the country's first Unitarian church (see no. 27). The sturdy belfry contains Boston's biggest bell cast by the Patriot Paul Revere (1735–1818) (see no. 16).

Walk along School Street passing the Old City Hall (1865–1969), where a pavement mosaic recalls Boston Latin School, America's first public school founded in 1635. At the corner with Washington Street is the gambrel-roofed former Old Corner Bookstore, Boston's oldest commercial building dating from 1718. In 1828 it became a bookshop, literary salon, and publishing house, where *Walden*, *The Scarlet Letter*, and *Uncle Tom's Cabin* were all published (it today contains a restaurant).

Across Washington Street is the Old South Meeting House. Completed in 1729, it is Boston's second oldest church and is where the Boston Tea Party was triggerered (see nos. 39, 42). From here

The Old State House is today surrounded by tower blocks

follow the Freedom Trail up Washington Street to reach the Old State House. Built in 1713 as a replacement for the First Town-House (1657), which had been Boston's first purpose-built town hall and the Colonial seat of government, this is today Boston's oldest public building. After the Declaration of Independence (1776), which was first proclaimed publicly here, it became the seat of state government. It remained as such until 1798, when it was replaced by the Massachusetts State House (see no. 28). Today it contains a museum.

The Freedom Trail continues north from here to Faneuil Hall, which once overlooked the Colonial-era docks (the coastline of 1630 is inscribed on the pavement). Beyond nearby North Street follow Union Street to reach the Blackstone Block, a maze of sett-paved alleys lined with brick buildings from the early 18th century. Remarkably this is the oldest extant city block in all America (see no. 33).

Other locations nearby: 33, 34, 36, 37

39 A World Famous Tea Party

MA 02210 (Downtown/Waterfront), the wall plaque commemorating the Boston Tea Party outside Independence Wharf at 470 Atlantic Avenue
T Silver Line 1, 2 to Courthouse or Red Line to South Station

Period-dressed actors recreate the Boston Tea Party

An interesting example of the landfill projects that have reshaped Boston's shoreline can be found outside Independence Wharf at 470 Atlantic Avenue (Downtown). Where the Evelyn Moakley Bridge makes landfall, a modest wall plaque informs passers-by that Griffins Wharf once stood here, where in 1773 the Boston Tea Party took place. In actual fact, the wharf was located 500 feet farther inland, the intervening area having since been reclaimed from the sea using material quarried from nearby Fort Hill.

Any retelling of the Boston Tea Party story should begin with the British East India Company. Created by Royal Charter in 1660, it once accounted for half the world's trade. Its influence on the American Colonies was considerable: the Company's London chapel, for example, set the pattern for New England churches; its flag inspired the Stars & Stripes; and its profits enabled Company President Elihu Yale (1649–1721) to found the university that bears his name.

The Company also precipitated the Boston Tea Party. Tea had been popular on the north-east coast of America since the 1650s but most of it was smuggled. By the 1770s the East India Company's rapid expansion elsewhere in the world had burdened it with huge running costs. One way to reduce these was to persuade the British government to pass the Tea Act of 1773, which enabled the Company to sell tea in America with a tax of three pence a pound.

As the ships carrying the first consignment of tea approached Boston, emotions in the town were already running high. Memories of the Boston Massacre (1770), when British troops opened fire on anti-British protesters, were still fresh (see no. 32). And they were kept that way by the Sons of Liberty, a Patriotic society that fought for the rights of colonists and opposed British taxation, which had commenced with the Molasses Act of 1764.

Public meetings were held at Faneuil Hall and the Old South Meeting House, where it was resolved that the tea would not be allowed to land. The first ship, *Dartmouth*, berthed at Griffins Wharf on November 28th, followed soon after by *Eleanor* and *Beaver*. By law, the *Dartmouth* should have unloaded within 20 days but the deadline passed with the tea still on board. Since Loyalist Governor Thomas Hutchinson (1711–1780) refused to allow the tea to return to England, an impasse ensued. Back at the Old South Meeting House, Patriot Samuel Adams (1722–1803) famously remarked that "This meeting can do nothing more to save the country".

It is likely that Adams' words were a secret signal to the Sons of Liberty to march down to Griffins Wharf and board the ships. Many others from the meeting followed and together they tossed 342 chests of tea into Boston Harbor. Except for the loss of a lot of tea (worth an estimated one million dollars in today's money) the crisis ended bloodlessly. For the British, however, it was a clear sign that revolution was afoot in the colonies. The bloody skirmishes at Lexington and Concord two years later, followed by the Battle of Bunker Hill, heralded the start of the American Revolutionary War (1775–1783) (see no. 4).

Modern day Patriots can throw replica tea chests into Boston Harbor at the Tea Party Ships and Museum, a floating attraction on Congress Street Bridge (an original tea chest is also on display). A re-enactment of the Tea Party takes place annually on December 16th, when the public join period-dressed actors as they march from the Old South Meeting House down to the water.

Other locations nearby: 40, 52, 53

40 From Expressway to Greenway

MA 02210 (Downtown/Waterfront), a walk along the Rose Fitzgerald Kennedy Greenway starting at the Fort Point Channel Parks on Congress Street
T Red Line to South Station

The North End in Colonial times was a promontory separated from the rest of the Shawmut Peninsula by a narrow tidal creek. Landfill projects during the 19th century ended the neighbourhood's isolation but in 1954 it was separated once again, when the elevated John F. Fitzgerald Expressway sliced through the area. Loathed by drivers and residents alike, this was replaced in 2003 by the 10 lane, 7.5-mile long O'Neill Tunnel. With the North End reconnected to Boston's Downtown, the land where the Expressway once ran has subsequently been transformed into a belt of parks called the Rose Fitzgerald Kennedy Greenway.

The ten-year project to shift the Expressway underground was known as the Big Dig. At the time it was the largest and most expensive urban building project in American history. Despite running wildy over budget and causing chaos in an already chaotic part of the city, most Bostonians are happy with the result. And they are equally happy with the 300 square acres of landscaped parks that now make up the Greenway.

This walk begins at the corner of Congress Street and Atlantic Avenue (although two parks can be found south of here, namely Dewey Square Park, which features a twice-weekly farmers' market, and Chinatown Park, with its waterfall and bamboo-style sculptures). Running north from Congress Street are the Fort Point Channel Parks. Planted in 2008 by the Massachusetts Horticultural Society, their alternative name of the New American Gardens reflects the New England species planted here. At Oliver Street note the dilapidated Northern Avenue Bridge on the right-hand side. Opened in 1908, this truss-built swing bridge once serviced the South Boston Waterfront and is currently awaiting replacement.

Beyond Oliver Street are the Wharf District Parks, so named because they front the Rowes, India, Central, and Long Wharves, part of Boston's redeveloped Waterfront. With their lawns and paved areas, these parks are designed with social gatherings in mind. Popular architectural features here include the *Harbor Fog* water sculpture at High Street, the Rings Fountain with sculptures by Ai Weiwei and the Mother's Walk around Milk Street, and, beyond State Street, the Harbor Islands Pavilion and Greenway Carousel, the latter featuring New England wildlife instead of horses.

Between the carousel and the harbour is Christopher Columbus Park, which contains the Rose Kennedy Rose Garden, a reminder that the Greenway is named after the daughter of Boston's first Irish-American mayor, John F. Fitzgerald (1863–1950), and the mother of President John F. Kennedy (1917–1963) (see no. 15). The park's creation and the preservation of the

Harbor Fog on the Rose Fitzgerald Kennedy Greenway

old waterfront warehouses hereabouts was lobbied for by prominent North End councillor and preservationist, Fred Langone (1922–2001).

The Greenway continues beyond the Carousel with the Armenian Heritage Park. Dedicated to the victims of the Armenian genocide, its abstract sculpture and labyrinth represent the immigrant experience.

This walk finishes with the North End Parks, which consist of several European-style gardens flanking the west side of the neighbourhood. The shallow canal recalls the water that isolated the North End in the 17th century.

Running along the Waterfront, parallel to the Wharf District Parks, is a section of the HarborWalk. When completed this 47-mile long shoreline path will run from Dorchester all the way to East Boston taking in countless recreational, cultural, and historic attractions along the way. It will also connect to inland walks, including the Walk to the Sea from the State House, the South Bay Harbor Trail from Roxbury, and the Neponset and East Boston Greenways.

Other locations nearby: 39

41 Boston for Bookworms

MA 02111 (Downtown/Downtown Crossing), a bookshop tour
beginning with the Brattle Book Shop at 9 West Street
T Green B/C/D/E Line to Boylston or Orange Line to Chinatown
or Red/Orange Line to Downtown Crossing

New York is regarded as America's literary heart – but it wasn't always so. During the 19th century Boston held that accolade, with authors such as Ralph Waldo Emerson (1803–1882) spearheading the free-thinking Transcendentalist movement, and *Uncle Tom's Cabin* by Harriet Beecher Stowe (1811–1896) turning the nation against slavery. Their legacy still resonates in the city's literary landscape today.

This tour of Boston's present-day bookshops begins with the venerable Brattle Book Shop at 9 West Street (Downtown). One of America's oldest and largest secondhand and antiquarian bookshops, it was founded as Burnham's Antique Book Store in 1825 on Cornhill (see no. 68). Writers including Emerson gravitated here, and the abolitionist J.J. Jewitt published the first edition of *Uncle Tom's Cabin* nearby. Remarkably the shop has been in the hands of the same family since 1949. They carry an impressive general stock of 250,000 titles spread over two floors, with a third floor for rarities and an adjacent outside lot for bargains. Their service is supplemented several streets north by another fine secondhand bookshop. Commonwealth Books at 9 Spring Lane is everything a good secondhand bookshop should be, with well-stocked shelves arranged in a series of cosily-appointed departments, a rare books area, and even a working fireplace.

Down in the South End are two very different types of bookshop. Ars Libri at 500 Harrison Avenue is located in the SOWA Art District and prides itself on holding the country's largest stock of rare and out-of-print books on art and architecture (see no. 64). The More Than Words Warehouse Bookstore around the corner at 242 East Berkeley Street is a non-profit social enterprise that employs young people struggling to get a start in life.

Over in Back Bay at 338 Newbury Street is Trident Booksellers. Noteworthy for being the largest of Boston's independents, it survives thanks in part to its magazine department, free wi-fi, and superb café. The competition is stiff though as witnessed by the branch of book behemoth Barnes & Noble not far away at 800 Boylston Street (another branch at 660 Beacon Street (Fenway–Kenmore) features the landmark neon *Citgo* oil sign on its roof). Also in Back Bay is Bromer Booksellers

Giant book covers hide storerooms at the Brattle Book Shop

at 607 Boylston Street, which specialises in antiquarian first editions, fine bindings, and miniature books.

Neighbouring Cambridge has long enjoyed a healthy bookshop culture thanks to the presence of Harvard and MIT, although even here several have recently fallen victim to rising rents and digital technology. Those left include the Harvard Book Store at 1256 Massachusetts Avenue. Opened in 1932 and facing Harvard Yard, it offers new and used titles, Harvard gear, and a print-on-demand service. More textbooks are available at the Harvard Coop Society at 1400 Massachusetts Avenue, founded by students in 1882, and Raven Used Books at 23 Church Street. A little farther out is the Bryn Mawr Book Store at 373 Huron Avenue, which funds scholarships with profits from its secondhand sales. And don't overlook the cheerfully-independent Porter Square Books at 25 White Street.

Cambridge's specialist bookshops include the Grolier Poetry Bookshop founded in 1927 at 6 Plympton Street, a tiny shop with an international reputation. There is also the MIT Press Bookstore at 301 Massachusetts Avenue for everything scientific, Ward Maps at 1735 Massachusetts Avenue for antique cartography, and several comic stores including Million Year Picnic at 99 Mount Auburn Street, Newbury Comics at 100 CambridgeSide Place, and New England Comics at 14A Eliot Street.

This tour finishes with the Boston Book Company, a splendid antiquarian shop at 705 Centre Street (Jamaica Plain), and the Lucy Parsons Center, a collectively-run Leftist bookshop at 358A on the same street.

Other locations nearby: 42, 43, 44, 45

42 Follow the Red-Brick Road

MA 02111 (Downtown/Boston Common), the Freedom Trail
beginning on Boston Common at the junction of Tremont
and West Streets
T Red/Green B/C/D/E Line to Park Street or Red/Orange
Line to Downtown Crossing

The idea for Boston's hugely popular Freedom Trail, which links a selection of the city's remarkable historic sites, was conceived in 1951 by local journalist Bill Schofield and historian Bob Winn. Within a few years thousands were walking it, prompting local businessman Dick Berenson to suggest it be marked permanently by means of a red-brick (or sometimes red paint) line. Since then annual footfall along the Freedom Trail has risen into the millions.

The Trail winds for 2.5 miles between Boston Common and the Bunker Hill Monument in Charlestown taking in the 16 locations listed briefly here (free maps giving more detail can be picked up from the Boston Common Visitor Center at 139 Tremont Street, where the Trail begins):

1) Boston Common is where in 1625 the first white settler, William Blaxton (1595–1675), established a farm before selling out to the Massachusetts Bay Colony (see no. 45).

2) Up on Beacon Street is the gold-domed Massachusetts State House embodying the country's ebullient mood following the Declaration of Independence (see no. 28).

3) Park Street Church is the first of several sites *not* associated with the Revolutionary War and is where William Lloyd Garrison (1805–1879) called for the nationwide abolition of slavery.

4) The Granary Burying Ground around the corner on Tremont Street is packed with Patriotic Bostonians, including Paul Revere (1735–1818) (see no. 32).

5) The nearby King's Burying Ground is the city's oldest and was used together with the King's Chapel by Boston's Loyalist population (see no. 38).

6) Outside the Old City Hall on School Street, the third of Boston's four City Halls, is a statue of Founding Father Benjamin Franklin (1706–1790), and a mosaic recalling America's first public school (see no. 38).

7) The former Old Corner Bookstore is another non-Revolutionary site and was once the epicentre of Boston's literary life (see no. 38).

8) The Old South Meeting House on Washington Street is where Patriots triggered the Boston Tea Party (see no. 39).

9) The Old State House on State Street was the seat of British Colonial-era government, and of state government after 1776 (see no. 38).

10) The site of the Boston Massacre (1770), when British troops fired on tax protesters, is marked in the pavement outside the Old State House (see no. 32).

11) Faneuil Hall, known as the Cradle of Liberty, is a highlight of the North End and is where Patriots gathered in protest against British taxation (see no. 43).

12) A remarkable survival is Paul Revere's house in North Square (see no. 16).

The Old South Meeting House on the Freedom Trail

13) It was Revere who arranged for the famous lantern signal from the steeple of the Old North Church on Salem Street alerting Patriots in Charlestown that the British were coming (see no. 14).

14) The man who hung the lanterns is buried in Copp's Hill Burying Ground, as is the owner of the shipyard where the venerable USS *Constitution* was built (see no. 12).

15) She is moored across the Charles River in the Charlestown Navy Yard having survived numerous British broadsides (see no. 3).

16) The Trail finishes at the Bunker Hill Monument, where the Patriots overcame defeat and eventually secured independence (see no. 4).

The Freedom Trail omits some Colonial-era sites for logistical reasons. In Downtown these include a wall plaque at 24 Winter Street marking the home of Patriot and statesman Samuel Adams (1722–1803). Additionly there are markers at Washington and Boylston Streets identifying the Liberty Tree, where the Sons of Liberty planned their anti-British activities, and a plaque at 470 Atlantic Avenue recalling the Boston Tea Party (see no. 39).

Other locations nearby: 29, 41, 43, 44

43 The Earliest Subway System

MA 02108 (Downtown/Theater District), the Tremont Street
Subway at Boylston Station
T Green Line B, C, D, E to Boylston

There is a photo from the early 1890s showing a steam train on Tremont Street. Belching out smoke, it is running along an elevated railway, with Park Street Church and the Old Granary Burying Ground to one side. Fortunately the photo is a fabrication created by those opposed to such an insensitive plan. It was clearly a successful piece of propaganda because the problem of reducing traffic on busy Tremont Street was solved instead by building America's first subway.

Congestion in Boston was inevitable following the introduction in 1853 of the horse-drawn streetcar. Within a few years lines built by competing companies were snaking their way across the city. Only in 1885 were they all consolidated under one company, the West End Street Railway, which rolled out the first electric streetcar in 1889, powered by a generating station at 540 Harrison Avenue (South End). It was the congestion caused by these vehicles (on a street already busy with wagons and pedestrians) that created the need for a subway.

Opened on September 1st 1897, the Tremont Street Subway is the world's third oldest rapid transit tunnel after London (1890) and Budapest (1896). A so-called 'cut-and-cover' construction, it originally served five closely-spaced stations – Boylston, Park Street, Scollay Square, Adams Square, and Haymarket – and was accessed through portals in the Public Garden, Canal Street, and Pleasant Street. The portals and the three northernmost stations were all subsequently swept away as the system (and the city) developed. What remains of the Subway between Charles Street and Court Street is now preserved as part of the Green Line.

To get a feel for the subway visit the two remaining stations at Boylston and Park Street. Although Park Street has been significantly altered below ground, it still retains its original Classical Revival entrances at pavement level. Boylston does, too, but more importantly its curving platform below ground still follows its original configuration. Another survival from the original Subway is that the Green Line still operates trolleycars powered by overhead wires rather than the more modern cars used on the city's other lines, which draw power from a third rail.

More vestiges of Boston's early streetcar system can be found along the Green Line west of Bolyston. There is the ornate wrought iron entrance at Copley Station, for example, built in 1915, when the Tremont Street Subway was extended along Commonwealth Avenue. Also from this phase of construction is the old Kenmore Square Portal, two stations farther west, which was abandoned in 1932 but never demolished.

Returning to Boylston, there is something else worth looking out for there. Preserved on a disused siding that once ran southwards to the Pleasant Street Portal (now covered over by the Elliot Norton Park) are two vintage streetcars. One of them, Car 5734, was built in 1924 and retired in 1959; the other, Car 3295, dates from 1951 and left service in 1986. Both were constructed for the Boston Elevated Railway, which was another solution to Boston's traffic conges-

A Green Line trolley departs from Boylston Station

tion. Inaugurated in 1901 using West End Street Railway lines, this system remained in service until the 1980s, with the last section demolished in 2004. It is difficult today to imagine that Boston ever had such a thing.

Boston's subway system today is managed by the Massachusetts Bay Transportation Authority (MBTA) and comprises three heavy-use rail lines (Red, Orange, and Blue), one light trolley line (the four-branch Green Line), and one bus line (the four-branch Silver Line). No route operates entirely underground, indeed only 26 out of the system's 133 stations are subterranean.

Other locations nearby: 41, 42, 44, 45

44 The Grand Lodge of Massachusetts

MA 02111 (Downtown/Theater District), the Grand Lodge of
Massachusetts at 186 Tremont Street
T Green Line B, C, D, E to Boylston

Other than all being Americans, what is it that connects George Washington, Davy Crockett, Henry Ford, and John Wayne? The answer is they were all Freemasons. Boston holds the distinction of being home to the Grand Lodge of Massachusetts, the state's governing body of Freemasonry, which is also the oldest in the western hemisphere.

With its ritualised meetings, hand grips, and penchant for symbolism, Freemasonry has always seemed arcane to the unitiated. Admittedly the origins of freemasonry still baffle historians. Some have fancifully suggested a re-emergence of the Knights Templar after their suppression in the 14th century. It seems more likely, however, that it stemmed from groups of European medieval masons working in freestone, who established secretive guilds to protect their skills (bakers, brewers, and other professions formed incorporations for the same reason). Later, with the admission of non-operative members to raise extra funds, they became builders in a philosophical sense and are known today for their charity work and espousal of good working practices.

The origin of Freemasonry in Massachusetts dates back to 1723, when London-born tailor and Freemason Henry Price (1697–1780) arrived in Boston and set up shop. A decade later he was appointed Provincial Grand Master of New England by the Grand Lodge of England, the world's oldest Grand Lodge (1717). This authorised him to constitute his fellow 'Brothers' into Regular Lodges, the first of which was the Grand Lodge of Massachusetts founded on Monday July 30th 1733 in the Bunch of Grapes Tavern on State Street (Downtown).

The Grand Lodge continued to meet at the tavern until 1821, when it leased the second floor of the Old State House. Then in 1830 the first purpose-built Grand Lodge was erected at the corner of Tremont Street and Temple Place. As the fraternity grew, so a larger building was acquired farther down Tremont Street at the junction with Boylston Street. This was destroyed by fire in 1864, as was its replacement in 1895. The present nine-storey building at 186 Tremont Street was constructed in 1899.

For many years it incorporated storefronts facing Tremont Stret.

After these were vacated in 1966, they were filled with mosaics depicting the seal of the Grand Lodge of Massachusetts (the busy beavers representing the industrious nature of the early masons), and motifs harking back to the organisation's origins as stonemasons, notably the set square, which also adorns the door handles, with a letter 'G' for the Great Architect (God).

A masonic set square door handle at the Grand Lodge of Massachusetts

For many years only Freemasons could enter the Grand Lodge. Fortunately in recent times non-members have been admitted as part of a guided tour, which takes in the six halls used by Freemasons for their various meetings and celebrations. Of these the Corinthian Hall is the most elaborately appointed, with its illuminated coffered ceiling and portraits of famous Freemasons. They include first President of the United States George Washington (1732–1799), polymath and Founding Father Benjamin Franklin (1706–1790), Dr. Joseph Warren (1741–1775), who served at the Battle of Bunker Hill, and the Marquess de Lafayette (1757–1834), who fought in the American Revolutionary War (1775–1783). The Gothic Hall is impressive, too, with its theatrically-appointed stage, gold leaf decoration, red carpet, and velvet chairs.

The tour also includes the grave marker of founder Henry Price and sometimes a glimpse of the extensive Masonic research library, with its various items of Masonic memorabilia, including aprons and jewels. A lock of George Washington's hair in a gold urn crafted by famous Boston Freemason, Paul Revere (1735–1818), is currently displayed at the Masonic Museum in Lexington.

Other locations nearby: 41, 43, 45, 46

45 A Stroll across Boston Common

MA 02108 (Downtown/Boston Common), a stroll across
Boston Common beginning at the Central Burying Ground
T Green Line B, C, D, E to Boylston

Boston Common formed part of the Shawmut Peninsula, the original landmass on which Boston was founded in the 1630s. Unlike the rest of the peninsula though, which was subsequently developed, Boston Common remained green. Today the 50-acre park separating Downtown from Beacon Hill is a magnet for those seeking a break from city life.

The Common's origins go back to 1625, when Boston's first white settler, William Blaxton (1595–1675), arrived and began farming here. Having settled with a group of colonists in modern-day Weymouth, Massachusetts two years earlier, he moved here alone when the colony failed. In 1630 John Winthrop (1587–1649) of the Massachusetts Bay Colony settled with a group of settlers in Charlestown but was frustrated by a lack of drinking water (see no. 1). Blaxton took the initiative by luring him across to the Shawmut, where a reliable spring existed. In 1634 Blaxton sold out to the settlers for 30 pounds and moved on.

Earmarked as public land ten years later, the Common's original purpose (according to an inscription outside the Park Street Station) was as a "trayning field" and "for the feeding of cattell". It served as a camp for British troops prior to the American Revolutionary War (1775–1783) and grazing continued here until 1830, when public park status was granted (see no. 16). This makes it the world's oldest.

Other purposes served by Boston Common are encountered if one takes a stroll from Boylston Station. On the left, for example, is the Central Burying Ground, opened in 1756 to alleviate pressure on Boston's earlier cemeteries (see nos. 12, 32, 38). Notable burials include artist Gilbert Stuart (1755–1828), whose portrait of George Washington adorns the dollar bill, Samuel Sprague (1753–1844), who participated in the Boston Tea Party, and British soldiers killed at the Battle of Bunker Hill (see no. 4).

To the right of the station is the Boston Massacre Monument commemorating those shot by Redcoats in 1770 during an anti-British protest (see no. 42). It is a reminder that the Common has long functioned as a place for memorials. A little farther north (beyond the bandstand

The Founder's Memorial records the origin of Boston Common

and a sandwich shop in a converted public convenience) is another: the Soldiers and Sailors Monument on Flagstaff Hill honours troops of the American Civil War (1861–1865). It overlooks the Frog Pond, now devoid of amphibians and used for ice skating.

Embedded in the grass towards Tremont Street is a plaque marking the former site of the Great Elm, which blew down in 1876. This is where the Puritans hung the Quaker Mary Dyer (1611–1660) in 1660 for defying a law banning her faith.

Closer to the Park Street Station is the Brewer Fountain, cast in Paris in the 1860s and gifted to the city by wealthy merchant, Gardner Brewer (1806–1874). The red-brick line in the pavement here is the famous Freedom Trail, which leads up to Beacon Street and a monument honouring the 54th Massachusetts Volunteer Infantry Regiment, the first black company raised in the Civil War (see no. 29).

Walk west now along the Beacon Street perimeter to reach the Founder's Memorial, which commemorates William Blaxton's role in establishing the Common (notice the Native Americans, who according to archaeological finds had been camping on the Common for thousands of years previously). Nearby is a modest stone marker recalling the Oneida Football Club, America's first, which played here during the 1860s. Walk down Charles Street, which separates Boston Common from the Public Garden, to regain the Central Burying Ground (see no. 69).

Other locations nearby: 43, 44, 46

46 The Home of Horror

MA 02116 (Downtown/Theater District), the Edgar Allan Poe
statue in Edgar Allan Poe Square
T Green Line B, C, D, E to Boylston or Arlington

'The Home of Horror' might seem a curious appellation for a relatively peaceful city like Boston. Of course the place has been associated with its share of horrible events from Colonial-era religious persecution to the race riots of the 1970s. But in this case the horrors are literary because Boston is writ large in the lives of two of the greatest horror writers.

The first is Edgar Allan Poe (1809–1849), born Edgar Poe on Carver Street (now Charles Street South) at the edge of Bay Village. As a child he lost both parents and was taken in by a Virginian tobacco merchant, John Allan, whose name he later adopted. Poe's relationship with Allan was never easy though and after a violent quarrel he returned to Boston, where in 1827 his first work *Tamerlane and Other Poems* was published. Although the work received little attention it included the themes of love, death, and pride, which would colour his later works.

Unable to support himself, Poe enlisted in the United States Army and was posted first to Fort Independence in South Boston and then Fort Moultrie in South Carolina (see no. 58). The experiences later inspired two short stories, *The Cask of Amontillado* and *The Gold-Bug*, in which respectively men take revenge by burying another alive, and a cryptogram leads to hidden treasure. They highlight Poe's talent as a master teller of both horror and detective stories.

After leaving the army in 1831, Poe lived with his aunt in Baltimore, where he won a short story competition with *MS. Found in a Bottle*, a harrowing seaman's tale about a ghost ship. As a result he secured a series of editing jobs and in 1836 married his cousin, Virginia Clemms. More short stories followed, including *The Fall of the House of Usher*, *The Raven*, and *The Tell-Tale Heart*. Although Poe's reviews improved his pay didn't and following his wife's early demise he collapsed mentally and died aged just 40.

Poe had a love-hate relationship with Boston and famously branded the city's cliquey Transcendentalists as 'Frogpondians' for their provincial didacticism. This probably explains why only recently a square was named in his honour at the junction of Charles and Boylston Streets (Downtown). It contains the life-sized sculpture *Poe Returning to Boston* showing the author striding away from Boston Common's Frog Pond towards his now-demolished birthplace, accompanied by a raven and a trail of pages spilling from his suitcase.

The other horror writer associated with Boston is H. P. Lovecraft (1890–1937). Born in Providence, Rhode Island, he was a reclusive child plagued by sleep paralysis and obsessed with *Grimm's Fairy Tales* and the stories of Poe. As a freelance journalist his own first short story *The Alchemist*, a dark tale concerning a family curse, was published in 1916.

The Edgar Allan Poe statue features a raven

Shortly after his mother's death in 1921, Lovecraft attended a journalists' convention in Boston, where he met and later married Sonia Greene, a widow and successful milliner. In 1924 they relocated to New York, where Lovecraft began writing stories such as *The Horror at Red Rock* and *The Call of Cthulhu* for the pulp magazine *Weird Tales*. Another story was *Pickman's Model*, an unnerving tale about something nasty in the cellar of a missing artist, which uses Boston's North End as its backdrop. Even the Boylston Street Subway gets a mention as being where "vile things were clambering up from some unknown catacomb through a crack in the floor"!

When Lovecraft's wife's business collapsed in 1926 and she sought work elsewhere, he returned permanently to Providence. He continued writing there but died young and in poverty.

Other locations nearby: 44, 45, 47, 69

47 A Theatre District Reborn

MA 02116 (Downtown/Theater District), a tour of
historic theatres beginning with the Colonial Theatre
at 106 Boylston Street
T Green Line B, C, D, E to Boylston

Centred on Boylston, Tremont and lower Washington Streets, Boston's
Theater District boasted some 40 playhouses during the 1920s. Inevitably the arrival of film saw many converted to cinemas and most were
eventually demolished. Fortunately half a dozen stayed in business
long enough to experience a renaissance. With their fabric now restored to former magnificence, they make an interesting thematic tour.

There were no theatres in Colonial-era Boston since the Puritans
banned such frivolity. Even after the American Revolutionary War
(1775–1783) this ingrained aversion meant that when Boston's first
theatre did open in 1793 it had to be called a "School of Virtue"! Indeed up until the mid-20th century, Boston's censors forbade performances that didn't meet their standards, hence the oft-heard expression "Banned in Boston". Despite this, Boston eventually became the
testing ground for Broadway-bound shows, premiering soon-to-be hits
such as *South Pacific, Oklahoma!*, *Porgy and Bess*, and *The King and I*.

This tour starts with the Colonial Theatre at 106 Boylston Street.
Opened in 1900 and incorporating sumptuous gilded decoration and
trompe l'oeil ceilings, its first production was *Ben-Hur*, which included
eight live horses for the famous chariot scene. Restored by Emerson
College, a communications and arts school, it is the city's oldest continuously-operating playhouse. Farther along Boylston Street at 162 is
a handsome building from the 1890s in the basement of which is Steinert Hall, a theatre abandoned in 1942 because of fire code restrictions.
Plans are afoot to reopen this long-forgotten space.

From here head south down Tremont Street to reach the Cutler Majestic Theatre at 219. Emerson College was also instrumental in restoring this 1903 *Beaux Arts* building, which features an auditorium with
a soaring red-and-gold Rococo ceiling. Further down Tremont at 246
is the Wilbur Theatre, which opened in 1914 and was the first theatre
to take inspiration from American Colonial-era architecture rather than
European styles. *A Streetcar Named Desire* starring Marlon Brando and
Jessica Tandy premiered here before moving onto Broadway.

Next door is the Boch Center Wang Theatre at 270 Tremont Street.
Opened as the Metropolitan Theatre in 1925, it has seats for over

The Boch Center Wang Theatre has a magnificent interior

3,600 people making it the largest theatre in New England. The jaw-dropping auditorium features gilded and sculpted arches reaching upwards past murals to a huge illuminated oculus. Its name honours both the wealthy Boch family that sponsors the theatre, and An Wang (1920–1990), a Chinese-American computer expert, who in the 1980s financed its restoration. Directly opposite at 265 is the Shubert Theatre, known as the 'Little Princess' for its white-and-gold interior dating from 1910.

Walk back up Tremont to Stuart Street, turning right to join Washington Street and head north to the Paramount Theatre at 559. This glitzy *Art Deco* theatre built in 1932 became an adult cinema in the 1970s, when the neighbourhood took a downturn, but was restored in 2010 as part of the revived Ladder District (the two main thoroughfares and side streets here resemble a ladder). The arched building at 545 once housed the Bijou Theatre, another victim of changing fire regulations, and beyond at 539 is the Boston Opera House, housed inside the lavish former B. F. Keith Memorial Theatre cinema built in 1928. This is where the Boston Ballet annually performs *The Nutcracker*, the world's most attended ballet production.

This tour finishes two doors further along with the Modern Theatre at 525, opened originally in 1876, converted later into a cinema (where Boston's first sound film, *The Jazz Singer*, was screened in 1928), and then reworked in 2010 as a combined theatre and hall of residence for Suffolk University.

Other locations nearby: 44, 45, 66, 69

48 The Only New England Chinatown

MA 02111 (Chinatown–Leather District), a walk through
Chinatown beginning at the Chinatown Gate at the junction
of Beach Street and Surface Road
T Green B/C/D/E Line to Boylston Street or Orange Line
to Chinatown or Red/Silver 1/2/4 Lines to South Station

Boston's Chinatown is a compact neighbourhood wedged into a dozen
city blocks between Downtown and the South End. What it lacks in
size, it makes up for in sheer energy. By day shopkeepers sell all manner of produce from live poultry to Mooncakes; by night restaurants
come alive with locals and visitors.

The demise of Chinatowns in Portland and Providence means that
Boston's is the only historic ethnic Chinese neighbourhood in New
England. All three were established by Chinese workers brought from
the West coast in the early 1870s to break a shoe factory strike in North
Adams, Massachusetts. Those staying on in Boston were drawn to a
reclaimed tidal flat, the former South Cove, where housing was cheap
(see no. 50). By 1875 they had established a niche for themselves in
garment manufacturing and laundering.

Chinatown today is a different place. During the 1990s, rising rents
and property sales brought about the demise of the garment trade. Although the majority of the population remains Asian-American (supplemented by Thais and Vietnamese), there is a fear that an influx of
non-Asian residents will bring gentrification. It is hoped that affordable housing projects will safeguard Chinatown's authenticity.

This walk begins at the junction of Beach Street and Surface Road
at the traditional Chinese gate (Paifang), where clusters of older residents gather to play Chinese chess. Gifted by the Taiwanese government in 1982, it carries a saying attributed to Sun Yat-sen: "All under
Heaven for the common good". Immediately on the right is narrow
Ping On Street, where the first Chinese immigrants settled.

Beach Street, a reminder of the neighbourhood's watery origins,
and the side streets branching off it are today a focus for Asian cuisine.
First turn left onto Hudson Street and visit the Happy Family Food
Market at number 11. The basement here is full of gurgling tanks con-
taining lobsters, crabs, and eels, all of which are sold live. Back up on
Beach Street at 67 is Hing Shing Pastry, the place for seed and nut-filled

Mooncakes (Ruby Foo's Den, Boston's first Chinese restaurant for non-Chinese customers, opened near here in 1929). Farther along at 60 is China King, renowned for its homemade Udon Chow Mein and Egg Foo Young, and at 48 is Wings Live Poultry selling chickens and ducks.

Continue to Harrison Avenue, once lined with clothing factories and laundries (a mural inside the Boston Chinese Neighbourhood Center at 38 Ash Street depicts a female garment worker). On the right at 36 is the Eldo Cake House selling pork buns and crushed pineapple rolls. On the left at 75 is Nam Bac Hong Chinese Herbs, where traditional remedies are dispensed from old wooden drawers. During the summer people queue outside New Dongh Khanh at 81 for tapioca-infused bubble tea. Back on Beach Street, Van's Fabrics at 14 is the last remnant of Chinatown's garment trade.

Chinese chess is a popular pastime in Boston's Chinatown

This walk finishes at the far end of Beach Street with the Empire Garden at 690 Washington Street. This traditional Dim Sum restaurant, which offers taro root dumplings from carts wheeled around the room, is housed inside the magnificent former Globe Theatre built in 1903.

Chinatown is at its most lively during Chinese New Year (usually late January) and the August Moon Festival, when the streets are alive with parading dragons and firecrackers. A Dragon Boat Festival is staged each June on the Charles River.

A modest wall plaque at the junction of Beach Street and Tyler Street marks where in 1761 eight-year old Phillis Wheatley (1753–1784) arrived on a slave ship. She was purchased by the Wheatley family and eventually became the first published African-American woman.

Other locations nearby: 49, 50

49 Last of the Old Fashioned Diners

MA 02111 (Chinatown–Leather District), the South Street
Diner at 178 Kneeland Street
T Red/Silver Line 1, 2 & 4 to South Station

There was a time when the classic American diner was the country's most popular 24-hour eating establishment. With its prefabricated architecture, affordable menu, and homely atmosphere, it attracted a broad audience from families and factory workers to barflies and lonely hearts. Despite giving way to fast food restaurants in the 1970s, those remaining have become icons of Americana.

The first diners in the 1870s were little more than horse-drawn wagons serving lunch to shift workers. Commercial production of seated wagons commenced in Worcester, Massachusetts in 1887. As demand for seats increased so wagons gave way to prefabricated structures, which were long and narrow to facilitate delivery by truck or train. Ease of construction and affordability meant that most were owner operated.

The South Street Diner at 178 Kneeland Street (Chinatown–Leather District) is Boston's only example. It was made in 1947 at the Worcester Lunch Car Company (WLCC), one of several manufacturers established to supply diners to industrialised cities on the eastern seaboard. The company shipped over 650 diners from 1906 until its closure in 1957.

WLCC diners were the first to be patented and the South Street Diner displays many original features, including a barrel-shaped roof and steel-framed enamel exterior panels. Inside there is a row of dining booths each furnished with leather banquettes, and running parallel across a tiled floor is a service counter lined with stools. The 25 cent children's pony ride on the pavement outside adds to the nostalgic feel.

The food and drink at the South Street Diner might as well have been patented too because it also follows a strict code: all-day breakfasts, steak and eggs, hamburgers, clubs and subs, apple pie, coffee, and 50s-style malted shakes. The clientele is really the only thing that's changed. Labourers and factory workers have been supplanted by families, tourists, and office staff from the converted former warehouses of the neighbouring Leather District (see no. 50). After hours the audience changes to students and clubgoers winding their way home.

The South Street Diner is a piece of vintage Americana

Not surpisingly the South Street Diner has attracted its share of celebrity guests, including actors Christopher Walken and Morgan Freeman, and rock singers Neil Young and Robert Plant. It has also featured in the film *21* (2008) and an issue of DC Comics' *Batgirl*. A particularly busy day is St. Patrick's Day, when the diner offers a Corned Beef, Cabbage and Guinness special!

Fans of WLCC diners will have to travel outside Boston to find further examples. The Deluxe Town Diner in Watertown, for example, was built the same year as the South Street Diner and looks much the same. The Rosebud Diner in Somerville is older and features a distinctive shovel nose and the Gothic script used originally by the company to render all their diners' names. The Salem Diner is different again being a rare example of a *Sterling Streamliner* built in the early 1940s by the J. B. Judkins Company to mimic the high speed *Burlington Zephyr* passenger train.

Although original diners are now an endangered species, there are numerous modern Boston diners that deliberately offer an old school vibe. They include Mul's Diner at 80 West Broadway (South Boston), where locals meet for blueberry pancakes, Mike's City Diner at 1714 Washington Street (South End), famous for its weekday roast turkeys, and the Galley Diner at 11 P Street (South End), which according to chef and fast food aficionado Anthony Bourdain serves the best corned beef hash and eggs in town!

Other locations nearby: 48, 50

50 The Leather District Preserved

MA 02111 (Chinatown–Leather District), a walk along
South Street in the Leather District
T Red/Silver Line 1, 2 & 4 to South Station

The Leather District is a neighbourhood that speaks eloquently of Boston's shifting demographics. Tightly defined by Essex Street, Atlantic Avenue, Kneeland Street, and Lincoln Street, it was originally developed in the early 19th century as a residential area. Later it became the centre of Boston's leather trade and is now home to offices, restaurants and stylish lofts. That there are no conventional visitor attractions here makes the neighbourhood all the more intriguing.

Like neighbouring Chinatown, the Leather District was once part of an area of tidal flats called South Cove (see no. 48). During the 18th century wharves were built out from the original shoreline here towards the deep water of the Fort Point Channel. The area's proximity to Boston's business district and harbour inevitably made it a target for further development and between 1806 and 1843 the area was drained and a terminal built for the new Boston and Worcester Railroad. The planned commercial development, however, was curtailed by the crash of 1837, and instead low-cost row housing was built for immigrants. The expendable nature of these homes facilitated the redevelopment of the area in the 1880s as the Leather District.

The boot and shoe industry had been a New England staple since Colonial times. When British trade restrictions in the early 19th century plunged the port of Boston into recession, manufacturing was centralised in shoe towns such as North Adams, Massachusetts. Buyers from these towns came to Boston to buy and sell, and by 1830 several had opened their own premises in the North End. The need for more space forced them southwards, first to Pearl Street (Downtown) and then, after the Great Boston Fire of 1872, to the area now known as the Leather District.

The neighbourhood is best appreciated on South Street, where it is immediately apparent why this is considered Boston's most intact and homogenous 19th century commercial district. The street is lined with red-brick buildings constructed in the first phase of development between 1883 and 1888. The building at 90–100 was the very first and sets the tone: five storeys high with a cast-iron frontage, brownstone detailing, and a flat roof. As such it fulfilled not only the practical requirements of the industry but also stringent fire controls. The ground floor with its large windows was used to showcase merchandise, the second floor was where business was transacted, the middle floors were for the storage of active merchandise, and the top floors used for slow-moving stock.

The narrow building opposite at 121–123 and the larger building farther down at 141–147 are important because their three-storey arches are influenced by the Romanesque Revival style pioneered by prominent American architect Henry Hobson Richardson (1838–1886) (see no. 75). Such 'Richardsonian Romanesque' fills an entire block to

The Leather District is an intact historic commercial district

the rear at 108–150 Lincoln Street, built during the second phase of construction between 1888 and 1893. It is also a feature of the former Fur Merchants Warehouse over at 717–719 Atlantic Avenue.

The Pilgrim Building at the far end of South Street at 208–212 is quite different. Dating from 1919, and the final phase of the Leather District's construction, it consists of a steel-framed skyscraper clad in a more contemporary Classical Revival pale-coloured brick. Similarly constructed is the huge Albany Building around the corner at 155–205 Lincoln Street, which once housed the United Shoe Machinery Company. Their departure from Boston in 1929 marked the end of the city's time as the centre of the New England shoe industry, as manufacturers moved south once again in search of lower costs.

Other locations nearby: 48, 49

51 Candy Capital of America

MA 02210 (South Boston), the former *NECCO Wafers* factory at the corner of A Street and Necco Court
T Silver Line 1, 2 to Courthouse

Boston and Cambridge were once home to 140 different candy companies. Indeed during the 1950s there were so many along Main Street in Cambridge that it was nicknamed Confectioners' Row. Although they have long since closed or relocated, some of their premises remain. Visiting them is a reminder that this was once the candy capital of America.

The oldest premises stand on the banks of the Neponset River in Lower Mills Village, Dorchester. This is where the country's first chocolate factory was established in 1764 by physician Dr. James Baker and Irish chocolatier John Hannon. When Hannon went missing in 1779 his widow sold out to Baker, whose successors took the *Baker's Chocolate* brand to national prominence. By the time the company relocated to Delaware in 1965, the original premises comprised 15 buildings, which have been subsequently converted into condominiums.

The first hard candy sold commercially in New England was *Gibraltar Rock* made in Salem in 1806 by English immigrant confectioners and they are still sold there today. Perhaps the greatest confectionary brand associated with New England though is *NECCO Wafers*. These were first manufactured in 1847 by English immigrant Oliver Chase, who invented a wafer-cutting machine for the purpose. Because the wafers were made in Boston, they were originally called *Hub Wafers*, after an old nickname for the city. They grew in popularity when Union soldiers carried them during the American Civil War (1861–1865).

In 1901 Chase merged with two other confectionary companies to become the New England Confectionery Company. This resulted in a re-branding of the wafers as *NECCO Wafers*. A year later the company moved into a custom-built, six-storey factory at the corner of A Street and Necco Court (South Boston). Subsequent expansion along Necco Street as far as the Fort Point Channel made it the largest confectionary plant in the United States.

For an impression of the inside of the factory take a walk up A Street to the Marriott Residence Inn at 370 Congress Street. That this modern hotel resembles the NECCO factory is no coincidence since it originally served as NECCO's molasses and sugar warehouse. The red-brick façade, white-tiled atrium, and 12-foot-high ceilings remain gloriously intact, and in the lobby are two huge cast iron doors from the old boilers.

In 1927 NECCO relocated across the Charles River to a completely new factory at 250 Massachusetts Avenue (Cambridge). From here in the 1930s the company supplied *NECCO Wafers* to Admiral Richard Byrd (1888–1957) for his famous flight to the South Pole. Wafer production peaked during the Second World War, when the government requested that the company provide confectionery for troops abroad. NECCO remained in Cambridge until 2003, when it relocated finally to Revere. The old buildings on Necco Street are now used by General Electric, whilst those in Cambridge are occupied by pharmaceutical company Novartis (across the road at

A part of the old *NECCO Wafers* factory in South Boston

181 Massachusetts Avenue is a new Novartis building created by designer Maya Lin (b. 1959), its remarkable perforated granite façade inspired by microscopic views of human bone).

Another former candy factory of note is Schrafft's at 529 Main Street (Charlestown). Established in 1861 to make gumdrops, the factory was built in 1928 to manufacture boxed chocolates. Closed in 1984, it is now offices, with confectionery memorabilia in the lobby and a *Schrafft's* neon sign still on the roof.

South Boston has a long history of manufacturing. During the 19th century the South Boston Iron Works was the largest in the country, where cannon used in the American Civil War (1861–1865) were cast. Around the same time there were more than 25 glass kilns in operation here, too. The main manufacturer today is Gillette, based since 1904 in a sprawling factory on West Second Street, where 1,300 employees produce four billion razor blades a year.

Other locations nearby: 40, 52, 53

52 Of Milk and Silk

MA 02210 (South Boston), the Boston Children's Museum
at 308 Congress Street
T Silver Line 1, 2 to Courthouse or Red Line to South Station

Between the 1830s and 1920s the Boston Wharf Company developed the eastern shore of the Fort Point Channel (South Boston), which had been reclaimed from tidal mudflats. It laid out streets and built redbrick warehouses and factories, initially for sugar and molasses then later for the wool trade. Boston's famous *NECCO Wafers* were manufactured here in the late 19th century and wool was marketed well into the 20th (see no. 51). Manufacturing and warehousing has long since been abandoned but the old buildings remain. To preserve their striking visual uniformity those on Congress, Summer, and A Streets have been designated the Fort Point Channel Historic District.

A range of tenants now occupy the old buildings. They include big-name companies such as General Electric, as well as members of New England's largest enclave of artists, the Fort Point Arts Community based in a cavernous former warehouse at 300 Summer Street (see no. 64). There are museums, too, including the Boston Children's Museum at 308 Congress Street.

The museum is easily identified by a 40-foot-tall wooden milk bottle outside. Built in 1933 as an ice cream stand, this architectural novelty originally stood in Taunton, Massachusetts. After being abandoned in 1967, it was purchased by the Massachusetts-based dairy company, H. P. Hood, which shipped it to Boston and presented it to the Children's Museum. Since then it's been known as the Hood Milk Bottle.

Behind the bottle is the Children's Museum, the country's second oldest after one in Brooklyn. Before opening here in 1979, the museum had a peripatetic existence. The idea for it was first mooted in 1909 by a group of local teachers keen to create a venue that would encourage children in their science studies. The first incarnation opened in 1913 in Jamaica Plain, where it consisted of a cabinet devoted to birds and another to minerals and shells, placed at children's eye level, with labelling in simple language.

A handful of branch museums followed and in 1936 the Jamaica Plain branch purchased its own building. Michael Spock, son of renowned pediatrician Dr. Benjamin Spock, served as director from 1962 to 1985, during which time he pioneered the concept of 'hands-on learning'. It was also during Spock's tenure that the museum moved to its current location, a former wool warehouse overlooking the Fort Point Channel. The following year, Boston's Japanese sister city Kyoto donated a wooden silk merchant's house to the museum. Dating from the late 19th century and called a *Machiya*, it is used in line with Spock's concept to educate children and adults alike about Japanese culture.

The museum comprises three floors of activity areas, including an art studio, contruction zone, and science playground. They are interspersed with artefacts drawn from the museum's extensive historical holdings, which encompass everything from Native American dress to 1950s games. Most importantly the museum is known for its groundbreaking

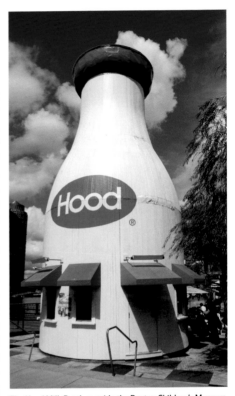

The Hood Milk Bottle outside the Boston Children's Museum

exhibits concerning cultural diversity, racism, and social inclusivity, including *Boston Black: A City Connects*.

In 2007, the museum completed a $47-million renovation and expansion project. This resulted in the Boston Children's Museum being hailed as the city's first 'green museum'. Features include green roofs, storm water reclamation, and building materials that are local and recycled. Also included was the glass-walled enclosure at the front of the museum, a new theatre, and the newly-landscaped Children's Wharf Park through which runs Boston's Harborwalk.

In 2013, the museum deservedly received the National Medal for Museum and Library Service in recognition of its significant contribution to the lives of individuals, families, and communities.

Other locations nearby: 39, 40, 51, 53

53 Boston on Fire

MA 02210 (South Boston), the Boston Fire Museum
at 344 Congress Street
T Silver Line 1, 2 to Courthouse or Red Line to South Station

South Boston's Fort Point Channel Historic District was designated in 2004. It comprises a series of former candy factories and wool warehouses erected on Congress, Summer, and A Streets during the late 19th and early 20th centuries (see no. 52). In amongst them is the Congress Street Fire Station, which today contains the Boston Fire Museum.

The station was built in 1891 for Fire Engine Companies 38 & 39 to a design by City Architect, Harrison H. Atwood (1863–1954). The unusually decorative building features a chunky granite entrance, giving way to light-coloured brickwork and tiles above. The all-important ground floor containing the engines (and until 1917 the nine horses to pull them) was kept free of columns by cleverly suspending the second floor from the roof trusses. Engine Company 38 was disbanded in 1947, and replaced in 1953 by Ladder Company 18. The station eventually closed in 1977 and a few years later the museum was established to preserve it.

The museum contains plenty of exhibits relating to the history of Boston firefighting. The oldest are 18th century leather fire buckets and Boston's first hand-operated Pumper from 1792. Among the larger exhibits is an American LaFrance Ladder Truck of 1860, an Amoskeag Steam Pumper from 1880, and a surprisingly elegant plum-coloured LaFrance truck built in 1926. The museum's display of early fire alarm telegraph systems is important because the world's first such alarm was transmitted in Boston in 1852. More mundane but no less important are the glass fire grenades, trumpets for directing firefighting operations, Lowrey hydrants, and a display of helmets, boots, and masks.

In the century following its founding, Boston suffered half a dozen serious fires. The title 'Great Fire' was first used to describe the conflagration of 1711, which destroyed the First Town-House, Boston's original purpose-built town hall and Colonial seat of government. In 1760, the title passed to a much larger blaze, which destroyed property between Pie Alley where it began, Long Wharf, and Fort Hill (today the junction of Oliver and High Streets).

The 1760 blaze was eclipsed dramatically by the Great Boston Fire of 1872, which has retained the title ever since. After starting at the

A vintage LaFrance fire truck at the Boston Fire Museum

corner of Summer and Kingston Streets, at the time the central business and retail district, it was fanned by high winds and spread north as far as State Street and east to Fort Hill. The upside of losing 65 acres of real estate (but miraculously only 13 lives) was that Boston's commercial heart was redeveloped using modern fireproof construction techniques. Also at this time the Italianate watch tower at 444 Harrison Avenue (South End) was erected alongside the city's new Fire Department Headquarters, which remained here until the 1950s, when it relocated to Roxbury (the tower is now part of the Pine Street Inn homeless shelter).

Another significant fire was the Cocoanut Grove Fire of 1942, when a nightclub on Piedmont Street (Bay Village) burned down. The thousand guests packing the 500-capacity building quickly blocked the main entrance causing chaos. A plaque at the site recalls the 492 people who died and the subsequent enforcement of stricter fire codes.

Boston's worst tragedy to befall firefighters themselves occurred in 1972, when nine lost their lives at the Hotel Vendome on Commonwealth Avenue (Back Bay). A memorial depicting a fireman's helmet and coat stands nearby.

A mural on the Inman Square Firehouse at 1384 Cambridge Street (Cambridge) depicts the crew of Engine No. 5, as well as Benjamin Franklin (1706–1790), who founded the country's first volunteer fire service.

Other locations nearby: 39, 51, 52, 54

54 Modern Art by the Water

MA 02210 (South Boston), the Institute of Contemporary Art
at 25 Harbor Shore Drive
T Silver Line 1, 2 to Courthouse

The South Boston Waterfront has undergone significant changes over the last two centuries. In the 1830s, the original tidal mudflats were reclaimed and used to build a series of piers to supplement Boston's existing port facilities (the area had been annexed by Boston in 1807). In the 1980s, by which time most of the piers had been abandoned, work began on redeveloping the area. The result is a revitalised neighbourhood of office blocks, hotels, and cultural attractions, serviced by Silver Line buses, Harbor Dock vessels, and the HarborWalk.

The 19th century version of the South Boston Waterfront comprised half a dozen piers and the 21st century version has made good use of them. Piers 1 and 2, for example, have been infilled to form the Fan Pier on which the John Joseph Moakley United States Courthouse sits. Designed by Henry N. Cobb (b. 1926), architect of the John Hancock Tower, it boasts several public art spaces, including an impressive rotunda containing *The Boston Panels* by Color Field artist Ellsworth Kelly (1923–2015). Pier 5 (Commonwealth Pier) is today the World Trade Center for conferences, and the landward end of Pier 7 (once part of the South Boston Naval Annex) is now occupied by the Blue Hills Bank Pavilion, an outdoor amphitheatre (see no. 57).

Perhaps the most arresting example of the redevelopment can be found on Pier 4. Here at 25 Harbor Shore Drive stands the Institute of Contemporary Art (ICA), which dazzles both inside and out. Designed by the architectural firm Diller Scofidio + Renfro and opened in 2006, the striking building at the water's edge is unlike any other in Boston. It consists of two glazed cubes, one on top of the other. The lower, smaller one has an outdoor public grandstand and performance space facing out across the harbour. The upper, larger cube is cantilevered so that it doubles as a roof for the space. The overall design when viewed from a distance echoes that of the gantry cranes once commonplace here.

The interior of the ICA is equally triumphant. The smaller cube contains an auditorium for performance arts and film screenings. The larger cube contains the ICA's permanent rotating art collection, including large-scale figurative works by Louise Bourgeois (1911–2010), sculptural textiles by Mona Hatoum (b. 1952), and photographs by Nan Goldin (b. 1953). Other features include the Founder's Gallery in

The Institute of Contemporary Art on the redeveloped South Boston Waterfront

the cantilevered section, the Mediatheque slung beneath it and a café with great night-time views.

It's worth noting that although the ICA was founded back in 1936 (as the Boston Museum of Modern Art) its permanent collection was only instigated when the ICA relocated here from 951–955 Boylston Street (Back Bay) (that address is now part of Boston Architectural College).

After visiting the ICA be sure to check out the new premises of the Society of Arts and Crafts at 100 Pier 4 Boulevard (Suite 200), which has been promoting the work of the city's artists since 1897.

The hinterland behind the South Boston Waterfront has also seen redevelopment, including the huge Boston Convention and Exhibition Center, which opened in 2004 on Summer Street. Attendees have an increasing choice of hotels, including the Seaport behind the World Trade Center, named one of America's greenest hotels. Not far away on D Street are two new parks, Eastport and South Boston Maritime. A very recent addition is the maritime-themed Our Lady of Good Voyage at 51 Seaport Boulevard, the first new Catholic church in Boston for over 60 years.

Other locations nearby: 52, 53, 55, 56

55 The Boston Fish Pier

MA 02210 (South Boston), the Boston Fish Pier
at 212 Northern Avenue
T Silver Line 1, 2 to World Trade Center

When work began in the 1980s on the redevelopment of the South Boston Waterfront, the area's old piers and warehouses north of First Street were long abandoned, and much of the area given over to bleak parking lots. These days it looks completely different, with smart office blocks and hotels, restaurants, cultural attractions, and parks all drawing a new audience to the area (see no. 54).

It is always heartening, however, when such drastic redevelopment nods respectfully to the past. Take for example the Commonwealth Pier, which was the world's largest when it opened in 1901. Able to accommodate the biggest vessels entering the Port of Boston, it was once a crucial element in the city's maritime infrastructure, where both freight and passenger traffic were handled. Today it has been successfully transformed into a waterside conference and exhibition centre.

Another example is Liberty Wharf farther east along Northern Avenue. This swanky row of restaurants began in the early 1920s as a seafood café over the road in what was then the Northern Avenue Fish Market. It was established by a young Greek immigrant, Jimmy Doulos, who arrived in Boston in 1915. The café flourished and in 1929 moved across the street, where as Jimmy's Harborside Restaurant – 'Home of the Chowder King' – it remained until 2007. It was then demolished by arrangement with the Doulos family and the new restaurants built to continue their waterfront dining legacy.

Throughout the redevelopment there has been one constant: the Boston Fish Pier. Opened in 1914 and operated by the Massachusetts Port Authority (Massport), it is the country's oldest working fish pier and remains at the heart of Boston's seafood industry. Admittedly with New England fish stocks now strictly managed, cod, mackerel and haddock is no longer landed here in the quantity it once was. Instead the pier's seafood dealers and processors draw around 75% of their catch from more distant oceans, which arrive by truck from the Conley Marine Terminal or Logan Airport. The rest still arrives by sea.

As high-end offices, apartments and attractions continue to encroach, the Fish Pier remains a defiantly blue collar place of work. The South Boston seafood industry supports more than 3,000 jobs and a good number of them are based in the buildings that run the length

Business as usual on South Boston's historic Fish Pier

of the pier. Behind the anonymous looking doors, hard-working sea-food processors wear fish-stained slickers and filleting gloves like their fathers and grandfathers before them.

Of course the seafood dealers on Fish Pier remain conscious of the fact that gentrification rarely takes living communities into account. Business is certainly up on previous years and the planned dredging of Boston Harbor will eventually allow large container vessels to land cargoes directly onto the pier. But still there is a need for the pier and its community to be protected. With this in mind state politicians are pushing for the Fish Pier to be added to the National Register of Historic Places. This would preserve its industrial character and protect it from unsuitable commercial development. Fingers crossed that this will happen.

For now the few public facilities on the pier are all related to the seafood business. They include the popular No Name Restaurant, which began life in 1917 as a seafood stall serving fishermen, and the Exchange Conference Center, housed in the former fish exchange at the end of the pier.

Each August since 2012 the Boston Fish Pier has hosted the Boston Seafood Festival. It is a great opportunity not only to enjoy seafood but also to learn about the sustainability of New England's fishing industry.

Other locations nearby: 53, 54, 56, 57

56 For Lovers of Craft Beer

MA 02210 (South Boston), the Harpoon Brewery
at 306 Northern Avenue
T Silver Line 1, 2 to Silver Line Way

The massive redevelopment of the South Boston Waterfront has been ongoing since the 1980s. Much of what's new lies either side of Seaport Boulevard and Northern Avenue. At the end of Northern Avenue is the Raymond L. Flynn Marine Park, which is largely reserved for maritime-related activities (see no. 57). Here amongst seafood warehouses and other marine enterprises is the Harpoon Brewery, a haven for lovers of craft beer.

Harpoon was founded in 1986 by a couple of college friends, who loved beer but found their post-Prohibition drinking choices still sorely limited. Inspired by holidays in Europe, and the rich brewing tradition they found there, they decided to start their own microbrewery. Within a year they had acquired part of a former naval warehouse at 306 Northern Avenue (South Boston), where they brewed the first *Harpoon Ale*. Fortunately they found a couple of Boston taverns willing to support their venture, including the Sevens Ale House at 77 Charles Street (Beacon Hill).

In 1988 they followed up with *Harpoon Winter Warmer*, the first seasonal craft beer brewed in New England. In 1993, and still technically a struggling company, they introduced *Harpoon IPA* as a refreshing summer tipple. The combination of an English-style ale using Northwestern US hops was an immediate success and transformed the company. As a result Harpoon moved into profit for the first time, expanded production, and hasn't looked back since.

The Harpoon Brewery today is a bustling concern that welcomes visitors both to its Boston premises and its sister concern in Windsor, Vermont. In Boston the brewery is easily identified by its giant fermenting silos, one of which is topped with a huge harpoon. When it first opened, the brewery was not easily accessible to visitors. That changed with the arrival of the T Silver Line in 2004. With visitor interest increasing, the brewery upgraded its visitor facilities to include a new entrance, a capacious Beer Hall, and a gift shop.

In the Beer Hall visitors can sample all the company's products on tap, including *Harpoon Ale* and *Harpoon IPA*, as well as *Harpoon UFO* (Un-Filtered Offering), a cloudy, unfiltered wheat beer introduced with great success in 1998. They can also view the goings-on in the brewery itself through large picture windows.

To fully understand the brewing process at Harpoon, however, it is recommended to join one of the company's informative daily tours. Everything is explained from the mashing of malted barley with water to convert starch to sugar, and heating and the addition of hops to add refreshing bitterness, to fermentation through the adding of yeast. The brewing process takes two weeks after which the beer is bottled, capped, and boxed for shipment. A tasting completes the tour.

A glance at Harpoon's website (www.harpoonbrewery.com) shows that great care is taken to ensure the business is environmentally sound. Note-

The Harpoon Brewery is a South Boston success story

worthy features include the thermodynamically efficient use of fuel through Cogeneration, on-site treatment of waste water, and supplying local farmers with spent grain for animal feed. The company, which has remained independent and is now employee-owned, also has a social conscience expressed through its charity races and annual Octoberfest and St. Patrick's Day festivals.

Afterwards, visit Yankee Lobster on the roundabout between Harpoon and the Blue Hills Bank Pavilion, where mouthwatering lobster rolls and clam chowder have been on the menu since 1950.

A world-renowned Boston brewery offering tours and tastings is the Samuel Adams Brewery at 30 Germania Street (Jamaica Plain). Established in 1984, it is named in honour of the Boston Patriot and maltster, Samuel Adams (1722–1803).

Other locations nearby: 54, 55, 57

57 Dry Dock Number 3

MA 02210 (South Boston), Dry Dock Number 3 on Tide Street
in the Raymond L. Flynn Marine Park
T Silver Line 1, 2 to Silver Line Way

Since the 1970s, the South Boston Waterfront has seen much of its original maritime infrastructure given over to new uses. That is certainly the case along Seaport Boulevard and Northern Avenue, where piers once used for landing fish, goods, and people are now overlooked by offices, hotels, and cultural attractions (see nos. 54, 55, 56). Beyond the roundabout on Northern Avenue, however, in the Raymond L. Flynn Marine Park, it is ships and the sea that still permeate life.

This area has gone by several different names over the years. Originally it was called Dorchester Flats (then Commonwealth Flats) reflecting the fact that the land was originally tidal mudflats at the tip of Dorchester Neck (reclaimed during the 19th century for use as state shipping terminals). The terminals never arrived though and instead the western part was used for Boston Wharf Company buildings and railyards. In 1920 the eastern part was purchased by the U.S. Department of Defense and used to build the South Boston Naval Annex (an extension of the Boston Naval Yard in Charlestown) and the South Boston Army Base (see no. 2).

During the Second World War the Army Base was used to warehouse and distribute military goods and supplies. The Naval Annex by this time consisted of seven piers north of Fid Kennedy Way, which were supplemented with dry docks, machine and paint shops, a barracks, and a power plant, the whole serviced by a railway known as Track 61. After the war the Annex was used to mothball aircraft carriers of the Atlantic Fleet and during the late 1950s there were 20 of them here, alongside numerous cruisers and destroyers. Active service vessels also continued to arrive for maintenance and repairs.

In 1974, when the Boston Naval Yard in Charlestown closed as an active naval installation, the South Boston Naval Annex and Army Base closed, too. The land was purchased in the 1980s by the City of Boston and renamed the Boston Marine Industrial Park (now the Raymond L. Flynn Marine Park). Like the rest of the South Boston Waterfront, it is slowly being redeveloped but the authorities have stated that they wish to preserve as much marine-related industry and fabric as possible.

A colossal ship undergoing repairs in Dry Dock 3

Four of the old piers were infilled during the 1980s using earth excavated during the construction of an MBTA Red Line extension, which means this area is currently of little historical interest. Two piers north of the Blue Hills Bank Pavilion, however, remain and enclose a now-abandoned dry dock installed in 1943. Vessels were once floated into here and the water then pumped out leaving them high and dry for hull maintenance and repairs.

To see a working dry dock, head south to Tide Street at the far end of Northern Avenue. Here can be found Dry Dock Number 3, one of the largest dry docks on the Eastern seaboard. Although public access is forbidden, there is a viewing balcony that permits an overview of the proceedings. Located seven miles from the open sea, the dock is used by the Boston Ship Repair Company to repair navy and other vessels up to 65,000 tons, with vintage cranes adding to the scene. The Cunard liner *Queen Elizabeth 2* was repaired here in 1992 after she hit an uncharted rock in Nantucket Sound.

Alongside the dock, on land formerly occupied by the Army Base, is the busy Black Falcon Cruise Terminal operated by the Massachusetts Port Authority. Over a hundred vessels call here during the cruise season, sailing thereafter either north towards Canada, south to Bermuda, or east across the Atlantic.

Other locations nearby: 55, 56

58 Pleasure Bay and Castle Island

MA 02127 (South Boston), a walk around Pleasure Bay to Fort Independence on Castle Island
T Red Line to Broadway then Bus 9 to Farragut Road and walk north along the Head Island Causeway to reach Castle Island (note: Fort Independence can only be visited as part of a guided tour on weekends 12am–3.30pm between Memorial Day and Labor Day)

Visitors are attracted to South Boston for different reasons, including the redeveloped South Boston Waterfront, the Fort Point Channel Historic District, and the Irish pub culture. Fewer take advantage of the neighbourhood's surprisingly scenic beaches running from City Point (the peninsula along East Broadway) down to Dorchester. To combine a beach walk with some history take the bus to the end of East Broadway and alight at Farragut Road (the statue here is David Farragut (1801–1870), first admiral of the United States Navy). From here it is just a few steps to reach a crescent of sand framing Pleasant Bay.

Turn left and walk along Head Island Causeway, which is a reminder that Castle Island, the goal of this walk, was once connected to the mainland by only a footbridge. Landfill projects during the 19th century gradually transformed the causeway into the peninsula seen today. Whilst walking note on the left-hand side the vast Conley Marine Terminal, the container facility for the Port of Boston, established here in 1966.

Continue to Castle Island, which takes its name from the sturdy Fort Independence that now hoves into view. History buffs eager to go inside will be pleased to know that excellent guided tours are available on weekends between Memorial Day (the last Monday in May) and Labor Day (the first Monday in September) from noon until 3.30pm.

The tour guides will explain how the island overlooking the mouth of Boston's Inner Harbor was ideal for deterring sea attack. The first fortification, known as 'The Castle', was an earthwork with three cannons, commissioned in 1634 by then Governor of the Massachusetts Bay Colony, Thomas Dudley (1576–1653). Rebuilt in timber (1644) then rebuilt again more substantially (1653), it was rebuilt yet again in 1673. A four-bastioned brick fort known as Castle William was completed in 1703 and armed with 72 cannons, providing a refuge for

A glimpse inside Fort Independence on Castle Island

British officials during times of unrest. This incarnation of the fort was torched by British troops evacuating Boston in 1776.

Rebuilt by Bostonians shortly afterwards as Fort Adams, it was renamed Fort Independence in 1778 and in 1803 rebuilt yet again. In 1827 Boston-born horror writer Edgar Allan Poe (1809–1849) was posted here for several months and legend has it that he based the plot of his story *The Cask of Amontillado* on real events wherein friends of an officer shot dead in a duel bury his killer alive in the dungeon (see no. 46).

The present five-pointed fort (the eighth and final fort on the site) was completed in 1851 under the direction of respected military engineer, Colonel Sylvanus Thayer (1785–1872), using granite shipped down the coast from Rockport. In 1962, when the fort was deemed no longer useful, Castle Island was deeded by the U.S. government to the City of Boston, since when it has become a popular visitor attraction.

After leaving the fort note the obelisk commemorating East Boston shipbuilder Donald McKay (1810–1880) and the Korean War Memorial (see photo on page 230). Then perhaps enjoy a hot dog at Sullivan's snack bar built in imitation of the Commandant's House that stood in front of the fort in the 19th century.

This walk can be extended by returning along East Broadway to reach Medal of Honor Park, where in 1981 the country's first Vietnam War memorial was erected. Thereafter continue down L Street to reach the 1930s-era Curley Community Center, home to the L Street Brownies, who have been swimming year-round in Dorchester Bay since 1902.

59 The Irish Find Their Place

MA 02127 (South Boston), Murphy's Law pub
at 837 Summer Street
T Red Line to Broadway then Bus 9 to the corner
of East Broadway and L Street and walk

Where better to learn about Boston's Irish history than in an authentic Irish pub. A good choice is Murphy's Law at 837 Summer Street (South Boston), opposite an abandoned Edison power plant awaiting reuse. No-nonsense bartending and cash-only service reign here, with the bonus that the annual St. Patrick's Day Parade passes along nearby East Broadway (the place also features in Ben Affleck's film *Gone Baby Gone*). So order a Guinness and let the story begin…

As the closest American port to Europe, Boston during the 19th and 20th centuries received many waves of immigrants. The first were Irish labourers, who began arriving in significant numbers during Ireland's Potato Famine (1845–1850): 37,000 in 1847 alone. Too poor to move inland, they initially settled near the waterfront on Batterymarch and Broad Streets, where they took unskilled work unloading ships, hauling carts, and cleaning stables.

Life for these early immigrants was harsh. Easy prey to unscrupulous landlords, families rented single rooms without water or sanitation. It was not uncommon for a single former merchant's house to be divided up into a tenement for a hundred immigrants, with those unable to find space occupying cellars and back yards instead. Disease was rife, with 60% of children dying in infancy, and few adults surviving more than six years after arrival.

Then there was the discrimination. Prim and proper Bostonians mocked the impoverished newcomers as they stepped ashore at Lewis Wharf. The working classes feared being undercut by the newcomers' willingness to work for less. Even Irish Catholicism was perceived as a threat by the predominantly Protestant host community and it was commonplace to see "No Irish Need Apply" signs posted when jobs were advertised. The Irish Famine Memorial at the corner of Washington and School Streets (Downtown) recalls the negative mood.

Despite this the Irish strove to establish themselves. They fought in the American Civil War (1861–1865) and afterwards provided the muscle behind America's industrial expansion, laying rail tracks and building boats, as well as waiting in restaurants and tending bars. They organised the first trade unions and conducted strikes when necessary

Landlady Peggy Kelly at Murphy's Law on Summer Street

for better working conditions. Single Irish women worked for wealthy families on Beacon Hill and did much to foster social welfare in newly-established Catholic parishes.

They settled extensively in the North End and East Boston, whilst those with a little more money, the so-called lace-curtain Irish, settled in Charlestown. Their eventual migration southwards into South Boston and eventually Dorchester was prompted by the arrival during the second half of the 19th century of new immigrants, namely Jews and Italians (see nos. 17, 26).

The Irish countered the discrimination against them through the ballot box. Being eligible to vote, the offspring of original immigrants joined the Democratic Party in droves, and the election in 1885 of Boston's first Irish Catholic mayor, Hugh O'Brien (1827–1895), saw them assimilated into the city's political life. By 1914 another Irish mayor, James Michael Curley (1874–1958), announced that "the day of the Puritan has passed; the Anglo-Saxon is a joke; a new and better America is here". For millions of Irish-Americans that 'better America' was fully realised in 1961, when Boston-born John Fitzgerald Kennedy (1917–1963) became the country's first Catholic president (see no. 15).

Boston's Irish diaspora has resulted in a plethora of Irish pubs. Other recommendations include the long-established J.J. Foley's at 117 East Berkeley Street (South End), the cosy Brendan Behan at 378 Centre Street (Jamaica Plain), and the Druid at 1357 Cambridge Street (Cambridge). For more Irish sites follow the Irish Heritage Trail (www.irishheritagetrail.com).

Other locations nearby: 60

60 When the Brits Left Boston

MA 02127 (South Boston), the Dorchester Heights Monument in Thomas Park
T Red Line to Andrew then bus along Dorchester Street

There are few places in Boston where the landscape remains unchanged from Colonial times. One of them is Dorchester Heights in South Boston. Despite being surrounded by urban sprawl, this grassy hill still commands the same expansive views of Boston Harbor and Downtown

that it did during the American Revolutionary War (1775–1783). A monument on top of the hill celebrates the fact that it was from here in 1776 that George Washington (1732–1799) forced the British out of Boston.

Back in the 18th century, the hill was one of several on a sea-girt promontory known as Dorchester Neck. After Boston annexed the islands in 1804, developers quarried them for landfill to help unify the area. Only one hill remained, which was made into a park in the 1850s to honour Colonel John Thomas, who defended the hill during Washington's siege. It was here in 1902 that the 115-foot tall Dorchester Heights Monument was erected to commemorate what happened here.

Cannon on Dorchester Heights were used to oust the British from Boston

Following the Battles of Lexington and Concord in April 1775, British Redcoats beat a tactical retreat to the narrow confines of Boston. With anti-British sentiment running high, thousands of New England militiamen followed them and occupied the surrounding countryside resulting in a standoff. In June British troops broke out and seized Bunker Hill but sustained huge losses in the process (see no. 4).

At the time Washington was on his way to Cambridge to take up command of the newly-formed Continental Army, which he did on July 3rd (see no. 97). The stand-off with the British, however, continued as each side assessed the other's firepower. Washington knew that to make a decisive move he needed artillery, so he dispatched Colonel Henry Knox (1750–1806) to retrieve cannon from Fort Ticonderoga in New York. With the help of 80 yoke of oxen, Knox successfully made the hazardous round journey arriving back in January 1776.

Washington made his move during the night of March 4th. As 800 American troops stood guard along the Dorchester shoreline, another 1,200 men rolled the 59 cannon into place on the summit of Dorchester Heights. So as not to alert the British, they deadened the sound of the wheels by wrapping them in straw. Working through the night they built a series of fortifications to protect the cannon and the men who would fire them.

By the time the British noticed what had happened Washington had gained the initiative. The British were faced with a wall of artillery that would have pulverised Boston had it been deployed. The British General William Howe (1729–1814) planned an attack but bad weather prevented his forces from crossing the water. Instead on March 17th, Howe, his troops, and a thousand Colonial loyalists were evacuated by the Royal Navy to Nova Scotia, abandoning Boston to Washington's forces and its Patriotic citizens. The 11-month long Siege of Boston was over, providing not only Washington with his first victory of the Revolutionary War but also the Thirteen Colonies that had declared independence with a huge morale boost. Since 1901 March 17th (Evacuation Day) has been observed in Boston as an annual holiday.

South Boston High School on the east flank of Dorchester Heights was built in 1901. It was the scene of racial tension in 1974, when African-American students were bussed in as part of an attempt to desegregate suburban schools. Black and white students clashed and parents marched to have the plan aborted. It was not until the 1980s and the upbeat mayorship of Ray Flynn (b. 1939) that the scars began to heal.

Other locations nearby: 59

61 Red-Brick and Cast Iron

MA 02118 (South End), the Francis Dane House
at 532 Massachusetts Avenue
T Green Line E to Northeastern or Symphony

Boston's South End neighbourhood stretches from the Massachusetts Turnpike (I-90) south-west along Tremont and Washington Streets to Roxbury. Originally a tidal mudflat, it was reclaimed from the sea from the 1830s onwards. The first inhabitants were members of Boston's burgeoning middle and upper classes, who began arriving here in the 1850s. Long gone now, having mostly relocated to neighbouring Back Bay after the financial Panic of 1873, their Victorian-style red-brick row homes remain gloriously intact.

South End's concentration of Victorian row housing between Dartmouth and Massachusetts Avenues is unmatched anywhere in the United States. Indeed so numerous are the houses and so homogenous the streets that in 1983 the entire area was listed on the National Register of Historic Places. This makes it the country's largest historical neighbourhood.

The row houses were built between 1850 and 1875 on a street plan drawn up much earlier by architect Charles Bulfinch (1763–1844). This explains why the layout resembles that of Beacon Hill, which Bulfinch helped lay out in the early 19th century (see no. 27). In the South End, however, his Federal-style townhouses are replaced by taller, bow fronted row houses. There are attractive Victorian-style garden squares here, too, such as Union Park and Worcester Squares, designed to attract well-to-do families. Blackstone and Franklin Squares sit on what was once Boston Neck, the narrow strip of dry land that originally connected the Shawmut Peninsula to the mainland (see no. 8).

The grandest of the squares is Chester Square. Despite being dissected by Massachusetts Avenue in the 1950s, it retains much of its 19th century charm. It seems fitting that since 1974 the house at number 532 has served as the headquarters of the South End Historical Society, which does so much to preserve the South End's architectural integrity.

The house was purchased newly constructed in 1860 by successful banker and boot manufacturer Francis Dane (1818–1875). The large sum he paid for the property reflected the desirability of the address at the time and the quality of its construction. The façade features a variety of window frames, deeply carved brownstone decoration, and a mansard roof. Inside is a large parlor-cum-dining room, with 13-foot-high ceilings, Carrara marble fireplaces, and ornate wood and plasterwork.

The iron balustrading on the front steps would originally have resembled that at number 534 but was probably lost during the early 20th century, when the South End's row houses were divided up for working class immigrants (see no. 62). It's worth noting that the South End features the country's largest collection of Victorian cast ironwork, much of which is botanical in form. An example of this so-called *Rinceau* work can be seen at 528.

Each October the South End Historical Society organises a self-guided walk-

The Francis Dane House typifies Victorian South End row housing

ing tour of Victorian private homes and public spaces (www.southendhistoricalsociety.org). All proceeds from the tour are used to support the Society's ongoing work, which has so far included the preservation of the Allen House, an ornate Victorian brownstone mansion at 1682 Washington Street. Built in 1859 for furniture dealer Aaron Hall Allen (1818–1889), it is built in an exotic blend of Italianate and French Second Empire styles. That the house was used between the 1870s and the 1950s by a succession of social clubs is further evidence of the South End's shifting demographics. The house has subsequently been adapted for use as apartments.

Whilst in the South End don't miss the Cathedral of the Holy Cross at 1400 Washington Street. Completed in 1875, this vast Gothic Revival building heralded the emergence of Catholicism in what had previously been a predominantly Protestant city and state.

Other locations nearby: 62

62 Wally's Café Jazz Club

**MA 02118 (South End), Wally's Café Jazz Club
at 427 Massachusetts Avenue
T Green Line E to Symphony**

By the early years of the 20th century, the Victorian row houses of Boston's South End were being carved up into lodging houses for working class immigrants. Members of the city's African-American community were among them, including the country's largest concentration of Pullman Porters attracted by the South Station, one of the world's largest rail hubs when it opened in 1899. In time the South End became a focus for the black middle classes and although many had relocated to Roxbury by the 1970s, they've left several indelible impressions.

One is Wally's Café Jazz Club at 427 Massachusetts Avenue. During the 1940s and 50s, the South End was a jazz hotspot, with myriad clubs introducing swing and blue notes to New England audiences. They included the High Hat, Savoy Ballroom, Chicken Lane, and Wig Wam, attracting the likes of Duke Ellington, Billie Holiday, and Sarah Vaughan. Another was Wally's Paradise opened in 1947 by Joseph L. 'Wally' Walcott (1897–1998), who had arrived from Barbados in 1910. Initially he ran a taxi service, counting James Michael Curley (1874–1958), Boston's colourful Irish-American mayor, among his customers. With Curley's help Wally was able to secure a liquor licence and then using his savings established his club.

Located originally at 428 Massachusetts Avenue, Wally's Paradise was the first New England nightclub owned by an African-American. It was also one of the first to be racially integrated. Amongst the legendary acts to tread the boards here were Charlie Parker, Art Blakey, Lena Horne, and Coleman Hawkins.

By the 1960s the music scene was changing but that didn't deter Wally's commitment to jazz. He sustained the club by inviting young musicians from Boston's various music schools to perform alongside veterans from the dwindling Big Band scene. The club moved across the road to its current location in 1979, where Wally continued to oversee business until his death in 1998 aged 101. Today the club is run by his children making it the country's oldest jazz club still in the same family. It features free live music every night and still maintains a tradition of providing local students with a stage on which to perform.

Another South End location with African-American ties is Charlie's Sandwich Shoppe at 429 Columbus Avenue, which has been serving meatloaf and turkey hash since 1927. During the era of segregation it was known for catering to African-American jazz musicians, indeed the country's top black musicians' union was based in the offices upstairs (it relocated in 1930 to 409 Massachusetts Avenue near the apartment rented in the 1950s by Dr. Martin Luther King Jr. (1929–1968), while he attended Boston University). As a youngster, Sammy Davis Jr. (1925–1990) tap danced in front of Charlie's for change.

A third location of African-American interest is Harriet Tubman Park at the junction of Columbus and Warren Avenues, which contains two important memorials. One is *Emancipation* (1913) celebrating the 50th anniversary of the Emancipation Proclamation by which slavery was abolished in the United States. The

Saxophonist Jonte Samuel continues Boston's South End jazz tradition

other is *Step on Board* (1999) honouring abolitionist Harriet Tubman (1822–1913) (see back cover photo). Having escaped slavery in 1939, she returned to slave territory 19 times to lead over 300 slaves to freedom via a network of safe houses known as the Underground Railroad. An exhibition about Tubman's life can be found in the Harriet Tubman Gallery at 566 Columbus Avenue (see no. 63).

Just beyond the park at 190 Warren Avenue is the former Concord Baptist Church, which has recently been converted into apartments. It was here that Martin Luther King Jr. served as guest minister.

Other locations nearby: 61, 83, 84

63   Tent City to Villa Victoria

MA 02116 (South End), Tent City on Dartmouth Avenue
and Villa Victoria on West Dedham Street
T Orange Line to Back Bay

The story of Boston's South End is the story of its immigrants. The first to arrive were members of the city's burgeoning middle and upper classes, who came in the 1850s to occupy red-brick row houses built on land reclaimed from tidal mudflats (see no. 61). The financial Panic of 1873, however, saw many relocate to Back Bay. They were replaced from the 1880s onwards by working class Irish Catholics, African-Americans, Jews, Lebanese and Greeks, all looking for work and affordable lodgings.

The row houses were modified accordingly to accommodate lodgers and multiple families (see nos. 59, 62). Since then more communities have arrived: Canadians in the 1930s, Hispanics in the 1940s, and in the 1990s, upwardly mobile young professionals, artists, and members of the LGBT community. All have left a mark on what is today a truly diverse neighbourhood.

It is no surprise that in 1891 one of the country's first Settlement Houses was established in the South End. Here reformist charity workers provided social services and recreational activities to people on low incomes, to engender a much-needed sense of community and neighbourhood pride. Several more followed and in 1960 a handful of them merged to form the United South End Settlements. An aspect of their work that can be appreciated by outsiders is the Harriet Tubman Gallery at 566 Columbus Avenue, where art is used to foster healthy neighbourhood relations despite disparate cultural and socio-economic backgrounds (see no. 62).

Urban gentrification often forces poorer and non-white residents to flee neighbourhoods. Fortunately the South End has maintained a healthy racial and income diversity due to its subsidised and publically-owned low income housing projects. The origin of one of these, Tent City, dates back to 1968, when the Boston Redevelopment Authority (BRA) was busy displacing poor minority tenants without relocation, and replacing their homes with upscale shopping malls and apartments. Their clearance of homes at the junction of Dartmouth and Columbus Avenues for a parking garage sparked a protest by several hundred demonstrators concerned about the neighbourhood's dwindling stock of affordable housing. By erecting tents they attracted

Mosaic detail in Villa Victoria's Plaza Betances

not only media attention but also public sympathy forcing the BRA to abandon their plans. As a result in 1988 a housing co-op of attractive apartment blocks was built for 269 mixed-income families. It was named Tent City in honour of the successful intervention.

An equally interesting housing project is Villa Victoria, a little farther south on West Dedham Street. Its origins also date to 1968, when African-Americans migrating out to Roxbury were being replaced by Puerto Ricans. To ensure the community had somewhere to live, the action group *Inquilinos Boricuas en Acción* (Puerto Rican Tenants in Action) was founded. They successfully acquired a plot of land and by 1976 had commissioned a series of apartment blocks for 435 low income Latino families. They are clustered around a square, Plaza Betances, named after the father of the Puerto Rican independence movement, Ramón Betances (1827–1898), who is depicted in a colourful wall mosaic here. The community stages cultural events at the Villa Victoria Center for the Arts at 85 West Newton Street.

The community's unofficial southern border is marked at the bottom of West Dedham Street by two large metal 'V's for 'Villa Victoria'. Nearby is a memorial commemorating the predominantly Puerto Rican 65th Infantry Regiment, which served bravely in Europe and the Pacific during the Second World War.

Other locations nearby: 65, 67

64 The SoWa Gallery District

MA 02118 (South End), the SoWa Artists Guild
at 450 Harrison Avenue
T Silver Line 4, 5 to East Berkeley Street

Newbury Street (Back Bay) is famous for its shopping. It first began attracting the well-heeled during the 1920s, and by the 1950s was lined with fashionable clothing boutiques. It has also long been a magnet for art establishments, including the Copley Society of Art, the country's oldest non-profit art association (1879), and the Guild of Boston Artists (1914) at 158 and 162 respectively. From the 1970s onwards these venerable art establishments were joined by trend-setting galleries such as Robert Klein, Barbara Krakow, and NAGA.

So much for the galleries – what about the artists? Rising rents and the nature of their work means that most have sought refuge in the city's various artists' communities. One of these is the self-styled SOWA Artists Guild, which as its name infers lies South of Washington Avenue (South End). Artists began arriving in the area during the 1990s, attracted by affordable accommodation in the neighbourhood's carved-up 19th century row houses (see nos. 61, 63). They were also drawn by the abandoned red-brick factory buildings straddling Harrison Avenue and Thayer Street, where goods as diverse as pianos and canned peas had once been manufactured. In a clutch of these warehouses at 450–460 Harrison Avenue, the SoWa Artists Guild now operates a non-profit association encompassing 70 studios, as well as 15 artist-run and independent galleries, such as Bromfield and Kingston.

SOWA's mission is to promote the diversity and individuality of its artists, whose work spans all types of media from painting and drawing to photography and sculpture. This it does through a variety of public events, notably the monthly SOWA First Fridays between 5 and 9pm, when visitors can see the artists at work in their studios. Some artists also open their studios in tandem with the SoWa Open Markets for crafts and farmers' produce staged each weekend from May until October between 10am and 4pm (the SoWa Vintage Market is held indoors at the same times, and also every Sunday). By whatever means the artists are exposed, what's important is that they can be accessed by everyone, and in a way that goes far beyond the traditional gallery experience.

The success of the SoWa Artists Guild has inevitably attracted other art and design-related businesses, and together they have created

The studio of artist Elena du Plessis at the SoWa Artists Guild

what is known today as the SoWa Art District. They include the incredible vintage clothing store Bobby from Boston at 19 Thayer Street, the Boston Sculptors Gallery at 486 Harrison Avenue, and Ars Libri farther along at 500, a bookshop that prides itself in holding the country's largest stock of rare and out-of-print art books. And don't forget the Food Truck Bazaar, which is open in conjunction with the SoWa Open Markets. It takes place on the forecourt of a colossal former power station at 540 Harrison Avenue built in 1896 to run Boston's first electric streetcars.

The largest and oldest artists' community in New England is the Fort Point Arts Community at 300 Summer Street (South Boston) (see no. 53). Established in 1980 and housed in a cavernous former warehouse, it is home to more than 300 artists. They showcase their work each autumn as part of the Boston Open Studios Coalition, which also includes United South End Artists, South Boston Studios, Fenway Studios, East Boston Open Studios, and the Artists Group of Charlestown (www.boston.gov). Boston's other artists' communities include the Cambridge Artists' Cooperative at 59 Church Street (Cambridge) and the Society of Arts and Crafts at 100 Pier 4 Boulevard (Suite 200) (South Boston).

Other locations nearby: 65

65 Recycling the Cyclorama

MA 02116 (South End), the Cylorama at the Boston Center
for the Arts at 539 Tremont Street
T Orange Line to Back Bay or Silver 4/5 Line to East Berkeley
Street or Union Park Street

Boston offers many impressive venues for the performing arts from pa-latial theatres to sleek concert halls. Undoubtedly the most unusual is the Cyclorama building at 539 Tremont Street (South End). Originally a 19th century visitor attraction, this extraordinary structure later served many other purposes and today it is a part of the Boston Center for the Arts (BCA), a nonprofit visual and performing arts complex.

Like the rest of the South End, the land on which the BCA sits was originally an area of tidal mudflats called South Bay. It was reclaimed from the 1830s onwards, and the first public building constructed was an evangelical church. Opened in 1877, the Moody and Sankey Tab-ernacle boasted a chorus led by conductor and organist Eben Tourjée (1834–1891), founder of the famous New England Conservatory.

The church didn't last though and a few years later the land was bought by wealthy Chicago businessman, Charles F. Willoughby. He engaged local architectural firm Cummings and Sears to build the Bos-ton Cyclorama. A popular form of entertainment in Europe and North America during the late 19th century, a cyclorama was a circular build-ing containing a huge life-like panoramic mural, usually depicting a battle.

The Boston Cyclorama was built in brick in the then popular Vene-tian Gothic style, with turrets and an enormous steel-trussed dome. Measuring 127 feet across, it was the largest dome in the country after the Capitol in Washington. Inside the building, the leading panoramic muralist of the day, Paul Philippoteaux (1846–1923), painted *The Battle of Gettysburg*. Measuring 377 feet in circumference and 42 feet in height, the huge canvas depicted Pickett's Charge, a turning point in the American Civil War (1861–1865), when Union forces defeated the Confederates.

When the Boston Cyclorama opened in 1884, visitors entered through a crenelated archway and proceeded along a long narrow pas-sage. At the far end, and with their eyes now accustomed to the low light, they ascended a staircase to a viewing platform seemingly in the midst of the battle. Model artillery, trees and soldiers placed between the viewer and the painting blurred the distinction between art and

The Cyclorama is today obscured behind a later frontage on Tremont Street

reality, the whole made even more real by a backlit painted sky. The effect must have been mesmerising.

In 1889 a new painting, *Custer's Last Fight*, was installed but by then the fashion for cycloramas (and the national pride they instilled) was waning. Subsequently the building's new owner, John Gardner (father-in-law of Isabella Stewart Gardner), converted it into an entertainment venue hosting boxing, riding, cycling and roller skating events.

A decade later the building became an industrial space used by the likes of the New England Electric Vehicle Company, the Buick Automobile Agency, and the Albert Champion Company. Champion pioneered the porcelain spark plug here in 1907 before relocating his company to Flint, Michigan.

In 1923 the Boston Flower Exchange acquired the building and added the skylight and the new entrance fronting Tremont Street. It occupied the building until 1970, when the Boston Redevelopment Authority designated the Cyclorama and surrounding buildings as the Boston Center for the Arts.

These days the Cyclorama is a vibrant and versatile venue not only showcasing performing and visual arts but also hosting commercial events. The basement contains intimate performance spaces and the adjacent new-build Calderwood Pavilion contains two conventional theatre spaces: the Wimberly and the Roberts.

After being dismantled, *The Battle of Gettysburg* mural was stored and then moved to Gettysburg itself. Since 2008 it has been displayed in a new cyclorama at the Gettysburg National Military Park Museum.

Other locations nearby: 63, 64, 67

66 Secrets of Bay Village

MA 02116 (Back Bay/Bay Village), a walk around Bay Village beginning on Fayette Street
T Orange Line to Tufts Medical Center

Bay Village is one of Boston's best-kept secrets. The city's smallest neighbourhood, it comprises a handful of city blocks bounded by Stuart, South Charles, Tremont, and Berkeley Streets. That Bay Village is primarily residential, supporting a population of only thirteen hundred, means it rarely makes the pages of mainstream guidebooks. But if it's tranquillity you're after, with some interesting history thrown in, then a walk through its leafy, gaslit streets is a must.

Like so much of central Boston, Bay Village is built on land reclaimed from water (in this case a shallow bay of mud flats on the western shore of Boston Neck) (see no. 8). The aptly-named Ephraim Marsh began drainage in 1814 and laid out the narrow streets in the 1820s. Thereafter he built the neighbourhood's first houses, including his own on Fayette Street, where this walk begins.

Although Marsh's house is no longer standing, it would have resembled those farther along at 33–39: modest yet refined three-storey, brick row houses. The distinctive Federal-style architecture echoes that of Beacon Hill, which is no surprise, since Marsh worked there as a contract builder. Additionally several Beacon Hill craftsmen settled and built homes for themselves in Bay Village.

From Fayette Street turn right onto Church Street. Initially the neighbourhood was called the Church Street District after a Presbyterian church built here in 1827. When the name fell out of favour, the area was renamed Bay Village to honour the neighbourhood's watery origins (tiny Bay Street at the end of Fayette Street does likewise).

At the end of Church Street is Melrose Street, which is also lined with brick row houses. It's worth walking the full length of this street to see evidence of a calamity that befell Bay Village in the 1860s. It was during this period that massive landfill projects to create the Back Bay and South End neighbourhoods left Bay Village at a lower level, causing its drains and sewers to fail. As the cellars of Bay Village flooded, so the City of Boston countered the problem by raising the streets by up to 18 feet. This explains the architectural anomalies encountered on Melrose and Fayette Streets, where ground floor windows are half buried beneath pavement level, and second floor doorways are reached by steps.

With the drainage problem resolved, the development of Bay Village continued apace. The creation of Back Bay meant that new land was now available beyond Arlington Street, where bow-fronted, Victorian-style homes were built along Cortes and Isabella Streets. The Our Lady of Victories Church on Isabella Street was added in 1880 by Marist Fathers from France.

Now follow Arlington Street northwards to its junction with Piedmont Street. Here stands the Castle, a granite structure built in the 1890s for the First Corps of Cadets. This private military or-

A Federal-style house on Fayette Street in Bay Village

ganisation was established in 1741 to guard the governor of the Massachusetts Bay Colony and latterly served in the Revolutionary, Civil, and Great Wars. After a stint as a library and a hotel convention centre, the building now houses a restaurant.

Piedmont and neighbouring Winchester Streets, where this walk ends, are different again. During the 1920s and 30s, close proximity to Boston's Theater District began attracting film distribution companies to Bay Village. To accommodate them, Federal-period houses were razed and *Art Deco*-style studios and warehouses erected in their place making Bay Village briefly the centre of Boston's film industry. They are used today as offices and apartments.

Other locations nearby: 47

67 Boston on Two Wheels

MA 02116 (Back Bay), the former Albert A. Pope bicycle
headquarters at 221 Columbus Avenue
T Orange Line to Back Bay

Boston is not only one of the most walkable cities in the United States
but also one of the most bike-friendly. Across Massachusetts there are
policies in place to make roads safer for cyclists, and the introduction of bike-share systems, such as Hubway, has increased accessibility
for those without bikes. All of which makes Boston a happier and a
healthier place to be.

Boston first found cycling fame in 1878, with the founding of the
Boston Bicycle Club, the nation's first. It is no coincidence that in the
same year Boston-born entrepreneur Albert A. Pope (1843–1909) began selling his *Columbia* bicycle, America's first commercially-produced, self-propelled vehicle. After seeing an imported English bicycle
two years earlier at the Centennial Exhibition in Philadelphia, Pope
shrewdly secured patents and contracted a struggling sewing machine
company to shift focus and undertake the manufacturing. By 1880 he
was selling 12,000 bicycles a year and on his way to becoming a house-
hold name.

Seeing the bicycle's potential to transform daily life, Pope promoted
cycling vigorously. Amongst other things, he established the League of
American Wheelmen to secure cyclists' road rights, financed courses
at MIT for road engineers, and even paid to have a stretch of Columbus
Avenue paved in his campaign for better road surfaces.

He chose Columbus Avenue because it was here at number 221
that he had his headquarters. The building contained offices for his
salesmen, warehousing for bicycles made at his factory in Hartford,
Connecticut, and a Riding Academy. Unfortunately in 1896 the building caught fire, with the loss of 1,700 cycles and thousands of tires. Not
one to be defeated though, Pope replaced it the following year with
the present seven-storey building. With its huge windows and ornate
façade (including 'A. A. P.' crests on the corners), it served Pope until
his death, after which the company moved away. The building today
contains luxury loft-style accommodation and a restaurant.

Boston lays claim to several cycling superlatives thanks to Pope. In
1882 seven men took 12 hours to ride *Columbia* bicycles from Worcester to Boston in the country's first 100-mile cycle race. In the same year
a *Columbia* was the first bicycle to be ridden across the United States,

a 103-day, 3,700-mile journey that finished in Boston. Then in 1894 Latvian immigrant Annie Cohen Kopchovsky (1870–1947) set out from Boston on a *Columbia* to become the first woman to cycle around the world. One of her sponsors was the Londonderry Lithia Spring Water Company of New Hampshire, which paid her to change her name to 'Annie Londonderry'!

By the time Albert Pope died in 1909, Henry Ford had rolled out his *Model T* heralding the automobile age. Boston's interest in bicycling remained though; indeed New England remains a centre for frame-building expertise. Typical is Geekhouse Bikes at 50 Terminal Street (Charlestown), a small company established in 2002 that specialises in superb custom-built steel and titanium bikes.

A crest marks the former headquarters of bicycle pioneer Albert Pope

Boston offers several other distinctive bike-buying options. Refurbished bikes dating as far back as the 1920s can be found at Cambridge Used Bicycles in the Cambridge Antique Market at 201 Monsignor O'Brien Highway (Cambridge). Bikes not Bombs at 18 Bartlett Square (Jamaica Square) is a non-profit organisation that reconditions thousands of used bikes for sale locally and for shipping abroad to developing countries. Both operations act as living reminders of Boston's position as the historic heart of the American bicycle business.

The Larz Anderson Auto Museum at 15 Newton Street (Brookline) includes a collection of historic bikes donated by a Boston dentist, who cycled across three continents.

Other locations nearby: 65, 68

68 The Salada Tea Doors

MA 02116 (Back Bay), the Salada tea doors at 330 Stuart
Street
T Green B/C/D/E Line to Arlington or Orange Line
to Back Bay (note: the doors are best seen when closed either
at weekends or after business hours)

When one thinks of Boston and tea it's usually the Boston Tea Party
that springs to mind (see no. 39). There are two other Boston tea tales,
however, that are less well known.

The first concerns the enormous Steaming Tea Kettle suspended
over the doorway of a Starbucks at 63–65 Court Street (Downtown).
This 1873 trade sign was originally commissioned by the Oriental Tea
Company and hung outside their shop on Court Street. In 1874 as part
of a promotional drive, the shop staged a contest to guess the kettle's
capacity. A large crowd gathered to hear the answer: 227 gallons, two
quarts, one pint, and three gills!

The surprisingly modern-looking building containing Starbucks
was actually built back in 1848. Known as the Sears Block, it is a rare
example of granite post-and-lintel construction, and forms an extension to the adjoining Sears Crescent, which once housed the publishing house of the abolitionist journal *The Christian Freeman*. The buildings are all that remains of Cornhill, one of Boston's oldest streets,
which was mostly razed in the 1960s to make way for the Brutalist I.
M. Pei-designed City Hall Plaza and Government Center.

Lost at the same time were parts of Court Street (including the Oriental Tea Company store) and the once-bustling Scollay and Pemberton Squares, which stood at the top of Tremont Street (the John Adams
Courthouse of 1893 is a rare survivor). In all a thousand old buildings
were demolished and 20,000 residents displaced in the name of urban
renewal. Fortunately the Steaming Tea Kettle was saved and re-hung in
1967 over what eventually became Starbucks.

The second tea-related location is a more serious affair. The Salada
tea doors are a pair of twelve-foot-high bronze doors at 330 Stuart
Street (Back Bay). They were installed in 1927 at what at the time were
the headquarters of the Salada Tea Company. The company's founder,
Peter C. Larkin (1855–1930), commissioned them to celebrate his industry's story.

Larkin, a Canadian businessman, founded the Salada Tea Company in 1892 in Montreal. A keen traveller, who specialised in find-

ing foodstuffs for import, he introduced the concept of packaging tea in foil to preserve its freshness (tea had previously been sold loose and lost its flavour in transit). This innovation proved a great success and quickly became the industry standard. It also helped establish Salada as a leading seller of tea not only in Canada but also in the northeastern USA.

To cope with American demand, Larkin opened the buildings on Stuart Street in 1917. Custom-designed by Boston architectural firm Densmore and LeClear, it included a blending and a packaging plant. Although the building has changed hands many times since then, the magnificent bronze doors by English sculptor Henry Wilson (1864–1934) remain in place.

Detail of the magnificent Salada Tea Doors in Back Bay

Comprising ten panels, they tell the story of tea: Ceylonese pickers harvesting, sorting and drying tea leaves; labourers and elephants transporting crates of tea; and tea being loaded onto ships for delivery to Europe and America. The scenes are accompanied by effigies of various Indian deities. The craftsmanship is exquisite and it is no surprise that the doors won a silver medal at the Paris Salon.

The stone door frame is also of interest. The work of French sculptor M. Caesar Caira, it includes stylised Asian women, elephant-shaped capitals, and a figure of Demeter, goddess of the harvest, and her children.

The Salada Tea Company is still in business today. In the USA it is a division of Redco Foods and in Canada a part of Unilever.

Other locations nearby: 67, 70

69 An Old Botanical Garden

MA 02116 (Back Bay), the Public Garden on Arlington Street
T Green Line B, C, D, E to Boylston or Arlington (note:
the Swan Boats are only operational between mid-Apr
and mid-Sep)

Boston's Public Garden has existed on Arlington Street (Back Bay) since the 1830s and opened to the public in the late 1850s. This makes it the country's second oldest public botanical garden after the United States Botanic Garden in Washington, which opened in 1850. Together with Boston Common, it forms the northern terminus of the Emerald Necklace, a string of urban parks created by landscape architect Frederick Law Olmsted (1822–1903) (see no. 91).

Until the early 1800s, the area occupied by the Public Garden was mudflats on the edge of Boston Common. The area had been used since 1794 by ropemakers, who gradually reclaimed the land using fill excavated from Mount Vernon (see no. 8). The City of Boston acquired this new land in 1824 and proposed it be used as a cemetery. This idea was rejected and instead in 1837 the Boston merchant, horticulturalist, and philanthropist Horace Gray (1800–1873) proposed the creation of a public botanical garden.

The early years of the garden were fraught with difficulties. Initially the land remained subject to tidal flooding but despite this a tree-lined boardwalk was laid out and a former circus at the corner of Beacon and Charles Streets was converted into a conservatory, where the country's first tulips were displayed. Unfortunately in the late 1840s Horace Gray lost much of his wealth and his conservatory succumbed to fire. Nearby Back Bay was also about to be reclaimed for housing and pressure mounted to build on the garden, too. Thankfully in 1856 it was agreed to save the garden and to use it instead as a way of encouraging Boston's well-to-do to relocate to Back Bay.

By the early 1860s the main features of today's 24-acre garden were in place, including the English-style landscaping by Boston architect George Meacham (1831–1917), the lagoon, and the iron railings. Several fountains and statues were also part of the original plan, including, on the Arlington Street side, the Ether Monument (1868), commemorating the first use of ether as an anesthetic, and a bronze equestrian statue of George Washington (1869) (see no. 22). The miniature suspension bridge over the lagoon was also constructed at this time.

The famous Swan Boats moored in the Public Garden

The most famous feature of the Public Garden is the Swan Boats, which carry people around the lagoon between mid-April and mid-September. They made their debut on the lagoon in 1877 and were built by Robert Paget, an English immigrant shipbuilder, who was inspired by Wagner's opera *Lohengrin*. Although the originals have long since been replaced, the Paget family are still in charge.

Since then many more monuments and memorials have been added to the garden. They include *Bagheera*, a fountain depicting the panther from Kipling's *Jungle Book*, a 16th century Japanese lantern from a garden in Kyoto, and a statue of Tadeusz Kościuszko, a Polish military engineer, who fought in the American Revolutionary War (1775–1783). Particularly popular are the eight bronze ducklings and their mother installed in 1987 at the north end of the lagoon. They are a tribute to Robert McCloskey's popular children's book *Make Way for Ducklings* (1941), which tells the story of a pair of mallards raising their family on the island in the lagoon.

Statues aside, one shouldn't forget that the Public Garden is primarily a botanical garden, and the plantings here are well curated. The beds flanking the central path are replanted each season, with other areas occupied by roses, bulbs, and flowering shrubs. There are also plenty of trees, notably willows around the lagoon and elms along the pathways. Look out for the solitary California redwood.

Other locations nearby: 46, 70

70　Heavenly Stained Glass

MA 02116 (Back Bay), a tour of some Back Bay churches beginning with Arlington Street Church at 351 Boylston Street
T Green Line B, C, D, E to Arlington

The Back Bay neighbourhood was created during the second half of the 19th century through the reclaimation of the Charles River tidal basin. With a grid iron of streets in place, the area filled quickly with mansions and row houses, cultural institutions, and churches. Arguably it is the churches that are the neighbourhood's greatest architectural asset, not least because they contain some heavenly stained glass.

This tour begins with Arlington Street Church at 351 Boylston Street. Back Bay's first public building, it was completed in 1861 to a neo-Classical design by architect Arthur Gilman (1821–1882), who drove a thousand wooden pilings into the reclaimed land to form a solid foundation (see no. 8). Above this rises the building's imposing brownstone exterior, with its 190-foot high bell tower.

The interior, with its arches and Corinthian columns, is modelled after a Baroque cathedral in Genoa. Note the box pews, which at one time were privately owned. Undoubtedly the greatest treasures, however, are the 16 stunning stained glass windows created by the studios of Louis Comfort Tiffany (1848–1933). They were designed by Frederick Wilson (1858–1932), Tiffany's chief designer for ecclesiastical windows, and he made full use of the company's glassmaking expertise, including its trademark opalescent *Favrile* glass to achieve a painterly effect and rippled 'Drapery Glass' to represent clothing.

Also completed in 1861 was the nearby Emmanuel Episcopal Church at 15 Newbury Street. Designed by Alexander Rice Esty (1826–1881) in the Gothic Revival style, it contains a fine stained glass window by Frederic Crowninshield (1845–1918) in which the allegorical figure of Piety from Bunyan's *The Pilgrim's Progress* points the way to Emmanuel's Land. Also here is the Leslie Lindsey Memorial Chapel designed by Scottish Gothic Revivalist architect Ninian Comper (1864–1960), which memorialises Lindsey and her husband, who married in the church and perished when the *Lusitania* sank in 1915.

Farther west at 67 Newbury Street is the Church of the Covenant. Completed in 1867 to a Gothic Revival design by British émigré architect Richard Upjohn (1802–1878), it is built of Roxbury puddingstone and for a time its soaring 236-foot high spire was Boston's tallest structure (see no. 79). During the 1890s the Tiffany Company was commissioned to redecorate the interior. Not only did they install 42 stained glass windows but they also painted the walls and ceilings, and designed numerous fixtures, including a jewelled chandelier topped with golden angels. The overall result is a superb display of Tiffany's talents when applied to a sacred space.

A solitary Tiffany window can be found at the First Baptist Church at 110 Commonwealth Avenue. One of the country's oldest Baptist churches, its original parishioners were forced by the Puritans to worship on Noddle's Island (see no. 6). Completed in 1872 to a de-

Tiffany's *The Good Shepherd* in Arlington Street Church

sign by Henry Hobson Richardson (1838–1886), the puddingstone exterior features an Italianate bell tower adorned with friezes by Frédéric Auguste Bartholdi (1834–1904) of Statue of Liberty fame. The church was Richardson's first ecclesiastical building before he designed his masterpiece, Trinity Church, which stands nearby on Copley Square (see no. 75).

This tour finishes with the New Old South Church at 645 Boylston Street, so called because the congregation of Downtown's Old South Meeting House relocated here after the building's completion in 1873 (see no. 38). Designed in the Gothic Revival style by Boston architectural firm Cummings and Sears, it features striped stonework, a 246-foot high *campanile*, and a lantern reminiscent of St. Mark's Basilica in Venice. Inside are polychrome walls and carved woodwork accompanied by English stained glass in the style of the 15th century.

Other locations nearby: 68, 69, 73, 74

71 The Mansions of Back Bay

MA 02116 (Back Bay), a tour of grand townhouses beginning
with the Gibson House Museum at 137 Beacon Street
T Green B/C/D/E Line to Arlington (note: Gibson House
Museum can only be visited as part of a guided tour)

Back Bay is the result of Boston's most ambitious land reclamation
project. During the second half of the 19th century hundreds of acres
of much-needed land were created here by infilling the Charles River
tidal basin (see nos. 8, 74). The man responsible, architect Arthur Gilman (1821–1882), imposed a gridiron of thoroughfares running east–
west from the Public Garden – Beacon, Marlborough, Commonwealth,
Newbury, and Boylston Streets – crossed by eight shorter streets named
alphabetically from Arlington Street to Hereford Street. The result is a
meticulously planned neighbourhood, with gaslit sidewalks lined with
elegant townhouses, churches, and shops, serviced by narrow alleys
to the rear.

A great draw for anyone interested in architecture is Back Bay's
townhouses. They are known collectively as 'brownstones' (after the
sandstone used in their façades), although some are made of brick
and other types of stone. They represent one of the country's best preserved ensembles of 19th-century urban design – and some are very
grand indeed.

This tour begins with the Gibson House Museum at 137 Beacon
Street, a rare example of a Back Bay townhouse open to the public. It
was built in 1860 for Catherine Hammond Gibson (1804–88), whose
husband, a successful sugar merchant, was lost at sea. Her move from
overcrowded Beacon Hill to the newly-fashionable Back Bay echoed
the journey made by many of Boston's well-to-do merchant class during this period.

The house was designed by Edward Clarke Cabot (1818–1901),
who was also responsible for the Boston Athenæum (see no. 30). His
façade features a sturdy brownstone ground floor, which gives way to
lighter red-brick upper storeys framing a brownstone bay window (a
common feature of Back Bay homes). The interior is thoroughly Victorian, with a grand entrance hall and dining room to impress visitors,
well-appointed parlours and bedrooms upstairs, and a kitchen, dumbwaiter, and coal shed in the basement.

That the house retains its interior is down to Gibson's grandson,
who opened it to visitors as early as 1936, at a time when similar

homes were being carved up into apartments. Officially a museum since 1957, it offers a unique glimpse into the lives of a well-to-do Boston family, including unusual features such as gold-embossed wallpaper and even a velvet tent for the pet cat!

A richly-furnished room in the Gibson House Museum

Drop down onto tree-lined Commonwealth Avenue to discover a different style of townhouse built around the same time. Numbers 3 and 5 were built in red-brick as a matching pair. In 1903, however, number 5 (known as the Gamble Mansion) was purchased by merchant Walter Baylies (1862–1936), who rebuilt it in white stone. He also added the striking single-storey Louis XV-style ballroom used in 1912 for his daughter's coming-of-age.

Farther west on Commonwealth Avenue, at the corner with Dartmouth Street, is the Ames-Webster Mansion built in 1882 for railroad and shovel manufacturing heir, Frederick Ames (1835–1893). His wealth is expressed in the building's two-storey conservatory and roof-top tower. Even grander is the Burrage Mansion at 314 Commonwealth Avenue built in 1899 for entrepreneur Albert Burrage (1859–1931). A heady fusion of Vanderbilt-style mansion and Loire chateau, it features carved oriel windows, gargoyles, turrets, and a conservatory to the rear.

This tour finishes across the road with the Oliver Ames Mansion, where Commonwealth Avenue joins Massachusetts Avenue. Built in the 1880s for Frederick Ames' cousin, businessman Oliver Ames (1831–1895), it is notable for its wealth of carved brownstone decoration.

It's worth calling in at nearby 346 Newbury Street as a reminder that during the 19th century this stretch of Boston's premier shopping street was stabling for the great homes just discussed.

Other locations nearby: 72

72 A Little Piece of France

MA 02116 (Back Bay), the French Cultural Center
at 53 Marlborough Street
T Green B/C/D/E Line to Arlington

The French Cultural Center at 53 Marlborough Street (Back Bay) has been at the centre of Francophone culture in Boston for more than half a century. During that time its goal has always been to preserve and promote French culture in the city through authentic social experience. This it achieves through its library, language courses, and communal activities.

The origins of the Center date back to the Second World War. In July 1940, in reponse to General de Gaulle's appeal for the French and their allies to unite for the liberation of occupied France, Americans founded the organisation France Forever. During the war it enrolled over 23,000 people of different nationalities, organised into 56 local chapters. One of the most active of these was the Boston Chapter led tirelessly by Belle P. Rand (1869–1956).

One of Rand's achievements was the setting up of a lending library of French books and periodicals. Anticipating the post-war dissolution of Forever France, she and her colleagues decided to make the library a permanent facility. Accordingly in December 1945 the French Library in Boston became a non-profit educational institution.

Bolstered by donations from the French Government through its Consulate in New York, the Library soon outgrew its original premises on Newbury Street. This prompted another strong-willed woman, Edna Allen Doriot (1901–1978), to spearhead a fundraising campaign that led in 1956 to the acquisition of new premises at 300 Berkeley Street. Later in 1961 Doriot arranged for the sculptor Katharine Lane Weem (1899-1989) to donate her brownstone mansion at 53 Marlborough Street to the Library, where it has been based ever since.

Doriot's work was continued after her death by her husband, General Georges F. Doriot (1899–1987), a French émigré and one of America's first venture capitalists. For their efforts the pair were named *Commandeur et Chevalier de la Légion d'Honneur*, one of the few couples ever admitted to the order.

In 2010 the Library was renamed the French Cultural Center to reflect the fact that there is now much more happening on Marlborough Street than just books. Admittedly the upstairs library is one of the largest private collections in the United States but today it is bolstered by films, music, and online resources. The Center's school (part of the Alliance Française network) offers French language classes for all ages. Cultural programming is broad and includes lectures and concerts staged in the elegant, wood-panelled ballroom. Political and artistic personalities often talk here, too, and seasonal celebrations include a Bastille Day street festival. Monthly art events are held in the gallery, and cooking demonstrations and wine tastings take place in the large working kitchen.

A Tricolour marks Boston's French Cultural Center

In recent years the Center has embarked on several important initiatives. These include *Accent on Success*, which provides free French language courses each year to 150 pupils in underprivileged Boston schools, and *Mosaïque*, which provides essential support for French cultural programming throughout New England.

After leaving the French Cultural Center note the First Church of Boston across the road at 66 Marlborough Street. This Unitarian Universalist Church was founded in 1630 as a Congregational church by the first Puritan settlers in Charlestown (see no. 1). The present building erected in 1968 occupies the burned-out ruins of a predecessor built when the church relocated here from the North End a century earlier.

There are several other cultural centres in Boston that welcome visitors. The Kaji Aso Studio at 40 St. Stephen Street (Fenway–Kenmore), for example, offers Japanese art, calligraphy, ceramics and poetry classes, and a tea ceremony each Sunday in the garden.

Other locations nearby: 71

73 A Masterpiece of Restoration

MA 02116 (Back Bay), RH Boston (The Gallery at the Historic Museum of Natural History) at 234 Berkeley Street
T Green Line B, C, D, E to Arlington or Orange Line to Back Bay

Most visitors to Boston's Museum of Science (West End) are too busy enjoying the interactive exhibits to muse on the building's history. If they did they would learn that the Modernist galleries only date back to 1951 (see no. 21). Before that the museum was housed in a grand neo-Classical red-brick and brownstone building at 234 Berkeley Street (Back Bay). This older structure was recently revamped as a flagship store for the California-based home furnishings company RH (Restoration Hardware) in what critics agree is a masterpiece of architectural restoration.

The museum's roots go back to 1830, when a group of men with shared scientific interests founded the Boston Society of Natural History. After using various temporary facilities to house their burgeoning collections, they settled in 1864 in Back Bay. As the New England Museum of Natural History, the building was only the second structure erected on what at the time was land newly reclaimed from the Charles River tidal basin. It was custom-designed by architect William Gibbons Preston (1842–1910), who founded it securely on a raft of thousands of wooden pilings driven down through the landfill to bedrock.

As a fervent historic preservationist – he helped save Boston's Massachusetts State House from demolition – Preston would have been horrified but ultimately be pleased with what later became of his building. Initially after being sold off, the building was re-purposed for use by various clothing retailers. False ceilings, partitions and mezzanines obscured much of Preston's original design, which had centred on a stately two-storey atrium containing a whale's skeleton lit by clerestory windows. Preston's graceful Corinthian pilasters and Romanesque archways were also obscured with little consideration for their aesthetics. Only in 2010, when the last clothing company moved out and RH acquired the building, did work begin on restoring Preston's original vision.

When the new store opened in 2013 as RH Boston (The Gallery at the Historic Museum of Natural History), it was a revelation to many. In conjunction with Backen, Gillam & Kroeger Architects, the atrium had been reopened from the ground floor all the way up to the newly-gilded, coffered ceiling. All the original plaster work and ornamenta-

The grand RH Boston furnishings' store was once a museum

tion had been painstakingly restored, and on the second floor a series of 18 foot-high mirrored archways reflected a dozen crystal chandeliers hanging overhead.

Other features are new additions and all the more novel for that. Pride of place goes to a traction-and-counterweight glass elevator inspired by an 1890s-era original in the Bradbury Building in Los Angeles. From the top it gives a wonderful overview of the newly restored interior.

Throughout the store are features that signal RH's evolution from a standard home-goods purveyor to a full-scale lifestyle brand. Browsing the various floors reveals room after room of tastefully curated living spaces: lounges, dining rooms, bedrooms all perfectly coordinated with effortlessly matched fixtures and fittings. There are some surprises here, too, including life-sized artifical olive trees, a rug room piled high with intricately woven carpets, and everywhere vistas luring visitors onwards to the next display.

The staff at RH Boston go to enormous lengths to use the building's unique backdrops to set off installations of the company's furniture and other merchandise in an inspiring way. Whether one buys something or not, the result is a shop that has become a unique, free-to-enter visitor attraction in its own right.

Other locations nearby: 68, 70, 74, 75

74 The Boylston Street Fish Weirs

MA 02116 (Back Bay), the Boylston Street Fish Weir diorama in the lobby of the former New England Life Insurance building at 90 Newbury Street
T Green Line B, C, D, E to Arlington or Orange Line to Back Bay

Completed in 1941, the New England Life building at 501 Boylston Street (Back Bay) is known today as the Newbry and serves as a commercial office building, with retail premises and a sports club at street level. An unexpected surprise for visitors is the series of dioramas depicting scenes from Boston's history in the lobby on the Newbury Street side of the building.

Commissioned by the New England Life Company, the four dioramas include the home of William Blaxton, Boston's first white settler, the filling of Back Bay in the second half of the 19th century, and the New England Museum of Natural History on nearby Berkeley Street, which today houses the RH Boston furnishings store (see no. 73). The structure shown under construction alongside the museum is the Rogers Building, part of the original Massachusetts Institute of Technology before its relocation in 1916 to Cambridge (the Newbry now occupies this site).

The fourth diorama is the most interesting of all as it depicts Boston in prehistoric times. It shows Native Americans attending a wooden fish weir on the Charles River in around 2,500 BC. Fish weirs – fence-like structures used to trap fish in tidal areas – have been used by indigenous peoples for thousands of years. Evidence for Boston's was first discovered in 1913 by engineers extending the city's subway system beneath Boylston Street. Buried 30 or so feet down in the glacial clay they found thousands of vertical wooden stakes. Archaeologists deduced they were the remains of an ancient fish weir constructed on ancient tidal mudflats.

More stakes were found by archaeologists in 1939 during the construction of the New England Life building. Here the stratigraphy was clearer, with the stakes overlaid by tidal silt and 20 feet of gravel added when the land was reclaimed during the 19th century (see no. 8). Further stakes were revealed in 1946 during the construction of the Old John Hancock Building at 200 Berkeley Street prompting archaeologists to posit a single huge fish weir made up of 65,000 stakes covering

The Boylston Street Fish Weir diorama on Newbury Street

more than two acres. It is this take on the evidence that is shown in the diorama.

Fast forward now to 1985, when the discovery of more stakes during construction work at 500 Boylston Street prompted a reappraisal of the archaeology. Radiocarbon dating, pollen analysis, and improved surveying techniques showed the remains to be parts of not one but several weirs built in different locations starting around 3,200 BC and continuing in use for over 1,500 years. They are thought to have measured 100–150 feet in length and been deployed to catch herring (known in North America as alewife) that spawn in late spring in the intertidal zone. The weirs were probably used by family clans of up to 50 members, who migrated each spring from their hunting camps to the coast in pursuit of seasonal food. The fish they caught in the weirs would not only have been eaten but also used to nourish soil for crops.

These days with climate change an important topic, it should be noted that the Boylston Street Fish Weir has something to say on the matter. Research has shown that the ocean level in Boston has risen over 10 feet in the last 6,000 years, and as the shoreline changed so the fish weirs were raised to accommodate it. Since skyscapers can hardly be raised, the only way to deal with future sea level rise in low-lying Boston will be to build a tidal barrier outside Boston Harbor and plans are already being drawn up to do just that.

Other locations nearby: 70, 73, 75, 76

75 One of America's Favourite Churches

MA 02116 (Back Bay), Trinity Church at 206 Clarendon Street on Copley Square
T Green B/C/D/E Line to Copley (note: there is an admission charge to visit the church, which includes guided and self-guided tours; free tours are available each Sunday at 12.15am in winter and 11am in summer)

In 1885 the American Institute of Architects (AIA) voted Boston's Trinity Church in Copley Square (Back Bay) the country's most important building. In 2007 as part of the celebrations marking the AIA's 150th anniversary, a public poll of America's favourite architecture revealed that the church was still in the top thirty. That it continues to appeal to both architects and the public alike says much about its design and decoration.

Although Trinity Church was completed in 1877, the Episcopalian parish it serves is much older. Founded in 1734, its members originally worshipped on Summer Street (Downtown Crossing). Only when that site was destroyed during the Great Boston Fire of 1872 did Rector Phillips Brooks (1835–1893) decide to relocate his parish to Copley Square. There he commissioned a church that would be like no other in America.

The architect chosen by Brooks was the Harvard-trained Henry Hobson Richardson (1838–1886). He had recently pioneered the eponymous Richardsonian Romanesque style, an impressive amalgam of French, Spanish, and Byzantine building elements, and in Trinity Church he deployed it to great effect. Before work above ground could commence, however, the land beneath had to be prepared.

Copley Square had only recently been reclaimed from a tidal basin, so to ensure a strong foundation 4,500 wooden piles were driven down through the landfill to bedrock (see no. 8). Two thousand of these were used to support four huge granite pyramids on which rests the 211 foot-tall Central Tower (the pyramids are still visible in the Undercroft). The other piles were used to support four wings radiating outwards from the tower, containing the nave, chancel, and transepts. The result is a building that still holds its own today despite being overshadowed since the 1970s by the far taller John Hancock Tower.

Brooks and Richardson decided that the sturdy arches and rough-hewn stonework of the exterior should be offset by a rich, polychrome interior. To achieve this they turned to artist John La Farge (1835–1910). Remarkably the murals inside Trinity Church were his first commission and rightly helped establish his reputation. When completed they covered an impressive 21,500 square feet.

With one exception, the church windows were all clear glass when the church was consecrated. Stained glass windows were soon commissioned though, including four designed by British artist Edward Burne-Jones (1833–1898) and executed by Arts and Crafts practitioner, William Morris (1834–1896). Another four were commissioned from La Farge,

A detail of Trinity Church in Copley Square

including his superb blue triptych *Christ in Majesty* above the entrance. It is made using his pioneering opalescent glass technique, in which coloured particles are suspended creating a milky, shifting effect (the technique was later patented by Tiffany).

An unusual feature in the chancel is the country's first freestanding altar (they usually backed onto a decorative screen), with seats at either end for Massachusetts' two bishops. One can picture the charismatic Brooks in his black gown here delivering one of the sermons for which he was famous (he is also remembered as the lyricist of the Christmas carol *O Little Town of Bethlehem*). Brooks and Richardson wanted Venetian mosaics in the apse behind the altar but they had insufficient funds. Only when the current altar was installed in 1938 were the mosaics finally added.

Upon leaving the church visit the tiny St. Francis Garden on Clarendon Street, which features a cloistered colonnade and fountain. The window tracery in one of the walls comes from the Church of St. Botolph in Boston, England, and is a reminder of whence the city's Puritan founders hailed.

Other locations nearby: 74, 76, 77, 78

76 All the Way from Lebanon

MA 02116 (Back Bay), the memorial to Kahlil Gibran
on the Dartmouth Street side of Copley Square
T Green B/C/D/E Line to Copley

William Shakespeare and the Chinese philosopher Lao-Tzu are the world's best selling prose poets. In third place is the Lebanese poet Kahlil Gibran (1883–1931), who wrote and illustrated his most famous work, *The Prophet*, in Boston. An eminently quotable treatise on the human condition, it has sold millions of copies worldwide and continues to inspire.

Gibran was born into a Maronite Christian family in the mountain hamlet of Bsharri in northern Lebanon. As the country was under Ottoman rule, he and his siblings were taken by their mother to America to avoid persecution. They arrived on Ellis Island in 1895 and headed north to Boston, where they settled into a Syrian-Lebanese community in Chinatown (see no. 48).

Gibran's mother became a seamstress, whilst he attended school to learn English. He also attended the Denison Settlement House art school, where his creative talents were encouraged by *avant-garde* photographer Fred Holland Day (1864–1933). So as not to forget his native aesthetic, however, Gibran returned to Lebanon aged 15 to study at a Maronite-run school. Upon arriving back in Boston in 1902 he found that one of his siblings had died, followed shortly afterwards by another, and then his mother. His remaining sister supported him though and in 1904 he was able to stage his first art show at Day's studio. It was there that he befriended Mary Elizabeth Haskell (1873–1964), a respected school headmistress ten years his senior.

With Haskell's patronage Gibran flourished. His first literary efforts were published in Arabic and in 1908 he studied art in Paris for two years. In 1918 his first English-language work, *The Madman*, a slim volume of aphorisms and parables was published, and in 1920 he led the Pen League of Arab Poets, which helped usher Arabic literature into the modern era. His greatest success though was *The Prophet*, which was published in 1923.

In *The Prophet* a fictional character called Almustafa is about to depart the foreign city of Orphalese after a long stay. As he does he is delayed by a group of locals, who beseech him to share his wisdom. What follows, through the voice of Almustafa, are Gibran's own views on such topics as love, marriage, family, work, and death.

The *Prophet's* fame spread initially by word of mouth, selling over a thousand copies in its first three months. Despite a cool critical reception, its easily-accessible truisms wrapped up in a cloak of Arabian mysticism appealed to Depression-era Americans desperate for escapism. By 1931, the year of Gibran's premature death in New York City from liver failure, it had been translated into 20 languages, and during the 1960s gained a new audience in America's freewheeling youth culture. It has never been out of print and Gibran's plea for cultural pluralism is as important today as it ever was.

Gibran is buried in the Mar Sarkis Monastery in Bsharri in accordance with his will, where today can also be found the Gibran Museum. He is remembered in Boston by a me-

A memorial to Lebanese poet and mystic Kahlil Gibran, who wrote his greatest work in Boston

morial on the Dartmouth Street side of Copley Square (Back Bay) in front of the Boston Public Library. Designed by Gibran's nephew and godson Kahlil George Gibran (1922–2008), a renowned sculptor who also lived and worked in Boston, it was unveiled in 1977 and features a bronze bas relief of a reflective Gibran clutching a copy of *The Prophet*.

Gibran was not the only Lebanese to leave a mark on Boston. Hannah Sabbagh Shakir (1895–1990) helped found the Lebanese-Syrian Ladies' Aid Society, which did much to help immigrants in Boston. She also opened a successful textile factory in Roxbury.

Other locations nearby: 74, 75, 77, 78

77 A Palace for the People

MA 02116 (Back Bay), the Boston Public Library
at 700 Boylston Street
T Green B/C/D/E Line to Copley

Two of Boston's best loved public buildings face each other across Copley Square (Back Bay). Trinity Church on Clarendon Street serves a parish of 3,000 households and attracts many visitors with its colourful interior (see no. 75). Boston Public Library at 700 Boylston Street serves a different congregation but is no less of a shrine. Over 3.5 million people visit annually to read books and to marvel at the magnificent art and architecture.

The idea to establish America's first public lending library was mooted in 1826 by George Ticknor (1791–1871), a Harvard professor and trustee of the Boston Athenæum, a private members' library on Beacon Street (see no. 30). The idea fell on deaf ears though and it was not until 1848 that a statute facilitated the library's creation using funds donated by Boston mayor, Josiah Quincy, Jr. (1802–1882).

The first Boston Public Library opened with 16,000 volumes in 1854 in a former schoolhouse on Mason Street (Downtown). It quickly outgrew these premises though forcing a move in 1858 to a new Italianate building on Boylston Street, where a quarter of a million books were held. That was outgrown too, and in 1880 the construction of the present building on Copley Square was approved.

The prestigious New York firm of McKim, Mead and White were chosen to design the library in a palatial Renaissance Revival style based loosely on the Bibliothèque nationale in Paris. Built of pink Milford granite and opened in 1895, it features huge arched windows and a red tile roof. Inside are bronze doors designed by acclaimed American sculptor Daniel Chester French (1850–1931), a magnificent marble staircase guarded by a pair of sculpted lions, the vast barrel-vaulted Bates Reading Room, and an open-air colonnaded courtyard based on the Palazzo della Cancelleria in Rome.

A key feature is the library's murals. Those in the Abbey Room, where books were originally collected by customers, are by Edwin Austin Abbey (1852–1911) and depict the Holy Grail legend. Most remarkable are those secreted away on the top floor in the dimly-lit Sargent Hall. Entitled *Triumph of Religion*, they are the work of John Singer Sargent (1856–1925), who used appliquéd jewels and plaster reliefs to imbue a three-dimensional appearance. With such luxury in mind –

The magnificent Bates Reading Room at Boston Public Library

and all for free – it is little wonder the library has been described as a 'Palace for the People'.

Since this is a library, we shouldn't forget the literature. With an extension, the Johnson Building, added in 1972, it is home today to almost 24 million items. This makes it the country's third largest public library after the Library of Congress and the New York Public Library. Amongst the rarities here are records of Colonial-era Boston, maps from the American Revolutionary War (1775–1783) (in the Norman B. Leventhal Map Center), the personal library of President John Adams (1735–1826), documents belonging to abolitionist William Lloyd Garrison (1805–1879), and materials relating to the trial of Italian-American anarchists, Sacco and Vanzetti (see no. 17).

Free art and architecture tours of the Library depart daily from the Dartmouth Street entrance. Additionally, a farmers' market is staged outside in Copley Square on Tuesdays and Fridays from mid-May to Thanksgiving.

The Johnson Building contains the library's main circulating collection and is the headquarters of Boston's 24 branch libraries. The East Boston branch was the country's first when it opened in 1869 (see no. 6). The North End branch at 25 Parmentier Street contains a fascinating model of the Venetian Doge's Palace built by local kindergarten teacher, Henrietta Macy (1854–1927).

Other locations nearby: 74, 75, 76, 78

78 The World's Oldest Annual Marathon

MA 02116 (Back Bay), the Boston Marathon finish line
at 665 Boylston Street
T Green B/C/D/E Line to Copley

The Boston Marathon takes place each year on Patriots' Day, a state holiday commemorating the Battles of Lexington and Concord, which heralded the American Revolutionary War (1775–1783). When the holiday was inaugurated in 1894 it was celebrated on April 19th, the day in 1775 when the battles took place. Since 1969 it has been shifted to the third Monday in April, which locals call Marathon Monday.

The Boston Marathon is the world's oldest annual marathon race. First staged in 1897, it was inspired by the revival of marathon running a year earlier at the first modern Olympic Games in Athens. Members of the Boston Athletic Association (BAA) participated in those games and inaugurated the Boston Marathon as a way of linking the American and Athenian struggles for liberty.

It is difficult today to imagine that only 18 runners participated in the first Boston Marathon. These days around 30,000 come from all over the world of whom almost half are women (remarkably women could not enter officially until 1972). Cheered along by half a million spectators, the race is New England's most watched sporting event.

Originally the route was 24.5 miles long. This was increased in 1924 to 26 miles and 385 yards so as to conform to the distance codified by the International Association of Athletics Federations. Accordingly the start line was moved from Ashland in Middlesex County to Hopkinton. There the race starts in staggered waves beginning with the mobility impaired around 8.50am, elite women at 9.32, and elite men at 10, followed by other successive waves until 11.15. To qualify runners must be over 18 and proven to have completed a standard marathon within the previous 18 months. Exceptions are made for the many charity runners, who between them raise more than $10 million a year.

From Hopkinton the course follows Routes 135, 16 and 30 as it winds its way into Boston. Along the way it passes through six Massachusetts' conurbations: Ashland, Framingham, Natick, Wellesley, Newton, and Brookline. The toughest part is the four Newton Hills, which begin at the 16-mile mark. The last of them near Boston College has been dubbed Heartbreak Hill because it comes at a point where a runner's glycogen stores are depleted.

The finish line is located on Boylston Street outside the Boston Public Library. Emblazoned with the BAA logo, it is painted from one side of the street to the other. The winner originally made do with a wreath woven from olive branches. Since the 1980s, however, corporate-sponsored cash prizes have lured professional runners. It was in the last few hundred yards of the race in 2013 that tragedy struck when two terrorist bombs killed three spectators and injured many hundreds more.

The church just beyond the finish line is nicknamed the Church of the Finish Line (its real name is the New Old South Church) (see no. 70). Two further Marathon-related sites can be found in Copley Square: a circle embedded in the pavement engraved with the names of previous winners and the sculpture *The Hare and the Tortoise* by Nancy Schön (b. 1928) to mark the hundredth anniversary of the race in 1996.

A Boston Marathon trophy displayed in the Adidas RunBase shop

Fans of the Boston Marathon should visit the Boston Marathon Adidas RunBase shop at 855 Boylston Street. This unique store combines runners' practical needs with a small museum containing the shoes, singlets, photos and trophies of famous runners, including seven-time winner Clarence DeMar (1888–1958), the first ever women's Olympic marathon champion Joan Benoit (b. 1957), and Johnny Kelley (1907–2004), who twice represented America in the Olympics.

Other locations nearby: 74, 75, 76, 77

79 View from the Skywalk

MA 02199 (Back Bay), the Skywalk Observatory on the
50th floor of the Prudential Tower at 800 Boylston Street
T Green Line E to Prudential or Green Line B, C, D to Hynes
Convention Ctr (note: ID is required to gain access to the
Skywalk Observatory, which is occasionally closed for private
events)

Boston is home to around 250 skyscrapers, 30 of which stand more than 400 feet high. The majority are clustered in Downtown's Financial District and in Back Bay, where they define those neighbourhoods' skylines. To get a bird's-eye view of them visit either *Building Boston*, a magnificent scale model of the city housed in the BSA Space at 290 Congress Street (Downtown), or the Boston Planning & Development Agency's Model Room on the 9th floor of Boston City Hall at One City Hall Square (Downtown). Whenever a new skyscraper is built, its miniature counterpart is added to these models.

Boston's first skyscraper was the 187-foot-high Ames Building, an office block completed in 1893 on Court Street (Downtown). In 1915 it was superceded by the 496-foot-high Custom House Tower on nearby McKinley Square (see no. 36). This remained Boston's tallest building until the building boom of the 1960s and 70s, when more than 20 new skyscrapers were constructed.

Of these, the John Hancock Tower at 200 Clarendon Street (Back Bay) was the tallest. Indeed the 790-foot-high, 60-storey tower completed in 1976 for John Hancock Insurance is still the tallest structure in Boston. Despite towering over much-loved older buildings, notably Trinity Church, the sleek, minimalist design of architect Henry N. Cobb (b. 1926) ensures it doesn't overshadow them.

Although more skyscrapers are currently under construction (or in the planning stages), only one – the South Bay Tower in Chinatown – is projected to exceed the height of the John Hancock Tower and then only by a few feet. That said, when viewed globally both appear way down the list of the world's tallest structures. Dubai's Burj Khalifa currently top of the pile at a staggering 2,722 feet high!

Not so long ago it was possible to visit a public observation deck at the top of the John Hancock Tower but this has been closed since the September 11th terrorist attacks. Fortunately there is another deck at the top of the city's second-tallest building, also constructed for an insurance company. The 749-foot-high, 52-storey Prudential Tower was completed in 1964 at 800 Boylston Street (Back Bay) – and if its rooftop masts are included it is actually taller than the John Hancock Tower. High up on the 50th floor is the Skywalk Observatory, currently the highest observation deck in New England, which offers a magnificent 360-degree view of the surrounding city, including Fenway Park and the grid-iron street layout of Back Bay. On a clear day it is possible to make out Cape Cod across Massachusetts Bay to the south and New Hampshire to the north. Look down and you might catch a glimpse of the Pru Garden, a 1.3-acre park that is nigh impossible to see at pavement level.

Copley Square and the John Hancock Tower from the Prudential Tower

Boston currently has two other public observation decks. One is at the top of the Custom House Tower already mentioned. The other is on the 14th floor of Independence Wharf at 470 Atlantic Avenue (Downtown). From here the view takes in Fort Point Channel and South Boston to the south, Boston Harbor, Logan Airport, and the islands to the east, and the Rose Fitzgerald Kennedy Greenway to the west (there is no direct view north).

> Standing alongside the John Hancock Tower is the Berkeley Building (or Old John Hancock Building), a 495-foot-high tower completed in 1947. The illuminated weather beacon on its summit can be decoded with the following rhyme: "Solid blue, clear view; flashing blue, clouds are due; solid red, rain ahead; flashing red, snow instead". It should be noted that flashing red during the summer months means a Red Sox game has been cancelled!

Other locations nearby: 63, 82

80 A Unique Tiffany Treasure

MA 02215 (Back Bay), the Ayer Mansion
at 395 Commonwealth Avenue
T Green B/C/D Line to Hynes Convention Ctr or Kenmore
(note: guided tours by appointment only)

Back Bay is defined architecturally by its smart row houses and mansions, interspersed with several churches adorned with Tiffany glass. Only in one building, however, do these design elements conspire to produce something unique. The Ayer Mansion at 395 Commonwealth Avenue is the world's only surviving example of a home created entirely by American interior designer, Louis Comfort Tiffany (1848–1933).

The mansion was built for businessman and art collector Frederick Ayer (1822–1918), who made his fortune several times over. Early on he pioneered new marketing strategies to promote his brother Dr. James Cook Ayer's patent medicines, including the hugely popular *Ayer's Cherry Pectoral*. As a result he was able to acquire several failing New England woollen mills, which he transformed into the successful American Woolen Company, which manufactured uniforms for the U.S. Army right up to the Korean War.

Ayer commissioned his mansion with his second wife, Ellen, in 1899 after returning from a trip to Africa and the East. Along the way they collected exotic art and furnishings, which they were keen to display effectively in their new home. The choice of Tiffany as designer was obvious because through his own travels he had helped make Orientalism a design facet of European Art Nouveau. At the Ayer Mansion he used the austere architectural forms employed by the Ayer's architect, A. J. Manning (1851–1919), as a foil for his own rich Orientalising designs.

Coming from Lowell, and therefore not part of Boston's tight-knit Brahmin society, the Ayers embraced their outsider status by building something unusually progressive for turn-of-the-century Boston. Instead of using Back Bay's ubiquitous brownstone or brick for the exterior, they chose unadorned light-coloured granite. Tiffany then emphasised the front door, bay window and cornice with colourful Moorish-themed stone mosaics. Other than at his own home, Laurelton Hall, it is the only time he employed mosaic work externally. Over the front door is one of Tiffany's trademark stained glass windows, which in Boston he normally reserved for churches (see no. 70).

If this wasn't enough to distinguish the Ayers as forward-looking and worldly, the mansion's interior certainly did. Completed in 1902, it reveals Tiffany's remarkable versatility as an all-round interior designer. He is responsible for everything from the glass mosaics and intricate woodwork to the light sconces and jaw-dropping globular chandelier in the stairwell, creating a wholly unified work of art.

Tiffany's *pièce de résistance* though is the remarkable staircase just off the entrance hall, where Ellen Mayer indulged her love of theatre. A set of semi-circular steps edged in mosaic rise proscenium-like through an uplit golden apse. At the top, where further stairs lead off either

The remarkable mosaic entrance hall at the Ayer Mansion

side, is an extraordinary mosaic mural of a Classical temple rendered in opalescent glass backed with metallic foil so as to appear back-lit. Framed by adjoining marble pilasters, it appears possible to walk right through it, and one can easily imagine Ellen Mayer giving an impromptu performance to her guests here.

With the demise of Frederick and Ellen Ayer, the mansion became offices. Fortunately the interiors remained largely intact and in 1964 the building was acquired by the Bayridge Residence & Cultural Center, a non-profit organisation providing accommodation for women attending local universities and colleges. With their approval, the Campaign for the Ayer Mansion is now restoring the mansion to its original glory, opening it twice monthly for guided tours.

The Ayers occupied the mansion with their children, including daughter Beatrice. In 1909 in the mansion's library she became engaged to the future General George S. Patton (1885–1945) of Second World War fame.

Other locations nearby: 81, 91

81 The Salem Witch Bureau

MA 02215 (Fenway–Kenmore), the Massachusetts Historical
Society at 1154 Boylston Street
T Green B/C/D Line to Hynes Convention Ctr (note: there is
a public exhibition space but library visits and building tours
are by appointment only)

Boston is America's oldest major city so it's no surprise to find the country's oldest historical society here, too. Founded more than 200 years ago, the Massachusetts Historical Society is a treasure trove of documents, paintings and artefacts illustrating the history of Boston, Massachusetts, and New England.

The Society was founded on January 24th 1791 by Boston-born clergyman and historian Jeremy Belknap (1744–1798), together with several likeminded colleagues. Determined to collect, preserve, and document items pertaining to early American history, they began by donating their own books, artefacts, and family papers. Only with the establishment of the New-York Historical Society and the American Antiquarian Society in the early 19th century did the focus of their collecting shift exclusively to New England.

The Society initially met in the attic of Faneuil Hall and subsequently at various other Downtown addresses. It moved into its current premises at 1154 Boylston Street (Back Bay) in 1899. Designed by City Architect, Edmund March Wheelwright (1854–1912), the flamboyant but sturdy building was described by *The Boston Herald* as "one of the surest storage batteries of historic knowledge in the city".

Since then the Society has continued to amass material, and today its holdings are vast. Among the 13 million documents are Massachusetts Bay Colony Governor John Winthrop's notes on the early settlement of New England, Paul Revere's account of his midnight ride, and a handwritten copy of the *Declaration of Independence* belonging to President Thomas Jefferson (1743–1826). A selection of items is always on public display on the first and second floors, including the only known portrait from life of legendary frontiersman Daniel Boone (1734–1820), an early 18th century weather vane by Shem Drowne (1683–1774) in the form of an Indian archer, and a bust of poet Henry Wadsworth Longfellow (1807–1882). The rest of the building is given over to library and temporary exhibition space.

One seemingly innocent object with a curious provenance is the so-called Salem Witch Bureau. Made of oak and white pine, with maple and walnut mouldings, this decorative chest of drawers is thought to have been made around 1680 at the Salem workshop of English immigrant woodworker John Symonds (1595—1671).

The so-called Salem Witch Bureau at the Massachusetts Historical Society

What makes this piece unique, however, is the documentation that accompanied it when it was left to the Society by General William H. Sumner (1780–1861), son of the Governor of Massachusetts, Increase Sumner (1746–1799). In his will Sumner described it as "the Witch Bureau, from the middle drawer of which one of the Witches jumped out who was hung on Gallows Hill, in Salem".

The 'witch' in question was Elizabeth Howe (1635–1692), an English immigrant who lived in the Puritan community of Topsfield, Massachusetts. In 1692 she was accused of afflicting fits on young village girls. According to one deposition, upon seeing Howe a girl "leaped over a chest" saying "There's that woman. She goes into the oven and out again". Quite how these cryptic words relate to the chest on display is unclear but they were enough to send Howe to the gallows. She was one of 14 innocent women executed during the Salem Witch trials, which were conducted by New England's Puritan ministers between February 1692 and May 1693. The hysteria they triggered is cited by historians today as a warning against the dangers of religious extremism and isolationism.

Local history of a more personal nature can be researched at the New England Historic Genealogical Society at 99-101 Newbury Street (Back Bay). Founded in 1845, it is the country's oldest and largest genealogical society.

Other locations nearby: 80, 82, 91

82 The Headquarters of Christian Science

MA 02115 (Back Bay), the Christian Science Center in the
Christian Science Plaza at the junction of Massachusetts
and Huntington Avenues
T Green E Line to Symphony (note: the Mapparium can only
be visited as part of a guided tour)

New Hampshire-born Mary Baker Eddy (1821–1910) was described by
one of her childhood tutors as having "some great future" ahead. It
turned out to be Christian Science, a religious movement she founded
on the premise that sickness is illusory and can be corrected by prayer.
Once America's fastest growing religion, the movement's world headquarters have been in Boston since 1894.

Eddy's success was born out of considerable hardship at a time
when women had few opportunities. Her father was a farmer and a
Protestant Congregationalist, with firm beliefs in the final judgement
and eternal damnation. Although Mary never got on with him and was
sickly, she was influenced by his insistence on prayer and aged eight
heard voices, which she took to be a religious calling.

As a teenager Mary was a thoughtful student and already question-
ing predestination. There must be a way, she thought, to use prayer to
improve one's health and to change the course of one's ultimate destiny. It would take a lot more misfortune, however, for her to formulate
these feelings into a faith. During the 1840s she lost her brother, first
husband, only child, and mother. Mentally exhausted, she credited
her recovery entirely to Christ. Several years of intense Bible study followed and in 1875 she published the book *Science and Health* containing the basic tenets of Christian Science.

Eddy's third marriage brought her to Boston and it was there in
1879 that she established the Church of Christ, Scientist "to rein-
state primitive Christianity and its lost element of healing". In 1894
using money raised from a college and a reading room, she opened
the movement's Mother Church. Built in the Romanesque style, it
stands today in the Christian Science Plaza at the junction of Massachusetts and Huntington Avenues (Back Bay). In 1906, with Christian Science flourishing, the church received a huge neo-Renaissance
extension, with a soaring dome, seating for over 3,000 worshippers, and a Boston-built pipe organ. Today both buildings appear to

The Christian Science Publishing House is home to the Mapparium

float side by side when viewed from the Reflecting Pool added in the 1970s.

Another building in Christian Science Plaza is the Christian Science Publishing House. Eddy founded the Society's publishing division in 1898 and it began publishing the popular *Christian Science Monitor* when she was 87. So successful was it that in 1930 the little-known Boston architect Chester Lindsay Churchill (1891–1958) was commissioned to design the present neo-Classical building, with its magnificently-appointed foyer and Mary Baker Eddy Library. It is in the Library that the unique Mapparium can be found (see front cover).

Churchill proposed this extraordinary three-storey high stained glass globe as a means not only of teaching geography but also to demonstrate the worldwide spread of Christian Science. He purchased the 608 half-inch-thick glass panels used in its construction from a company in England and shipped them to New York, where the maps were drawn onto them. It then took eight months to paint and fire the panels, after which they were brought to Boston, fitted into a bronze frame, and illuminated from the outside.

By passing though the Mapparium on a footbridge, visitors are able to view the world from the inside, which provides them with a more accurate perspective of the world than is possible using traditional flat maps. It is interesting to see how many countries and borders have altered since the Mapparium opened in 1935.

Some ten million people have now passed through the Mapparium. This would have pleased Mary Baker Eddy despite the number of adherents to her movement having declined in recent times.

Other locations nearby: 79, 81, 83, 84

83 World Class Acoustics

MA 02115 (Fenway–Kenmore), some classical music venues
including Symphony Hall at 301 Massachusetts Avenue
T Green Line E to Symphony

Boston has a great reputation for Classical music. Not only is it home to the world-renowned Boston Symphony Orchestra (BSO) but also to numerous chamber and choral ensembles. Each has its preferred venue and together they make Boston a magnet for music lovers.

The BSO was founded in 1881 by broker and banker Henry Lee Higginson (1834–1919) to provide a "full and permanent orchestra, offering the best music at low prices". Its first home was the Boston Music Hall at 1 Hamilton Place (Downtown), built in 1852 using money from the Harvard Musical Association. Single tickets were 25 cents and Higginson's subsidies ensured the best European conductors.

When in 1900 the building was threatened with road and subway construction, the BSO relocated to the custom-built Symphony Hall at 301 Massachusetts Avenue (Fenway–Kenmore) (the Boston Music Hall survived but was later rebuilt as the live music venue, the Orpheum Theatre). Symphony Hall was designed by prominent architectural firm McKim, Mead & White, who also designed Boston Public Library (see no. 77). At Higginson's request, they based the long, high hall with seating for 2,600 concert-goers on the second Gewandhaus in Leipzig, which Higginson had visited and admired.

To ensure the best acoustics, the firm engaged Harvard physicist Wallace Clement Sabine (1868–1919). His scientifically-derived recommendations – including shallow balconies to avoid trapping sound, coffered ceiling and Classical statue-filled niches to channel sound to every seat, and sloping stage walls to focus sound – mean Symphony Hall is still one of the world's best-sounding classical venues. Indeed so precise were Sabine's specifications that when the stage floor was replaced in 2006, the new floor was built using identical maple boards and hand-cut nails, so as not to alter the original acoustics.

To appreciate the acoustics firsthand attend a BSO concert between September and April (in summer the BSO ships out to the Tanglewood Festival in Lenox, Massachusetts). Alternatively in May and June try a concert by the Boston Pops, a pared-down version of the BSO, which plays light classics and show tunes (they play a free concert every Fourth of July at the Hatch Shell, an outdoor venue on the Charles

The Boston Symphony Orchestra in Symphony Hall

River Esplanade). Guided behind-the-scenes tours of Symphony Hall are also available (www.bso.org).

Across Huntington Avenue at 30 Gainsborough Street is the 1,019-seat Jordan Hall. Opened in 1903, it too boasts superb acoustics. The building is the principal performance space of the New England Conservatory, the country's oldest independent school of music founded in 1867. One of its trustees, a member of the family that established the Jordan Marsh retail chain, financed the building. The semi-professional Boston Philharmonic Orchestra and several other ensembles also perform here, as well as at Harvard University's Sanders Theatre.

North of Symphony Hall at the junction of Boylston Street and Massachusetts Avenue is Berklee, the world's largest independent college of contemporary music encompassing everything from bluegrass to hip hop. Its numerous venues include the Berklee Performance Center (a former cinema at 136 Massachusetts Avenue) and Café 939's Red Room at 939 Boylston Street, the country's only student-run, all-ages night club. Since 2016, Berklee has operated in tandem with the Boston Conservatory for performing arts based at 8 Fenway.

Pop and rock acts as varied as James Taylor, Donna Summer, The Pixies, and local heroes The Dropkick Murphys are all connected with Boston. At 330 Newbury Street is the former Synchro Sounds studio, where in 1981 new wave band The Cars recorded their hit album *Shake it Up*. In a previous incarnation as Intermedia Studios, Aerosmith recorded their eponymous debut album here in 1972.

Other locations nearby: 62, 82, 84

84 National Braille Press

MA 02115 (Fenway–Kenmore), National Braille Press
at 88 St. Stephen Street
T Green E Line to Northeastern or Symphony (note: guided
tours by appointment only)

It is oft-quoted in American literary lore that the country's first printing press was set up at Harvard College in 1638. Less well-known is the fact that in 1927 America's premier braille publisher, National Braille Press, was founded in Boston. Guided tours of this unique facility offer a fascinating insight into the production of books for the blind and visually impaired.

Braille is a written code in which characters are represented not by printed letters but by patterns of raised dots felt with the fingertips. Its origins can be found in the tactile military code *Ecriture Nocturne* (Night Writing) developed by French army captain Charles Barbier de la Serre (1767–1841), to enable soldiers to communicate silently at night. Requiring up to a dozen embossed dots to represent a single letter, the system ultimately proved too complicated and was rejected.

Instead in 1821 Barbier introduced his code to the Royal Institution for Blind Youth in Paris. There he encountered Louis Braille (1809–1852), a bright 15 year-old student, who suggested ways to reduce the number of Barbier's dots and to assign a specific pattern of dots to each letter of the alphabet. This made it easier and faster to scan with the fingers. Although Barbier's aristocratic upbringing prevented him from acknowledging Braille's important recommendations, without them his system would have gone no further. Indeed it is Braille's improved system introduced in 1827 (and subsequently improved further) that is used today.

Fast forward 60 years and the arrival in New York City of Italian immigrant Francis B. Ierardi (1886–1967). A baby at the time, he lost his sight aged twelve in an explosion. He cleaned shoes to supplement the family income and in 1901 relocated to Watertown in Massachusetts to attend the Perkins School for the Blind. During the First World War, whilst employed as a social worker, he realised how dependent the blind were on the sighted to read them the news. As a result he decided to publish the first Braille weekly newspaper.

Despite difficult economic conditions, Ierardi secured funding and a reliable source of copy. Assisted by volunteers and working evenings, he hand-published the first issue of *The Weekly News* on March 17th,

Running one of the presses at National Braille Press on St. Stephen Street

1927. It was an immediate success and as circulation grew so did the need for bigger premises. Half a dozen different buildings were occupied until 1946, when what had become National Braille Press settled at its current premises at 88 St. Stephen Street (Back Bay).

National Braille Press today is a non-profit publishing house committed to encouraging braille literacy. Tours of the facility follow the complex process by which a braille book is produced. First the original written text is transcribed into braille code using special software. Each character or 'cell' contains up to six raised dots arranged in two rows of three, permitting up to 64 variants. This is then proofread against the original and sometimes against an audio version. Next the electronic file containing the code directs a Plate Embossing Device to emboss braille dots onto zinc plates (shapes and images are added using special embossing tools and plastic cut-outs). The plates are then run on converted Heidelberg letter presses to produce braille pages, which are finally collated into finished books ready for shipping.

Braille usage has declined for a number of reasons although National Braille Press is quick to point out that braille remains just as relevant in the digital age. Notably braille literacy remains uniquely important for developing reading skills among blind and visually impaired children, enabling them to actively engage in work, family, and community affairs.

Other locations nearby: 62, 82, 83

85 Fine Arts and Quiet Spots

MA 02115 (Fenway–Kenmore), the Museum of Fine Arts
at 465 Huntington Avenue
T Green Line E to Museum of Fine Arts

As with most big museums, Boston's Museum of Fine Arts can be daunting to visit. Its half a million objects embracing everything from Egyptian mummies to minimal Mondrians, are displayed in a labyrinth of galleries stretching literally for miles. But don't be put off. There are several quiet spots, where visitors can recharge their batteries.

When the museum first opened in 1876 it was located on Copley Square (Back Bay) drawing most of its holdings from the Boston Athenæum on Beacon Street (Beacon Hill). To this day certain works still commute between the two (see no. 30). It moved to its current location, a three-storey *Beaux Arts* building at 465 Huntington Avenue (Fenway–Kenmore), in 1909. Since then the collection has grown enormously – and the building has been expanded to accommodate it.

Today the original building on Huntington Avenue contains the museum's Art of the Ancient World galleries (including a world class collection of Egyptian artefacts), a Musical Instruments gallery (featuring one of the world's first saxophones), and several galleries covering the Art of Asia, Oceania, and Africa. A highlight is the collection of Chinese furniture in Gallery 285, including inlaid lacquered tables and finely-carved teak day beds. Here can also be found one of the museum's best quiet spots. The Buddhist Temple Room in Gallery 279 was built in 1908 by Japanese and American craftsmen inspired by the 8th century monastery of Hōryū-ji, one of the oldest in Japan. Its minimalist décor and subdued lighting evoke the dignified simplicity of such temples and encourage contemplation of the wooden Buddhas displayed.

The rear of the Huntington Avenue building connects at several points with the museum's various extensions: the I.M. Pei-designed West Wing (renamed the Linde Family Wing for Contemporary Art) to the left and the new Art of the Americas Wing on the right. There are myriad treasures here for art lovers, with more than a few showstoppers that draw the crowds. If viewing fatigue sets in retreat to the Shapiro Rotunda on Level 2, which is adorned with murals and bas reliefs by American artist John Singer Sargent (1856–1925). Having spent much of his professional life as a portraitist, he changed format here by creating murals with Classical themes and scenes from Greek my-

The Buddhist Temple Room in the Museum of Fine Arts, Boston

thology to reflect the museum's collections (he apparently modelled Apollo on a black elevator operator, Thomas McKeller, who worked at the Fairmont Copley Plaza Hotel, where Sargent kept rooms). The adjacent Colonnade is dimly lit and contains comfortable leather armchairs creating the ambience of an old fashioned members' club.

Beyond the Rotunda is the Evans Wing for Paintings, which opened in 1915 as part of the original museum masterplan. It today contains the museum's Art of Europe galleries, where just about every European artist of note is represented from Gauguin to Van Gogh (don't miss the 17th century Dutch dolls' house in Gallery 242, the 12th century Catalonian chapel fresco in Gallery 254A, and the 16th century Spanish alabaster tomb effigy in Gallery 218).

After exiting the building onto Fenway visit the museum's Japanese garden open April to October. Based on 15th century Japanese temple gardens, it is named Tenshin-En in honour of one of the museum's former Asiatic curators. A so-called *Karesansui* garden, it depicts landscapes in miniature through the use of boulders, raked gravel, and well-tamed shrubs. A lovely quiet spot to finish one's visit.

New England's largest free contemporary art space, the Bakalar and Paine Galleries, can be found in the South Building of the Massachusetts College of Art & Design Galleries at 621 Huntington Avenue.

Other locations nearby: 86, 88

86 One Woman's Remarkable Museum

MA 02115 (Fenway–Kenmore), the Isabella Stewart Gardner Museum at 25 Evans Way
T Green Line E to Museum of Fine Arts or Longwood Medical Area

Isabella Stewart Gardner (1840–1924) was a remarkable woman. America's first female art collector, she married well but it was only after her husband's death that she created Boston's extraordinary Isabella Stewart Gardner Museum. It is the country's only public museum in which both the collection and the building containing it are products of the same mind.

Gardner led a colourful life. The daughter of a successful linen merchant, she was born in New York City, where her education exposed her to art and music. Aged 16 she moved to Paris, where two events changed her life: she became classmates with Julia Gardner, member of a wealthy family of Boston shipowners, and she experienced Renaissance art during a visit to the Museo Poldi Pezzoli in Milan. She vowed that should she ever inherit money she would create such a museum, too.

In 1858 after returning to New York she visited the Gardners in Boston, and was introduced to Julia's brother, John 'Jack' Lowell Gardner (1837–1898). The two married in 1860 and moved into a spacious home at 152 Beacon Street (Back Bay). In 1863 Isabella gave birth to a son but he succumbed to pneumonia. She then suffered a miscarriage, and with no further children possible became depressed.

The answer to Isabella's woes was to travel, and in 1867 she and Jack spent a year exploring Europe. She returned to Boston reinvigorated and began establishing her reputation as a socialite. A dozen further trips followed, including the Middle East and Asia, and each time the couple returned with artworks. By the 1890s, with the help of an inheritance from Isabella's father, they had accumulated a world-class collection of paintings and sculpture, as well as ceramics, metalwork, tapestries, and furniture.

Fate stepped in again in 1898, when Jack suddenly died. For the last few years of his life the couple had struggled to display their burgeoning collection on Beacon Street. Now Isabella dealt headlong with her grief by realising her dream of building a museum. She purchased land in the Fenway area and hired New England architect Willard T. Sears (1837–1920) to help her.

Opened in 1903, Fenway Court (as the museum was known originally) was unlike any other museum building in America. Relatively plain from the outside, the four-storey structure faces inwards onto a glass-roofed courtyard inspired by the palaces of Renaissance Venice. Gardner spent a year arranging the collection (predominantly her beloved 15th and 16th century Italian Renaissance works) according to her own aesthetic, with each object displayed to foster a love of art rather than its study. In her will she stipulated that the museum would only remain open after her demise if this arrangement was preserved, and with the exception of a new entrance this has been honoured.

This covered courtyard is at the heart of the Isabella Stewart Gardner Museum

Undoubtedly the courtyard, with its statuary, plants, and Roman mosaic is a highlight. Equally appealing though is the adjacent Spanish Cloister used to great effect in framing the flamenco painting *El Jaleo* by John Singer Sargent (1856–1925). On the second floor is the Tapestry Room hung with 16th century works from Brussels, and the Short Gallery containing Anders Zorn's effervescent *Isabella Stewart in Venice*. The superb collection of 17th century Northern European paintings here was diminished in 1990, when several works were stolen leaving only empty frames.

The tour concludes on the third floor, where the ceiling of the Veronese Room features *The Coronation of Hebe*, and the Gothic Room contains Sargent's *Portrait of Isabella Gardner* (nicknamed *Saint Isabella* because of its apparent halo). The fourth floor is now offices but originally contained Isabella's private quarters.

Other locations nearby: 85, 87, 88

87 The Skull of Phineas Gage

MA 02115 (Fenway–Kenmore), the Warren Anatomical
Museum on the 5th floor of Harvard Medical School's
Francis A. Countway Library of Medicine at 10 Shattuck
Street
T Green Line E to Brigham Circle (note: photography is
prohibited in the museum)

"Mortui Vivos Docent" (The Dead Teach the Living). These are the words of anatomist and surgeon Dr. John Collins Warren (1778–1856), who made medical history by operating on the first patient anesthetised with ether (see no. 22). Over the course of a long career, he inevitably assembled a large teaching collection of anatomical and pathological specimens. These he presented in 1847 to Harvard Medical School, together with an endowment to ensure they be used to teach future medical students.

Today the specimens form the core of the Warren Anatomical Museum, which can be found on the 5th floor of Harvard Medical School's Francis A. Countway Library of Medicine at 10 Shattuck Street (Fenway–Kenmore). That the School lies away from Harvard's traditional Cambridge home is also down to Warren, who as its first dean orchestrated the move in 1810.

Until the 1920s the Museum served as an important resource for the study and teaching of medicine at the School. Since then it has increasingly become a historical collection chronicling the story of medical practice. The holdings today number around 15,000 items from kidney stones to lantern slides, including the Boston Phrenological Society's collection of skull castings.

Since 1861 the Museum has also included a display of artefacts for the enlightenment of the public. These tend to be striking objects such as a pair of conjoined fetal skeletons, *papier-mâché* models of eyes by French anatomist Louis Auzoux (1797–1880), and a disarticulated skull known as a Beauchêne Skull. By far the most engaging exhibit is the skull of Phineas P. Gage (1823–1860), a railroad foreman remembered for surviving an accident in which an iron rod passed clean through his head!

The accident happened in 1848, when Gage was directing a work gang blasting rock for the new Rutland & Burlington Railroad just south of Cavendish, Vermont. Having drilled a hole into the rock and added explosive powder, Gage was adding inert sand with a tamping iron. Distracted suddenly by the men working behind him he turned and as he did the 3 foot seven inch-long tamping iron sparked against the rock and ignited the powder prematurely. Rocketting out of the hole, the iron entered the left side of his face at jaw level, moved upwards behind his left eye, pierced the left frontal lobe of his brain, and exited through the top of his skull. As Gage collapsed, the iron landed 80 feet away!

Incredibly Gage was talking within a few minutes of the accident, and with assistance walked to a nearby cart, which took him back to his lodgings. There he was attended by a physician, John Harlow (1819–1907), who patched him up and set him on the road to recovery. Despite some inevitable memory loss and an altered personality, Gage eventually

The severely-damaged skull of Phineas Gage in the Warren Anatomical Museum

returned to work as a long distance stagecoach driver. Only 11 years later in 1859 did he begin suffering the epileptic fits that would claim his life.

In 1866 Harlow acquired Gage's skull and the tamping iron that damaged it, and in 1868 donated them to the Museum. Today they represent an important early case in which doctors were able to associate damage to certain areas of the human brain with specific changes in behaviour.

Those in need of fresh air after the museum should head south to the Kevin W. Fitzgerald Park on St. Aphonsus Street (Roxbury). It was originally called Puddingstone Park after the conglomerate quarried here in the 1840s, which was used to build the twin-spired Basilica of Our Lady of Perpetual Help nearby.

Other locations nearby: 86

88 Where Orthodox Meets Modern

MA 02215 (Fenway–Kenmore), the Holy Trinity Orthodox Cathedral at 165 Park Drive
T Green Line D to Fenway or E to Museum

The first Orthodox Christians to arrive in the New World did so in 1768. They were Greeks helping settle the colony of St. Augustine in Florida, America's oldest city. Next to arrive were Russian fur traders in the 1740s doing business in the Aleutians and Alaska, which were both then part of Russia. The greatest number, however, were immigrants seeking freedom and opportunity during the 19th and 20th centuries. Arriving from Greece, Russia, the Balkans, and the Middle East, they brought with them a rich liturgy and a penchant for icons, incense, and *a capella* singing.

Whilst many Orthodox Christians in America trace their ancestry with pride, they are no longer classed as an 'immigrant' church. Its five million adherents are today grouped into a dozen well-established ecclesiastical jurisdictions, the largest of which is the Greek Orthodox Archdiocese of America. Falling under the sway of the Ecumenical Patriarchate of Constantinople, it was born out of the country's first permanent Greek Orthodox community established in 1892 in New York City. In Boston this jurisdiction is represented by the magnificent Annunciation Greek Orthodox Cathedral of New England built in 1923 at 514 Parker Street (Roxbury), as well as the St. John the Baptist Hellenic Orthodox Church established a year later in a former 19th century Protestant church at 15 Union Park Street (South End).

Another Orthodox jurisdiction is the Orthodox Church in America, which traces its roots back to 1794, when eight Russian Orthodox monks opened a mission on Kodiak Island in Alaska. When the United States purchased Alaska from Russia in 1867, it became a diocese of the Russian Orthodox Church and over succeeding decades its numbers were augmented by immigrants from Eastern Europe and Western Russia. These included Albanians escaping Ottoman persecution, who arrived in 1908 and now worship at St. George Cathedral, a former Unitarian church at 523 East Broadway (South Boston).

Another group, fleeing the disintegrating Russian and Austro-Hungarian Empires, worship at the Holy Trinity Orthodox Cathedral at 165 Park Drive (Fenway–Kenmore). This parish was established in 1910

New England meets Russia at the Holy Trinity Orthodox Cathedral

and like the Albanians initially lacked the funds to build a new church. Instead they acquired an existing Congregational church in Roxbury and rearranged its interior to accomodate traditional Orthodox furnishings. The desire for a thoroughly Orthodox structure persisted though and in 1948 the commission for the current building was given to architect Constantin Pertzoff (1899–1970).

A White Russian immigrant and a parishioner, Pertzoff had graduated from Harvard Graduate School of Design at a time when Bauhaus Modernism was all the rage. Unlike many of his compatriots, he was thoroughly assimilated into American society and was married to a niece of Boston philanthropist and art collector, Isabella Stewart Gardner (1840–1924). This enabled him not only to donate funds for the new church but also to acquire the building plot for a good price.

Pertzoff's church consecrated in 1960 was a unique synthesis of Russian Orthodoxy and New World Modernism. It consists of a traditional barrel-vaulted cruciform nave but one rendered in wood like an upturned New England fishing vessel. His Modernism is also apparent in the light yellow brick on the outside (as opposed to traditional Boston red-brick), the airy, uncluttered interior, and the use of sconces like those used by Bauhaus pioneer Walter Gropius (1883–1969) at Harvard Law School (see no. 96). It's only a pity that Pertzoff's original space-age cupola was replaced in 1994 by a more traditional onion dome. The Divine Liturgy sung each Sunday at 9.30am is memorable (the cathedral doors are open for an hour before and after).

Other locations nearby: 85, 86

89 Boston for Stargazers

MA 02215 (Fenway–Kenmore), the Judson B. Coit
Observatory above the Astronomy Department on the
5th floor of Boston University's College of Arts and Sciences
at 725 Commonwealth Avenue
T Green Line B to BU Central or BU East (note: Public
Open Nights are held most Wednesday evenings weather
permitting, with priority given to those who have booked
in advance)

Boston is a great place for stargazing because the city boasts three astronomical observatories open to the public. Space on open days is limited though so get there early (ideally book in advance), and ensure beforehand that the weather is fine by checking www.cleardarksky. com.

The first permanent observatory in America was installed in 1828 in a church steeple at Yale University. Its demolition in 1893 means that the country's oldest observatory today is Hopkins Observatory built in 1836 at Williams College, Massachusetts. Boston enters the frame in 1839, when the Harvard College Observatory was founded, with a Boston clockmaker, William Cranch Bond (1789–1859), appointed its first director.

As well as working for free, Cranch initially provided his own equipment, which was set up in Harvard Yard. Only in 1843, when a sun-grazing comet provoked sufficient public interest in astronomy, was Harvard able to raise the funds necessary to build the observatory seen today. Here in 1847, a 15-inch Great Refractor was installed, which for the next 20 years was the country's most powerful telescope. It enabled Bond to identify the innermost ring of Saturn and to pioneer astrophotography. Both the telescope and the observing chair used by Bond can be seen on Observatory Nights on the third Thursday of each month (except June, July, and August), preceded by a lecture at 7.30pm in the Phillips Auditorium.

Modern by comparison is the Gilliland Observatory on the roof of the Museum of Science at 1 Science Park (West End) (see no. 73). It is open on Friday evenings between 8.30 and 10pm, and visitors are encouraged to prepare themselves beforehand by attending the museum's Hayden Planetarium, which shows *The Sky Tonight* at 7pm. The scale model sun outside the planetarium marks the start of the perfectly-scaled Community Solar System Trail (a model of Pluto stands on the platform of the T Riverside Station on Grove Street in faraway Newton!).

Boston's third centre for astronomy is the Judson B. Coit Observatory atop Boston University's College of Arts and Sciences at 725 Commonwealth Avenue (Fenway–Kenmore). Used by the University's Department of Astronomy, as well as its Astronomical Society, it is named after the New York-born mathematician and astronomer, Judson B. Coit (1849–1921).

Astronomical news at the Judson B. Coit Observatory

In 1882, shortly after receiving his PhD on *The Orbit of Eta Cassiopeia*, Coit was appointed Assistant Professor of Mathematics at Boston University's College of Liberal Arts, where he included astronomy in his lectures. Since the college initially had no astronomical equipment, he took his students to Boston Common, where he paid for them to use a public pay telescope. From 1907 onwards the College was located on Boylston Street (Back Bay), where Coit was instrumental in creating the university's own observatory on the roof. He was made the university's first Professor of Mathematics and Astronomy in 1915.

When the College of Liberal Arts relocated to the Boston University campus on Commonwealth Avenue, it was renamed the College of Arts and Sciences. The observatory went with it and can be found today on the roof of the Astronomy Department's 5th floor. Public Open Nights are staged most Wednesday evenings (8.30pm in spring/summer; 7.30pm in autumn/winter) but be aware that space is at a premium, with priority given to those who have acquired tickets in advance (www.bu-edu/astronomy/).

Boston University's Marsh Chapel was the setting in 1962 for the Good Friday Experiment during which psychologist Timothy Leary (1920–1996) tested whether the use of psychedelic drugs would facilitate religious experiences in divinity students. The experiment proved positive.

90 A Vintage Baseball Stadium

MA 02215 (Fenway–Kenmore), Fenway Park at 4 Yawkey Way
T Green B/C/D Line to Kenmore then walk down Brookline
Avenue

Baseball is a religion for many Bostonians and the Red Sox are their saints. It seems right therefore that their place of worship is Fenway Park, an architecturally unique stadium that lays claim to being America's oldest Major League ballpark. Indeed whenever relocation to a newer, more capacious stadium is mooted, nostalgia-minded fans ensure that the team stays put!

The Boston Red Sox came into being in 1901, as one of eight teams comprising the new American League of Professional Baseball Clubs. Known originally as the Boston Americans, the team's first home was the Huntington Avenue American League Baseball Grounds. Here in 1903 several games in the first ever World Series between the American and National Leagues were played, with the Boston Americans defeating the Pitsburgh Nationals. Although the site is now occupied by the Northeastern University, a stone still marks the home plate alongside a statue of Cy Young (1867–1955), who pitched the first game.

In 1908 the Boston Americans were renamed the Red Sox on account of the red hose they began wearing at the time. It was also around this time that team owner John Irving Taylor (1875–1938) set about trying to find them a new home. In 1911 he secured a plot on what later became Yawkey Way and began building Fenway Park.

Completed in 1912, Fenway Park is a reminder of just how quirky early ballparks could be. That it was shoehorned into a constrained, asymmetrical space explains its famously unruly dimensions. These include the shortest right-field line in Major League Baseball and the shallowest outfield bounded in part by a 37-foot high left-field wall known as the Green Monster (built to avoid breaking windows on Lansdowne Street!). Almost directly opposite the home plate the wall forms a triangular area that further disturbs the usually smooth arc of most outfields.

To find out more about the history of Fenway Park join one of the hour-long daily tours. They include a chance to sit in the seats atop the Green Monster from where it is just possible to see the solitary red seat in the right-field bleachers marking the longest home run of 502 feet hit in 1946 by Ted Williams (1918–2002). Other features include the manually-operated scoreboard and the yellow-painted right-field foul pole known as Pesky's Pole. The tour guide will also explain

A capacity crowd at Fenway Park

the Curse of the Bambino invoked when Red Sox owner Harry Frazee (1880–1929) sold young pitcher Babe Ruth (1895–1948) to the New York Yankees, allegedly to finance his girlfriend's Broadway career. It would be 86 long years until the curse lifted allowing the Red Sox to win the World Series in 2004 and again in 2007.

Such successes have inevitably ensured high attendances at Fenway Park and although tickets for games are affordable they sell out fast. The season runs from April to October but don't worry if you can't get a ticket. Just pull up a seat at the Bleacher Bar at 82a Lansdowne Street, which has a floor-to-ceiling window looking out onto the center field. Afterwards try McGreevy's at 911 Boylston Street (Back Bay), a replica of the 3rd Base Saloon, America's first sports bar opened in 1894, where the Red Sox Royal Rooters fan club once drank.

Boston's other baseball team, the Braves, played at the South End Grounds across from the Huntington Avenue Grounds (now Ruggles Sation) until relocating to Braves Field in 1915, where they stayed until departing for Milwaukee in 1953. That site is now occupied by Boston University's Nickerson Field athletic stadium.

Other locations nearby: 91

91 Olmsted's Emerald Necklace

MA 02215 (Fenway–Kenmore), Back Bay Fens Park
T Green Line B, C, D, E to Kenmore

Boston, like Manhattan, was once much smaller and originally fringed with marshes. Throughout the 19th century, as their populations burgeoned, both cities created much-needed new land by infilling tidal flats. In Manhattan, as the streets grew busier so did the need for green space, where citizens could escape the bustle. The answer was Central Park designed by landscape architect Frederick Law Olmsted (1822–1903) and opened in 1858.

Bostonians were rightly envious, with one complaining that "to be behind in these matters would not only be discreditable to our city, but positively injurious to our commercial property." As a result, when in 1883 Olmsted opened the world's first professional office for landscape design in Brookline, Massachusetts, he was commissioned to design a green space for Boston, too.

When Olmsted commenced work on his Boston design he took into account several existing green spaces, namely the Colonial-era Boston Common, and the 19th century Public Garden and Commonwealth Avenue Mall (see nos. 45, 69). Designed in 1856 by Back Bay architect Arthur D. Gilman (1821–1882) and inspired by Parisian boulevards, the Mall is a tree and statue-lined greenway running the length of Commonwealth Avenue as far as Charlesgate. Here Olmsted began adding his own green links in what would become known as the Emerald Necklace.

Olmsted's first contribution was Back Bay Fens Park (Fenway–Kenmore). With the Back Bay neighbourhood largely reclaimed and building well underway there, the Fens remained a fetid swathe of marshland. Olmsted tamed the aptly-named Muddy River, which flowed through the Fens from Jamaica Pond, creating a gently-meandering stream, flanked with managed banks of reeds to clean the water whilst retaining a sense of wilderness. Where the river flowed under Boylston Street on its way to the Charles River, Olmsted's colleague, architect Henry Hobson Richardson (1838–1886), built a mock medieval bridge in locally-quarried puddingstone.

Nearby at the corner of Boylston Street and Park Drive are the Victory Gardens, the country's oldest community gardens, established during the Second World War. Another noteworthy green space is the Kelleher Rose Garden below Agassiz Road, which boasts 200 varieties.

Reeds and a rustic bridge in Back Bay Fens

It was laid out in 1931 by Olmsted's protégé, Arthur Asahel Shurcliff (1870–1957). Nearby is a 17th century Japanese temple bell, salvaged by sailors of the USS *Boston* after the Second World War, as well as a cluster of veterans' war memorials.

Where the Park swings north-west it is overlooked on the south side by the Museum of Fine Arts, the Isabella Stewart Gardner Museum, and a couple of Boston's smaller colleges (Simmons and Emmanuel). On the other side stands the modernist Holy Trinity Orthodox Cathedral and the hulking Landmark Center, formerly the Sears, Roebuck and Company Mail Order Store (see no. 88). Also on this side, at the junction of Peterborough Street and Park Drive, is Ramler Park. Created in 2004 out of a former parking lot, it is an example of the ongoing greening-up of Boston.

From the Landmark Center, Olmsted's taming of the Muddy River continues south-west along a series of greenways, namely Riverway, (marking the Boston–Brookline border), Jamaicaway (which encompasses Leverett Pond, Olmsted Park, and Jamaica Pond), and Arborway.

The next link in Olmsted's Emerald Necklace is located at 125 Arborway (Jamaica Plain). The spectacular Arnold Arboretum is a 265-acre, Harvard-managed collection of over 15,000 trees and shrubs. Highlights include the Larz Anderson Bonsai Collection along the Chinese Path, and the collection of centenarian trees, including a silver maple planted in 1881, which at 120-feet tall is the garden's tallest plant. Spring highlights include lilacs, magnolias, and rhododendrons: autumn highlights include New England's famously blazing colours

A serene and watery vista in Back Bay Fens

courtesy of over a hundred species of maple. An overview of the arboretum can be had by climbing the 240-foot high Peters Hill.

The final and southernmost link in the Emerald Necklace is Franklin Park (Dorchester), which lies just beyond the Forest Hills Cemetery (see no. 106). Olmsted's son and successor, John C. Olmsted (1852–1910), claimed that this 527-acre park was perhaps his father's greatest achievements. With its miles of trails for walkers and cyclists modelled on pastoral English countryside, it is easy to forget that bustling Boston lies only a few miles away.

In the eastern corner of the Park at 1 Franklin Park Road (Roxbury) is Franklin Zoo. Olmsted drafted plans for a zoological garden for native species but when it finally opened in 1912 it was far more exotic. Today it contains everything one would expect of a modern zoo, with exciting themed areas such as the Serengeti Crossing, where zebra roam rolling hillsides, and the African Tropical Forest, a vast indoor savanna containing gorillas and hippos. Historians will be delighted to find some original relics here, too, including a huge, wrought-iron walk-through aviary and some abandoned bear pens in the woods beyond the nearby stadium. On Pier Point Road can be found the ruined Overlook Shelter, Olmsted's only architectural commission, which once served as changing rooms and seating for the Playstead sports field below.

From Arborway it is possible to return to Copley Place (Back Bay) by means of the Southwest Corridor Park, a 4.7-mile long greenway completed in 1990 along a 19th century rail corridor. It is popular with walkers, cyclists, and community gardeners.

Olmsted's Brookline home and office, *Fairsted*, is preserved as the Frederick Law Olmsted National Historic Site at 99 Warren Street. The archive contains thousands of landscape designs from the White House to Yosemite Valley.

Other locations nearby: 81, 90

92 Great Dome and Infinite Corridor

MA 02139 (Cambridge), an architecture tour of the Massachusetts Institute of Technology begining with the Rogers Building at 77 Massachusetts Avenue
T Red Line to Central then walk down Massachusetts Avenue

The Massachusetts Institute of Technology (MIT) was founded in 1861 in response to the increasing industrialisation of the United States. Originally based in Boston's Back Bay, it relocated to its current home on the reclaimed mudflats of East Cambridge in 1916. Since then it has expanded to cover 168 acres and risen to international prominence as a centre for theoretical and practical research in the physical sciences and engineering. It has been dubbed the most innovative square mile on the planet.

Unlike the architecture of Harvard University, which is comparatively strait-laced, the buildings at MIT are rendered in a plethora of progressive styles reflecting the freethinking nature of the place. After all, the students and staff here pioneered everything from microwave radars and black box flight recorders to computer spreadsheet programmes and electronic ink.

This tour takes in a selection of buildings representing the four broad phases of campus construction. It starts with the Rogers Building at 77 Massachusetts Avenue built during the first phase (1916–1939). Named for MIT founder William Barton Rogers (1804–1882), it serves as an entrance to the so-called Infinite Corridor, a pedestrian thoroughfare traversing the entire

This chapel is one of several noteworthy buildings at MIT

East Campus. Together with the ceremonial Great Dome beyond, the Rogers Building was designed by the architect William Welles Bosworth (1869–1966). Both are neo-Classical in appearance in line with the then-fashionable City Beautiful Movement and are made of reinforced concrete clad in limestone. This was a first for a non-industrial – much less a university – building in the United States.

Return now to Massachusetts Avenue and cross to the other side. Here half-obscured by trees is the MIT Chapel built during the second phase (1940–1959). Designed by Finnish architect Eero Saarinen (1910–1961), it consists of a moated red-brick cylinder topped with a sculpted aluminium belfry. The windowless interior is illuminated by floor-level slits reflecting light upwards from the moat and by a skylight casting light downwards onto the altar through a twinkling metallic curtain. Saarinen also designed the tent-like Kresge Auditorium beyond.

Now drop down onto Memorial Drive and head east to the Walker Memorial Building. Turn left to reach the circular McDermott Court, which is overlooked by the towering Green Building. This is one of several buildings designed by MIT graduate I. M. Pei (b. 1917) during the third phase (1960–1990). The 21-storey tower is the only structure to break with MIT's architectural tradition of horizontality. The sculpture *Big Sail* in front of the tower is one of many artworks adorning the campus. Pei also designed the Wiesner Building a little farther east on Ames Street, which contains the MIT List Visual Arts Center, a contemporary art museum.

From here walk north up Ames Street then cut across to Vassar Street passing Frank Gehry's Stata Center, which dates from the fourth phase (1990 to the present) (see no. 94). Other contemporary structures here include the Brain and Cognitive Sciences Building by Charles Correa (1930–2015) at number 42, and beyond Massachusetts Avenue the extraordinary Simmons Hall by Steven Holl (b. 1947) based on a sea sponge (between the two is the fortress-like Metropolitan Storage Warehouse, built in 1895 and being converted into student housing).

MIT students are famous for their pranks, which include placing a replica police car on top of the Great Dome. They also created the curious markings on the pavement of Harvard Bridge. Known as Smoots, they represent the height of Oliver R. Smoot (b. 1940), who was used as a human measuring tape in 1958 as part of a fraternity pledge. A plaque on the Boston side of the bridge marks where in 1908 Harry Houdini (1874–1926) performed one of his famous escapes.

Other locations nearby: 93, 94

93 The Wright Brothers Wind Tunnel

MA 02139 (Cambridge), the Wright Brothers Memorial Wind Tunnel at the MIT Department of Aeronautics & Astronautics in the Guggenheim Aeronautical Laboratory (MIT Building 33) at 125 Massachusetts Avenue
T Red Line to Central then walk down Massachusetts Avenue (note: tours of the Wind Tunnel are by appointment only)

Unlike Old Cambridge, an agricultural village that grew into Harvard University, East Cambridge developed around industry. During the 19th century it was home to the likes of the New England Glass Company, and the Kendall Boiler and Tank Company, whose machine shop still stands at 275 3rd Street. By the first decades of the 20th century the area was New England's main industrial zone, with Carter's Ink Company, the Atheneum Press, and the New England Confectionery Company all based here (see no. 51). The Ford Motor Company built the world's first vertically-integrated assembly plant at 640 Memorial Drive, Kodak occupied a Modernist factory farther along at 784, and Polaroid had its hedquarters in Kendall Square.

It therefore seems fitting that around the same time the Massachusetts Institute of Technology (MIT) relocated to this part of Cambridge from Back Bay (see no. 92). And it was good it did because when East Cambridge began losing its industrial base during the Great Depression, MIT picked up the baton, transforming East Cambridge into a world class research centre for physical sciences and engineering.

For a flavour of what goes on at MIT scrutinise the information panels in the Kendal/MIT T station and then visit the MIT Museum at 265 Massachusetts Avenue (it will relocate in 2020 to a new state-of-the-art space in Kendall Square). Home

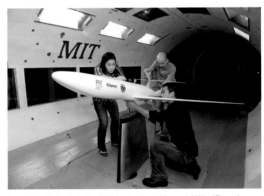

Preparing for tests in the Wright Brothers Memorial Wind Tunnel

to over a million artefacts, the museum conveys the vast scope of interests pursued at MIT since its founding in 1861. Here can be found everything from slide rules and stroboscopes to cathode-ray tubes and thermometers. Of particular interest is the world's largest collection of holograms, quirky kinetic sculptures by former artist-in-residence Arthur Ganson (b. 1955), and drawings from the Architects Collaborative founded by Walter Gropius (1883–1969) (the Hart Nautical Collection documenting New England ship building resides nearby at 55 Massachusetts Avenue).

For obvious reasons most departments at MIT are off limits to the public. The Department of Aeronautics & Astronautics (AeroAstro for short), however, is different in that it offers guided tours by appointment. Located in the Guggenheim Aeronautical Laboratory (MIT Building 33) at 125 Massachusetts Avenue, the tour's highlight is a peep inside the Wright Brothers Memorial Wind Tunnel. Built in a shipyard in 1938 (which explains the submarine-like door!) it offers a maximum test speed of 400mph.

The study of aeronautics at MIT began in 1897 – three years prior to the Wright Brothers' pioneering flight – when mechanical engineering student Albert J. Wells built a model wind tunnel as part of his thesis. By 1916 MIT was offering the country's first course in aeronautical engineering and a full-size wind tunnel was built on Vassar Street, the first structure on MIT's new Cambridge campus. The Guggenheim Aeronautical Laboratory opened alongside it in 1928, and a decade later the present wind tunnel was installed to facilitate advanced aerodynamic research.

During the Second World War, the department became a national centre for aeronautical research and testing, with the wind tunnel running 24 hours a day testing military aircraft designs. Charles Stark Draper (1901–1987) pioneered Inertial Navigation here, making the world's first inertially-navigated long-distance flight in 1953. Later in 1959, with the space race underway, 'Astronautics' was added to the department's name. President Kennedy's famous committment to landing astronauts on the moon was based on a NASA plan devised by one of Draper's students, and the resulting Apollo mission could not have taken place without the inertial guidance systems developed here.

The Charles Stark Draper Laboratory is today a not-for-profit research organisation based at 555 Technology Square (Cambridge), where several of Draper's inventions are displayed in the foyer.

Other locations nearby: 92, 94

94 Cambridge Deconstructed

MA 02139 (Cambridge), the Stata Center at 32 Vassar Street
Red Line to Kendall/MIT

East Cambridge is an area dominated by the campus of the Massachusetts Institute of Technology (MIT), as well as numerous new technology companies and laboratories (see no. 93). The architecture here, comprising repurposed factories and progressive 20th century new builds, is very different to the gridiron Victoriana of Back Bay across the water. Yet there is one architect who has left a distinctive footprint in both areas. He is Canadian-born Frank Gehry (b. 1929), a pioneer of the controversial postmodern style known as Deconstructivism.

Deconstructivism first appeared in the early 1980s and is characterised by a deliberate lack of symmetry, continuity and harmony. By manipulating a structure's façade through the use of non-rectilinear shapes, which distort and dislocate the whole, an impression is given of a building in the process of fragmentation. Loved and loathed in equal measure, Deconstructivism represents controlled chaos.

Gehry's work at 360 Newbury Street in Back Bay is something of a hybrid. The yellow brick part of the building was constructed in 1920, and used from the 1960s until the mid-1980s by the musical instrument retailer, E. U. Wurlitzer. When they moved out, the unex-

The Stata Center at MIT was designed by architect Frank Gehry

ceptional building was reworked by Gehry into something more unusual. Honouring the original façade, he added a wildly flaring rooftop awning to echo a less extravagant existing canopy at pavement level, and extended the building to the rear in concrete in a surprisingly harmonious manner. The building won a Parker Award for most beautiful new building in Boston and was later converted from offices to high end condominiums.

Across the river in Cambridge, Gehry was later commissioned to design an entire building in the Deconstructivist style. The Stata Center at 32 Vassar Street opened in 2004 to house MIT's Computer, Information and Intelligence Sciences departments. It was financed by MIT graduate Ray Stata and his wife, Maria, as well as the likes of Bill Gates of Microsoft.

Before discussing it, however, it should be noted that the Stata Center replaced Building 20, which had been erected in 1943 to house MIT's Radiation Laboratory. It was here that the microwave radars used by the United States during the Second World War were developed, as well as the world's first long range radio navigation system. After the war, it served as an incubator for Noam Chomsky's work on generative grammar, Amar Bose's research on loudspeakers, and early aspects of what became the hacker culture. It was this sort of unfettered free thinking in a building that was flexible rather than beautiful that led William J. Mitchell (1944–2010), Dean of MIT's School of Architecture and Planning, to suggest Gehry design the replacement building.

The Stata center is classic Gehry. It consists of several orange brick blocks between which are disarticulated silver elements, exploding outwards and colliding with each other. Even the windows are bursting forwards. Multiple entrances lead to a broad main corridor called Student Street, which runs the length of the building. Used by students as a makeshift market space, it also gives access to an information point and a café open on weekdays to the public. Above the fourth floor, the building splits into two distinct structures: the Gates or G Tower and the Dreyfoos or D Tower.

Like the work of other Deconstructivist architects, including Zaha Hadid, Daniel Libeskind, and the Coop Himmelb(l)au cooperative, the Stata Center has its devotees and detractors. Those in favour say its chaotic appearance is a metaphor for the daring research that occurs here: those against highlight the irony of housing a scientific department in a building that deliberately reverses structural algorithms.

Other locations nearby: 92, 93

95 The Founding of Newe Towne

MA 02138 (Cambridge), a walk around Old Cambridge
beginning at the First Parish Church at the junction
of Massachusetts Avenue and Church Street
T Red Line to Harvard

Like Boston, Cambridge was founded in 1630 by Puritans of the Massachusetts Bay Colony. Looking to create a self-contained religious community, they chose the area around Harvard Square because it was the first convenient Charles River crossing outside Boston. In the following spring they set about building permanent structures prompting the settlement's name, Newe Towne.

This milestone dates from the early days of Cambridge

The settlers built their first meeting house in 1632 at the corner of Mount Auburn and Dunster Streets. From here Minister Thomas Shepard (1605–1649) suggested the founding of a training college for clergy, its students benefitting from his preaching. Initially called Newe College, it was soon renamed for English minister John Harvard (1607–1638), who bequeathed a much-needed library and half his wealth (see no. 96). Harvard and Shepard were both alumni of England's Cambridge University, and in 1638 Newe Towne was renamed Cambridge to honour their valuable contributions.

The subsequent growth of Cambridge from agricultural village to bustling educational hub means that little of Old Cambridge remains. What has survived is covered by this walk, which begins at the junction of Massachusetts Avenue and Church Street. Here stands the fifth and final incarnation of Thomas Shepard's meeting house. Built in 1833 and known as the First Parish in Cambridge, it is where for many years Harvard staged its annual commencement ceremonies.

Alongside the church is the Old Cambridge Burying Ground opened in 1633. The headstones are typical for the period, with inscriptions extolling the piety of the deceased and winged skulls for ghoulish decoration. Because this was for many years the only burial ground in Cambridge, it contains not only settlers and soldiers but also landowners, slaves and Harvard presidents.

An interesting old milestone can be found in the corner of the cemetery, where Massachusetts Avenue joins Garden Street. It marks the Boston Post Road, a 17th century mail route connecting Boston with New York City. Its inscription is a reminder that until the construction in 1792 of the Longfellow Bridge, it was necessary to ride eight miles through Brookline, Roxbury, and across Boston Neck to reach Boston.

On the opposite side of the cemetery is another historic church, Christ Church, built in 1761 to a design by Englishman Peter Harrison (1716–1775), the first formally-trained architect to work in the British colonies. He also designed Boston's King's Chapel, and it was members of that Loyalist congregation living in Cambridge, who founded this church in 1759. This explains why the deliberately English-looking clapboard church was attacked by Patriot dissidents during the American Revolutionary War (1775–1783). In 1967 Martin Luther King Jr. (1929–1968) spoke out against the Vietnam War here.

Now take the alley down the side of the church to reach Farwell Place. The charming Federal-style houses dating from the early 19th century are rare reminders of Harvard Square's former residential character. They are complimented at 56 Brattle Street by the Dexter Pratt House built in 1808 for the village blacksmith (see no. 105). Brattle Street was once known as Tory Row because Loyalist worthies had their Colonial-era mansions here. One of them, Brattle House at number 42, was built in 1772 for Major General William Brattle (1706–1776), the wealthiest man in the Massachusetts Bay Colony.

Continue onwards to Brattle Square and cross onto Mount Auburn Street to reach the tree-filled Winthrop Square, where this walk finishes. Back in the 1630s, this was the marshy shore of the Charles River, where local farmers gathered to sell their produce. A battered stone at the centre of the square bears the name 'Newtowne'.

Other locations nearby: 96, 97

96 The Athens of America

MA 02138 (Cambridge), a walk around Harvard Yard
beginning at Johnston Gate on Massachusetts Avenue
T Red Line to Harvard

Among students graduating Harvard College in 1796 was one William Tudor (1779–1830). Co-founder of the Boston Athenæum, member of the Massachusetts Historical Society, and editor of the *North American Review*, he christened Boston 'The Athens of America' for its contribution to American learning. That contribution began in 1636 with the founding of Harvard College, America's oldest university.

This walk begins at Johnston Gate on Massachusetts Avenue. The church opposite belonging to the First Parish in Cambridge is a convenient reminder of Harvard's origins. It was established by Puritans of the Massachusetts Bay Colony, when they founded Cambridge as a religious community in 1630

Harvard's Johnston Gate and the First Parish church beyond

(see no. 95). Their minister Thomas Shepard (1605–1649) suggested the creation of a training college for clergy called Newe College. It was renamed Harvard College in 1639 in honour of its first benefactor, John Harvard (1607–1638), who bequeathed half his wealth and a much-needed library.

A statue of John Harvard can be found by passing through Johnston Gate into Harvard Yard, the oldest part of the Harvard campus. As student-led tours gleefully point out, however, the statue doesn't resemble Harvard at all; additionally it wrongly cites Harvard as founder, and even gives the wrong date! Such errors aside, John Harvard's contributions were invaluable and helped set the college on its way to eventually becoming an internationally-renowned university.

Ranged around the statue are all the things traditionally associated with Harvard: tree-lined footpaths, freshman dormitories, trim lawns, and scholarly libraries. The immediate surroundings actually comprise the Old Yard, the farmer's field on which the first college buildings were erected. Of these – the wooden Old College and the brick-built Indian College – nothing remains above ground (see no. 99). What can be seen are several old dormitories illustrating Harvard's transition from training college to university. Massachusetts Hall (1720), for example, is Harvard's oldest surviving structure. It appears modest when compared with the grandiose Matthews Hall built around the corner a century later. Another early survival is the Georgian-style Holden Chapel (1744), Harvard's first place of worship.

Behind the John Harvard statue is University Hall (1815). Designed by Charles Bulfinch (1763–1844), it was the first building to challenge Harvard's traditional red-brick style (see no. 27). Beyond it is the New Yard dominated by the colonnaded façade of the Widener Library. One of 73 campus libraries, it is named after Harvard graduate and *Titanic* victim Harry Elkins Widener (1885–1912), whose mother financed it in his memory. Its 3.5 million books on 60 miles of shelves make it the world's greatest university library (although not open to the public, one can visit the neighbouring Houghton Library and its collection of rare books on a guided tour each Friday at 2pm).

The enormity of the Widener is offset by the delicate spire of the Memorial Church (1932) opposite, honouring alumni lost during the First World War. It is complemented across Cambridge Street by Memorial Hall (1878) (which contains the Sanders Theatre) honouring students lost during the American Civil War (1861–1865).

Beyond Memorial Hall, the Harvard campus sprawls northwards to encompass Harvard Law School and its Gropius Complex (1950), the first modern building on the campus. Southwards beyond Massachusetts Avenue are several upperclassmen residences, including Lowell House (1930) on Holyoke Place, with its beautifully-kept courtyards.

Nearby at 96 Winthrop Street is the clubhouse of the Hasty Pudding Club, America's oldest collegiate social club, established by Harvard undergraduates in 1795. The Club's thespian wing, the Hasty Pudding Theatricals, perform in Farkas Hall at 12 Holyoke Street.

Other locations nearby: 95, 97, 103

97 Legend of the Washington Elm

MA 02138 (Cambridge), the Washington Elm on Cambridge Common
T Red Line to Harvard the walk north along Massachusetts Avenue onto Garden Street

Cambridge Common is a triangle of public land just west of Harvard Yard. Bounded by Massachusetts Avenue, Garden Street, and Waterhouse Street, it has been used by the local community since 1630, when the first English immigrants arrived from Charlestown and began grazing their cattle. Harvard College commencements were subsequently staged here, as were local militia exercises and public debates.

These days Cambridge Common is a park where people relax and occasionally scrutinise some interesting monuments. Most obvious of these is the steeple-like memorial erected in 1870 to Cambridge troops lost during the American Civil War (1861–1865) (the statue of President Abraham Lincoln (1809–1865) was added in 1887). Nearby is a sculpture of three emaciated figures recalling the Irish Potato Famine (1845–1850), which drove so many people across the Atlantic to Boston. Another statue towards Waterhouse Street depicts John Bridge (1578–1665), a Puritan who settled in Cambridge in 1632 and established the first church school.

An especially interesting clutch of monuments can be found half way along Garden Street. They include a tree sur-

Legends have grown up around the Washington Elm on Cambridge Common

rounded by railings known as the Washington Elm. According to an accompanying inscription it was under this tree that General George Washington (1732–1799) first took command of the American Army on July 3rd 1775. Washington had arrived in Cambridge on July 2nd during the Siege of Boston, the opening phase of the American Revolutionary War (1775–1783) (see no. 60). He initially set up his headquarters in the Benjamin Wadsworth House in Harvard Yard (moving shortly after to an abandoned mansion on Brattle Street) and the next day took command of the newly-formed Continental Army. The tree, however, is too young to have been growing at that time and although the soldiers did camp on Cambridge Common there is no documentary evidence for Washington commissioning them there.

A delve into the archives reveals the truth. The original Washington Elm actually stood at the junction of Garden and Mason Streets. Planted around 1700, it was one of half a dozen elms along the west side of the 'Cow Commons', as Cambridge Common was originally known. In 1923 an attempt to prune the ancient tree caused it to collapse and die. That said, however, it remains a moot point whether Washington commissioned his troops on Cambridge Common at all, with historians now suggesting it most likely occurred in Harvard Yard.

Still the legend of the Washington Elm persists and it explains why other monuments have gravitated here. They include a relief of Washington reviewing the troops, memorials to two Polish captains hired to lead revolutionary forces, and cannon abandoned by the British at Fort Independence, when they evacuated Boston in 1776. More recently five black slabs have been installed to commemorate Prince Hall (1735–1807), an African-American community leader in Boston, who campaigned for the abolition of slavery and founded the African Masonic Lodge.

Across Garden Street is a gate leading into Radcliffe Yard, a lovely garden at the heart of Radcliffe College founded in 1879 to give women access to the then exclusively-male domain of Harvard. The two colleges merged in the 1970s.

Two more monuments can be found nearby. Northwards at the junction of Garden Street and Concord Avenue is one of many copies of Alice Ruggles Kitson's *The Hiker*, commemorating the citizen soldiers who took part in America's Manifest Destiny expansion, including the Spanish-American War (1898). South at the junction of Garden Street and Massachusetts Avenue is a road traffic island with bronze hoof prints recalling Patriot William Dawes (1745–1799), who in 1775 accompanied Paul Revere on his famous midnight ride to Lexington (see no. 16).

Other locations nearby: 95, 96

98 A Garden of Glass Flowers

MA 02138 (Cambridge), the Harvard Museum of Natural
History at 26 Oxford Street
T Red Line to Harvard (note: entry includes access to the
Peabody Museum of Archaeology and Ethnology)

Most university museums are academic by nature. Their serried ranks of cabinets and dry scientific labelling rarely grab the layperson's attention. By contrast the Harvard Museum of Natural History at 26 Oxford Street (Cambridge) has gone all out to make its holdings accessible to all. Every bit as thrilling as its public counterparts in New York and London, the museum annually delights a quarter of a million visitors.

Despite Harvard being the country's oldest university, the Harvard Museum of Natural History only opened in 1998. Its goal, however, is to highlight the collections of three far older Harvard research collections: the Museum of Comparative Zoology (founded in 1859 by renowned Swiss-born zoologist and geologist Louis Agassiz (1807–1873)), the Herbaria and Botanical Museum (founded 1842 and 1858 respectively), and the Mineralogical and Geological Museum (1784 and 1901).

The museum currently displays around 12,000 specimens drawn from these collections accompanied by a programme of hands-on educational activities aimed at connecting families and young visitors with some very intriguing objects. Those from the Comparative Museum

An exquisite glass
flower displayed in the
Harvard Museum
of Natural History

of zoology include the massive skeleton of a Right whale, the world's largest turtle shell, and the only mounted skeleton of a Kronosaurus. From the Museum of Mineralogy and Geology come meteorites, rare gems, and an enormous amethyst crystal.

Many visitors consider the museum's most unusual exhibits to be drawn from the Botanical Museum. The Ware Collection of Blaschka Glass Models of Plants (*Glass Flowers* for short) is a unique collection of highly realistic glass botanical models. Created between 1887 and 1936, they were commissioned as a teaching collection by the first director of the Botanical Museum, George Lincoln Goodale (1839–1923). Comprising 847 life-sized models (representing 780 species and varieties of plants across 164 families), and well over 3,000 more of various plant parts and anatomical sections, the collection numbers around 4,400 individual pieces in total.

The models were created by Leopold Blaschka (1822–1895) and his son Rudolf (1857–1939) at their studio in Hosterwitz, near Dresden, Germany. When Goodale first came across their work they had already developed a thriving business creating glass models of marine invertebrates. Aware that pressed botanical specimens faded and *papier-maché* models were crude, Goodale asked the Blaschkas whether they would make botanical models in glass for Harvard. When they agreed, Goodale secured funding from one of his former students, Mary Lee Ware (1858–1937), and her mother, Elizabeth, who were already benefactors of Harvard's botany department. The collection was dedicated to Elizabeth's dead husband, Dr. Charles Eliot Ware (1814–1887), a prominent Boston physician and a great nature-lover.

It has been said that the Blaschkas employed secret techniques to create the glass flowers. In reality, the techniques they employed were common at the time. It was just their skill and enthusiasm as glassmakers and their extraordinary attention to detail that made them remarkable. Their primary technique was that of Bohemian lampworking, whereby glass is heated over a gas torch fanned by air from a foot-powered bellows. Tools are then used to pinch, pull, and cut the hot glass into shape, and wire supports inserted where necessary (other models were blown in the traditional way). Some models were made using coloured glass, whilst others were painted later in the process. Their lampworking table today forms part of the *Glass Flowers* exhibit.

The Blaschkas also provided models of marine invertebrates to the Museum of Comparative Zoology, and a selection of these are displayed in a separate exhibit called *Sea Creatures in Glass*.

Other locations nearby: 99, 100

99 Harvard's Indian College

MA 02138 (Cambridge), Peabody Museum of Archaeology
& Ethnology at 11 Divinity Avenue
T Red Line to Harvard (note: entry includes access to the
Harvard Museum of Natural History)

Boston has existed for less than four centuries. Founded by outsiders, it is often cited as America's oldest major city. Such an accolade, however, obscures the fact that the land on which it stands was occupied for thousands of years previously by Native Americans. That these indigenous people used the land only seasonally means they've left few remains (the discovery of prehistoric fish weirs during construction work in Back Bay was a rare find indeed (see no. 74)).

Fortunately the presence of Harvard University has helped make up for this paucity. Since the late 19th century it has been

Decorated beadwork sash of the Wampanoag tribe in the Peabody Museum of Archaeology & Ethnology

home to the Peabody Museum of Archaeology & Ethnology, which boasts one of the country's great collections of Native American artefacts. The museum was established in 1866 with money given by the wealthy Massachusetts-born financier, George Peabody (1795–1869). Known as the Father of Modern Philanthropy, he helped establish his young country's international credit, and gave generously to public causes at home and in England.

The building housing the museum at 11 Divinity Avenue was opened in 1877 and today houses well over a million archaeological and ethnological artefacts. It is no surprise that the emphasis is on the

Americas but there are also significant collections from Africa, Asia, Europe, and Oceania. The Oceanic holdings are interesting because they were collected by Boston's 18th century maritime merchants during voyages across the Pacific.

The Americas are broken down into three distinct regions. South America is represented by Incan metalwork, Nazca pottery, and Amazonian feather headdresses. From Central America come Mayan stone stelae from Copán and offerings from the sacred well at Chichén Itza. The holdings from North America include Northwestern bird-beak masks and totem poles, dolls made by the Arizona Hopi, and artefacts collected in the early 1800s by the Lewis and Clark Expedition.

A unique exhibit called *Digging Veritas* concerns the story of Harvard's Indian College. When it opened in 1636, Harvard was America's first university – but it struggled financially. Some help came from the English Society for the Propagation of the Gospel in New England, which provided funds for American Indian education. Their hope was that graduates would proselytize their home communities with the Gospel. Harvard in turn agreed to waive tuition fees for these students and to accommodate them.

That accommodation took the form of the Indian College. Erected in 1655, where Matthews Hall stands today, it was the first brick building in Harvard Yard, and only the second educational building after the Old College (see no. 96). Five students from the Wampanoag and Nipmuck tribes were educated here but only one ever graduated, and he died shortly after of consumption. It is a sobering fact that up to 90 % of the local Native American population succumbed to epidemics introduced by European settlers.

Despite the education of Native Americans being enshrined in Harvard's 1650 Charter, the Indian College didn't last long. Cultural relations became strained when the Wampanoag began resisting Colonial expansion, and in 1670 the building was used instead as a printing works, where the country's first Bible was printed in the Algonquin language. The building was demolished in 1698 and it was not until the 1970s that Native Americans returned to Harvard, where today a plaque at Matthews Hall honours their shortlived predecessors.

Across from the Peabody at 6 Divinity Avenue is the Harvard Semitic Museum founded in 1889. Representing the university's archaeological activities in the ancient Near East, the artefacts here include amulets and figurines from Egyptian tombs, examples of Babylonian cuneiform writing, and stone votive figurines from prehistoric Cyprus.

Other locations nearby: 98, 100

100 A Monster of a Computer

MA 02138 (Cambridge), the Collection of Historical Scientific Instruments in the Putnam Gallery at the Harvard University Science Center at 1 Oxford Street
T Red Line to Harvard

Founded in 1636, Harvard University is America's oldest. Over the last century its public face has been its museums, with three devoted to art, and four to science and culture (see nos. 98, 101). One of the least well-known is the Collection of Historic Scientific Instruments (CHSI) established in 1948, its mission to preserve signicant modern instruments rendered obsolete by new technologies.

The CHSI is housed in the Putnam Gallery in the Harvard University Science Center at 1 Oxford Street (Cambridge). Visitors will discover that the collection actually has its roots in a *Wunderkammer*, or cabinet of wonders, assembled during the 17th century. Only when this was lost in

A small part of the Mark I computer at the Harvard University Science Center

a fire a century later was the nucleus of the present collection put together. One of the chief contributors was the Boston-born polymath Benjamin Franklin (1706–1790), who acquired numerous instruments during his time in Europe helping establish America's international relations. Over the years these have been augmented by donations from various Harvard departments, as well as private benefactors.

The CHSI today numbers around 20,000 objects spanning the 15th to the 21st centuries. A superbly-curated selection of these represents astronomy, horology, navigation and surveying. In amongst the myriad microscopes and timekeeping devices are four objects of particular note: a French astrolabe of the 1400s; a clockwork orrery built in the 1770s by Boston clockmaker Joseph Pope; a 19th century longcase clock once connected by telegraph to railway stations across New England to prevent train crashes; and the control panel of the 1950s-era Harvard cyclotron used in nuclear and particle physics.

Calculating is another discipline represented in the CHSI. By far the largest exhibit in this category is America's first programmable computer, the Mark I. This monster of a computer, which sits out in the foyer, was conceived in 1937 by Harvard graduate student, Howard H. Aiken (1900–1973), to solve advanced mathematical problems encountered in his work as a research physicist.

Aiken proposed modifying existing, commercially-available technologies and coordinating them from a centralised control system. To do this he needed the support of a major manufacturer and with the backing of Harvard began approaching various companies. He eventually secured interest from International Business Machines (IBM), which at the time was a successful manufacturer of calculating machines and punch card systems.

Over a period of five years, engineers at IBM in Endicott, New York developed the Mark I's systems using IBM components. But by the time the finished machine was delivered to Harvard in 1944, America had entered the Second World War. As a result it was used by the U.S. Navy Bureau of Ships for military purposes. It quickly proved Aiken's vision correct though, as its ranks of difference engines and punch cards made quick work of calculations that hitherto would have required whole teams of human calculators.

The Mark I remained in operation until 1959, when it was superceded. Rather than destroying it, however, half the parts were given to IBM and the Smithsonian in Washington. The remaining half is that displayed in the CHSI today, and it is incredible to compare it with the tiny digital devices used today to make similar calculations.

A memorial in front of the John F. Kennedy Federal Building at 15 Sudbury Street (Downtown) commemorates the world's first telephone call. It was made in 1875 by Scottish immigrant Alexander Graham Bell (1847–1922) in an attic workshop on what was then Court Street. Of related interest is the *Art Deco* façade of the former New England Telephone Building at 185 Franklin Street (Downtown) adorned with a giant golden bell.

Other locations nearby: 98, 99

101 Bozzetti, Bauhaus, and Buddhism

MA 02138 (Cambridge), the Harvard Art Museums
at 32 Quincy Street
T Red Line to Harvard

The Harvard Art Museums at 32 Quincy Street (Cambridge) comprise three distinct public collections, as well as four research centres, which together represent the oldest fine arts research, training, and conservation facility in the United States. The museums – the Fogg, Busch-Reisinger, and Arthur M. Sackler – contain a quarter of a million objects ranging in date from antiquity to the present day, and spanning the globe from Western Europe to Asia. What follows is a description of three exhibits that caught this author's eye.

The oldest and largest component of the Harvard Art Museums is the Fogg Museum established in 1895. A celebration of Western art, it includes paintings, sculptures, and decorative arts from the medieval period onwards, being particularly strong on the Italian Renaissance, British Pre-Raphaelite, and French Impressionist periods.

Something rather special can be found tucked away on Level 2 in Room 2520 (European Art – 17th Century). It is a terracotta mock-up or *bozzetto* modelled by Baroque sculptor Gian Lorenzo Bernini (1598–1680) for his work *Angel with the Crown of Thorns*. Made around 1688 in Lazio, it is one of 15 Bernini *bozzetti* held at the museum, a large number considering their ephemeral nature. Throughout his long and productive life, Bernini probably made thousands of *bozzetti*, each normally

This Marcel Breuer chair is displayed in the Fogg's Busch-Reisinger Museum

about *due palmi* (two palms) high, from which he or others would then have created full-scale versions in marble or bronze. Note Bernini's measurement marks at the base of the throat.

The Busch-Reisinger Museum, founded in 1901 as the Germanic Museum, is North America's only museum dedicated to the art of the German-speaking countries of Central and Northern Europe. Until 1991, it was housed in the Adolphus Busch Hall at 27 Kirkland Street, where a collection of medieval casts are still displayed. Works at Quincy Street cover the Austrian Secession, German Expressionism, and the Bauhaus design school, the latter resulting from a partnership with Bauhaus founder, Walter Gropius (1883–1969), who chaired Harvard's Department of Architecture from 1937 until 1952.

A vintage piece of Bauhaus design here is the Club Chair (B3) by Hungarian-born Marcel Breuer (1902–1981), which can be found on Level 1 in Room 1520 (Modern and Contemporary Art – Art in Germany Between the Wars). Inspired by his own bicycle handlebars, former own Bauhaus student Breuer pioneered the use of tubular steel in furniture design, and his B3, which dates to around 1930, still appears modern today.

The Arthur M. Sackler Museum, the youngest of the Harvard Art Museums, opened in 1985 and is dedicated to Asian, Indian, Islamic, and Byzantine art. Originally located across Broadway in what is now the History of Art and Architecture Department, it occupies part of the new Renzo Piano Wing on Quincy Street. Highlights here include examples of Rajput art, Classical Greek vases, and one of the best collections of carved jade outside China.

On Level 2 in Room 2740 (Buddhist Art – The Efflorescence of East Asian and Buddhist Art) is a battered but intriguing sculpture. Despite lacking its head, forearms, and lower legs, the figure's majestic pose and simple monastic robes identify it clearly as the Buddha. It was carved from limestone during the Dvaravati period (7th–8th century AD), when Buddhism arrived in Thailand together with Indian sculptural styles. The artist's subtle modelling and achievement of a balance between light and shadow is exquisite.

Up on Level 4 is the Forbes Pigment Collection, a remarkable reference collection of 2,500 colours assembled by the Straus Center for Conservation. Although not open to the public, the tubed specimens can be seen from across the atrium.

Other locations nearby: 102, 103

102 Big Screen Boston

MA 02138 (Cambridge), the Harvard Film Archive
Cinematheque in the Carpenter Center for the Visual Arts
at 24 Quincy Street
T Red Line to Harvard

The American cinema industry was born in 1893 in New York City, when people queued to see the first moving pictures on a peephole *Kinetoscope* pioneered by Thomas Edison (1847–1931). The first commercially successful film screening followed two years later in the same city using Edison's *Vitascope* projector. Within weeks the *Vitascope* was appearing in cities across America. In Boston it premiered at B. F. Keith's Theatre, a vaudeville playhouse that once stood on Washington Street.

Boston's first dedicated cinema opened in 1906. The Theatre Comique on Scollay Square offered half hour shorts followed by several illustrated songs all for 10 cents. Unfortunately both theatre and square were later swept away during urban renewal (see no. 68). Boston's other early cinemas are all lost, too, having been demolished or else converted to another use. Fortunately there are a few more recent survivors in the suburbs, including the Somerville Theatre (1914) at 55 Davis Square (Somerville), the *Art Deco* Coolidge Corner Theatre (1933) at 290 Harvard Street (Brookline), and the Brattle Theatre (1953) at

A pianist accompanies
a silent film at the
Harvard Film Archive
Cinematheque

40 Brattle Street (Cambridge). The Exeter Street Theatre (1914) at 26 Exeter Street (Back Bay) uniquely occupied what was once America's first spiritualist church built in the 1880s and is today a school.

A singular venue is the Harvard Film Archive Cinematheque in the Carpenter Center for the Visual Arts at 24 Quincy Street (Cambridge). Completed in 1962, the Carpenter Center is the country's only building designed by Swiss architect Le Corbusier (1887–1965). He made good use of a confined plot by creating a roughly figure-of-eight concrete structure, with winding ramps on both sides.

The Harvard Film Archive (HFA) has been located in the Carpenter Center since its founding in 1979 and is today one of the world's most important university-based motion picture collections. Each evening between Friday and Monday it screens a selection from its 25,000+ holdings in the 200-seat Cinematheque located in the basement of the building. These include Hollywood movies and world cinema, documentaries and avant-garde works, American independent films, animations, educational films, and newsreels. It is a great opportunity to watch rarely-seen film in its original format on the big screen (for the current screening calendar visit hcl.harvard.edu/hfa/).

Access to the HFA itself is restricted to Harvard staff, students, and visiting scholars. They come not only to study films but also the HFA's large collection of ephemera, including posters and stills spanning the history of film-making from the silent film era to today.

Film buffs will want to check out Boston's various annual film festivals, as well as Boston University's Howard Gotlieb Archival Research Center in the Mugar Memorial Library at 771 Commonwealth Avenue (Fenway–Kenmore). This unlikely repository of Hollywood memorabilia contains Fred Astaire's dancing shoes!

Boston became a film star in its own right in 1906 with the travelogue *Seeing Boston by Streetcar*. Since then it has provided the backdrop for numerous successful feature films, including *The Thomas Crown Affair* (1968) and *Love Story* (1970). Fans of the late Robin Williams (1951–2014) still gravitate to the bench in the Public Garden where he philosophised with Matt Damon in *Good Will Hunting* (1997). Another memorable scene in that film takes place in the L Street Tavern at 650 East 8th Street (South Boston). Southie also provided the backdrop for Ben Affleck's *Gone Baby Gone* (2007), as well as Martin Scorsese's *The Departed* (2006) and *Black Mass* (2015) with Johnny Depp, which both reference real-life Irish-American mobster James 'Whitey' Bulger (b. 1929). Other Boston-based films include Clint Eastwood's *Mystic River* (2003) and Affleck's *The Town* (2010). Several of the locations used in these films are covered by Boston TV and Movie Sites Tours (www.onlocationtours.com/boston-tours).

Other locations nearby: 101, 103

103 Where Retro Rules in Boston

MA 02138 (Cambridge), a selection of long
established stores including Leavitt and Peirce
at 1316 Massachusetts Avenue
T Red Line to Harvard

Powerful retail chains are transforming our high streets, with online shopping driving old fashioned independents out of business. Fortunately in Boston and Cambridge several long established stores are clinging on, preserving local colour and an old fashioned sense of service.

Take for example the jeweller Shreve, Crump and Low at 39 Newbury Street (Back Bay). Although this company has only been based at its current address since 2012, it was founded way back in 1796 making it the country's oldest purveyor of luxury goods. They fashioned the original Davis Cup for tennis and the Cy Young Award for baseball. Almost as old is the Brattle Book Shop at 9 West Street (Downtown) established in 1825 (see no. 41).

L. J. Peretti Co. at 2½ Park Square (Downtown) has been selling imported and house-blended tobaccos since 1870, as well as the pipes in which to smoke them. The company once had its own cigar factory nearby, where 50 hand rollers created some of the finest cigars in New England.

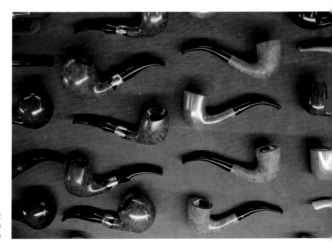

Pipes for sale at
Leavitt and Peirce
in Cambridge

Most long established stores have relocated since their opening. De Luca's Market, however, Boston's oldest grocery store, has remained at 11 Charles Street (Beacon Hill) since it first opened in 1905. Despite humble beginnings it is now famous for its meats, breads, and cheeses numbering John F. Kennedy and Admiral Byrd among its celebrity customers.

Two old stores reflect the North End's Italian heritage. They are V. Cirace & Sons at 173 North Street, a grocer established in 1906, that turned to spirits after receiving Boston's first licquor license following prohibition, and Polcari's Coffee at 105 Salem Street, which opened in 1932 (see no. 17). Boston's oldest mercantile sign by the way, from an inn of 1694, can be seen embedded in the wall over the door of Cirace's. Spirits of a different kind can be encountered at the Original Tremont Tearoom at 333 Washington Street (Downtown), America's oldest psychic salon established in 1936!

Three stores from the 1940s are worthy of mention here. Dorothy's Boutique at 190 Massachusetts Avenue (Back Bay) has been selling fancy dress costumes and accessories since 1947. The Bromfield Pen Shop at 5 Bromfield Street (Downtown) opened in 1948 and continues to retail fountain pens and ink despite the arrival of digital technology. And opened the same year is Boston's oldest hardware store, Charles Street Supply Co., at 54 Charles Street (Beacon Hill).

Over in Cambridge there is another long established store that must be mentioned. Leavitt and Peirce at 1316 Massachusetts Avenue has been a fixture of the Harvard retail and sporting scene since it opened in 1884. Since then it has sold an eclectic mix of smoking supplies, toiletries, and games, with a chess parlour on the balcony. Aficionados queue on the ground floor for house-blend 'Cake Box' tobacco, cigars, snuff, and smoking paraphernalia. Vintage display cases containing antique shaving kits and silver hip flasks impart an old school feel to the place, as does the Harvard sporting memorabilia on the walls. Before the Internet, sporting fixtures were pasted in the windows.

A couple of streets away at 82 Mount Auburn Street, dressy shoppers might care to visit J. Press, which has been satisfying the sartorial needs of the Harvard community since 1932.

Cambridge is also the place to go for modern stores selling vintage and retro items. Over a hundred of them can be found at the huge Cambridge Antique Market at 201 Monsignor O'Brien Highway. Elsewhere there are specialists, including Oona's at 1210 Massachusetts Avenue for clothes, Cheapo Records at 538 Massachusetts Avenue for vinyl, and numerous vintage comic stores (see no. 41).

Other locations nearby: 96, 101, 102

104 A Night in a Monastery

MA 02138 (Cambridge), the Society of St. John the
Evangelist Episcopal Monastery at 980 Memorial Drive
T Red Line to Harvard (note: accommodation and retreats
by appointment only)

When Boston's bustle gets too much there is help at hand. Why not
retreat to a Cambridge monastery? The Society of St. John the Evangelist Episcopal Monastery overlooks the Charles River at 980 Memorial
Drive. With its sturdy walls and Italianate arches, it might appear aloof
but step inside and the monks will welcome you into an unexpected
sanctuary.

The monastery's location so near to Harvard University may seem
curious at first glance. The proximity, however, is intentional. The Society's first monastery was
built in 1866 near Oxford
University in England,
where it was hoped that
the monks might provide
spiritual guidance to the
students (the Society was
the first Anglican (Epis-
copalian) religious order
for men founded since the
English Reformation). The
same rationale underpins
the location in Cambridge.

The Society's North
American congregation
was established in Boston
in 1870, as part of the Protestant Episcopal Church in
the United States of America. Work on the Cam-
bridge monastery com-
menced in 1924 to a de-
sign by Ralph Adams Cram
(1863–1942), an architect
renowned for his ecclesi-
astical buildings. The land

Entrance to the Society of St. John the Evangelist Episcopal
Monastery

on which it sits was purchased with a bequest from local art patron and philanthropist Isabella Stewart Gardner (1840–1924) (see no. 86).

In the mid-1930s Cram designed new living quarters for the monks, and the original monastery building became a Guesthouse. At the same time he designed the impressive new monastery Chapel dedicated to St. Mary and St. John, rendered in Cram's favoured French Romanesque Revival style. With its columns of Indiana limestone, marble floors and stained glass, it conveys the essence of an early Christian basilica.

The monks at the monastery today are chiefly involved in local and regional ministries, preaching and offering spiritual guidance not only to students but also prisoners, the homeless and the sick. They have also developed a successful line in hospitality, offering short-term accommodation and retreats in their Guesthouse to those in search of peace and tranquillity.

All sorts of retreats are possible – from an individual self-guided experience for a single night to a group retreat for several days under the guidance of the monks. For overnight visitors the Guesthouse offers a dozen or so single bedrooms, each modestly appointed and named after a saint or apostle. The homely communal areas include a refectory, kitchen and meeting rooms.

With polite signs promoting quiet, and mobile phones banished to the perimeter fence, life at the monastery follows a gentle rhythm. The monks are always on hand for prayerful conversation and the sharing of meals though, and passers-by are encouraged to use the Chapel and the contemplative gardens. The monks have thus struck a successful balance, preserving a sense of old fashioned sanctuary, whilst also engaging energetically with the world outside.

Those in Cambridge with only five minutes' free for respite should visit Harvard Divinity School at 47 Francis Avenue. Here outside Rockefeller Hall beneath a grove of ancient oak trees are stone benches perfect for reading and relaxation. And nearby is a contemplative garden at the centre of which is a labyrinth based on one in Chartres Cathedral.

There are many other interesting places of worship in Cambridge. On Magazine Street alone, which runs south from Central Square to the river, there are half a dozen. They include the brick-built First Baptist Church at number 5, with its soaring neo-Gothic spire, the stocky Sts. Constantine and Helen Greek Orthodox Church at 14, the whitewashed First Korean Church at 35, and the clapboard Congregation Eitz Chaim at 136.

105 Under a Spreading Chestnut Tree

MA 02138 (Cambridge), the Longfellow House–
Washington's Headquarters National Historic Site
at 105 Brattle Street
T Red Line to Harvard then walk along Brattle Street

Around the time of the American Revolutionary War (1775–1783), Brattle Street, the road connecting Old Cambridge and Watertown, was nicknamed Tory Row. It was here that a group of well-to-do Loyalists built seven mansions. Not surprisingly these Tory estates were either sold or confiscated during the Revolution. The mansions, however, still stand albeit now encroached upon by later development. Two of them are open to the public.

Walking west from Brattle Square, the first of the mansions is the Brattle House at 42. It was built in 1772 for Major General William Brattle (1706–1776), the wealthiest man in the Massachusetts Bay Colony. He was forced by an angry mob to flee following his involvement in the so-called Powder Alarm, when British troops emptied a local powder store to prevent it being used by Patriots.

The Brattle House today is occupied by the Cambridge Center for Adult Education, which also uses the Dexter Pratt House farther along at 56. Whilst not one of the seven mansions, this building is nevertheless of interest. It was built in 1808 for village blacksmith Torrey Han-

Glorious weather at the Longfellow House on Brattle Street

cock, who sold it in 1827 to fellow blacksmith Dexter Pratt. He worked here until his death in 1847 and provided inspiration for the poem *The Village Blacksmith* (1841) by celebrated American poet Henry Wadsworth Longfellow (1807–1882). The poem references a "spreading chestnut tree" beneath which Pratt worked with "his brawny arms... strong as iron bands". Although the tree is long gone, its existence and the smithy is recalled by an iron sculpture of a tree and an anvil.

The second mansion is the Henry Vassall House at 94 Brattle Street. Built in 1746, it became the medical headquarters for the Continental Army after its Loyalist owner abandoned it in 1775. Vassall's nephew, John Vassall, another well-to-do Loyalist, built the third and most important mansion farther along at number 105. As its name suggests, the Longfellow House–Washington's Headquarters National Historic Site has important associations both with the Revolutionary War and 19th century American literature.

Built in 1759, this mansion was abandoned when anti-Tory sentiment rose at the outbreak of the Revolutionary War, its owner fleeing with his wife first to Boston and then England. The mansion was then requisitioned by General George Washington (1732–1799), who used it as his headquarters during the Siege of Boston (see no. 60).

After the war, the mansion was bought by Andrew Craigie (1754–1819), who had been the Continental Army's first Apothecary General. When he died leaving his wife in debt, she took boarders to make ends meet. One of these was Henry Wadsworth Longfellow, who arrived in 1837, whilst a professor of modern languages at Harvard. In 1843 he married Fanny Appleton, whose father, a wealthy industrialist, purchased the mansion for the couple as a wedding gift. Longfellow subsequently spent the rest of his life here.

The mansion remains much as it was in Longfellow's day, when Cambridge was home to an influential group of poets known as the Fireside Poets. Now a National Historic Landmark it can be visited during the summer months, with its lovely garden open all year round. A highlight in Longfellow's study is an armchair made from the wood of the famous "spreading chestnut tree" after it was cut down.

The four other mansions on Tory Row are the Lechmere-Sewall House at 149, the Hooper-Lee-Nichols House at 159, which as one of the oldest houses in New England (1685) is also open to the public, the Fayerweather House at 175, and the Thomas Oliver House at 33 Elmwood Avenue, once part of Brattle Street.

106 The Original Garden Cemetery

MA 02138 (Cambridge), Mount Auburn Cemetery
at 580 Mount Auburn Street
T Red Line to Harvard then either walk (25 minutes)
or take Bus 71 or 73 to Aberdeen Avenue (note: maps
showing the location of important graves are available
at the entrance)

Far out on the western edge of Cambridge, straddling the border with Watertown, is Mount Auburn Cemetery. With its neo-Classical monuments set in acres of beautifully landscaped grounds, it couldn't be more different from Boston's stark Colonial-era burying grounds. Considered America's first landscaped garden cemetery, it was laid out in the 1830s and did much to soften the country's traditionally bleak view of death and the afterlife.

It was Massachusetts-born Jacob Bigelow (1787–1879) who first proposed the idea of a garden cemetery. As a medical doctor he knew of the health risks attached to burying the dead in overcrowded church crypts, and as a botanist he saw virtue in spacious, out-of-town burial grounds like Père Lachaise in Paris. With assistance from the Massachusetts Horticultural Society, and a design from its first President, Henry Dearborn (1783–1851), the cemetery was inaugurated in 1831.

As much a park as a necro-

The Washington Tower offers views across Mount Auburn Cemetery

polis, Mount Auburn quickly became a visitor attraction. Sixty thousand people passed through the cemetery's impressive Egyptian Revival gate in 1848 alone. This prompted New England's first horse-drawn trolley company to build a terminus at the cemetery in 1853. The Greek-style pavilion across the road from the gate was added in 1870 to cater for funeral receptions and now contains a monumental mason. It was superceded in the 1890s by the much larger sandstone building that stands just inside the gate.

The cemetery sprawls for a glorious 175 acres. Ten miles of roads and paths wind through tranquil woodlands, alongside ponds, over knolls, and through dells. Each landscape element is used to provide a sympathetic backdrop to the graves of the 98,000 people buried here (see photo on page 4). Visitors can either wander at leisure or else sign up for one of several thematic guided tours (www.mountauburn.org). For an overview, head to the 62-foot Washington Tower at the centre of the cemetery. Erected in the 1850s and named after the first American president, it offers breezy views of the cemetery, Cambridge, and Boston beyond.

Rightly much is made of the fact that there are over 9,000 trees at Mount Auburn, encompassing hundreds of different species. Additionally there are thousands of shrubs to add texture and fragrance to the scene, many of which are tagged with botanic labels. Such diversity attracts wildlife, with over 220 species of bird recorded by ornithologists, who have long been drawn here. A breeding colony of spotted salamanders occupies the pond in Consecration Dell.

It is no surprise that Mount Auburn has its fair share of resting luminaries. They include poet Henry Wadsworth Longfellow (1807–1882), author of *The Bostonians* Henry James (1843–1916), art patron Isabella Stewart Gardner (1840–1924), founder of Christian Science Mary Baker Eddy (1821–1910), architect Charles Bulfinch (1763–1844), and polymath Oliver Wendell Homes Sr. (1809–1894). Also here is Jacob Bigelow, whose creation of Mount Auburn is celebrated by the flamboyant Bigelow Chapel built in the 1840s.

Mount Auburn became the model for many other suburban American cemeteries, including Mount Hope in Bangor (1834) and Laurel Hill in Philadelphia (1836). In Boston a second garden cemetery, Forest Hills, opened in 1848 at 95 Forest Hills Avenue (Jamaica Plain). Like Mount Auburn, its layout was drafted by Henry Dearborn, who at the time was Mayor of Roxbury. Famous Bostonians buried here include poet e.e. cummings (1894–1962), playwright Eugene O'Neill (1888–1953), and inventor of the fountain pen, Lewis Waterman (1837–1901). A Lantern Festival is held in July and a Mexican Day of the Dead festival takes place in November.

Opening Times

Correct at time of going to press but may be subject to change.

101 Merrimac Street (West End), Mon–Fri 7am–6pm

Abiel Smith School (Beacon Hill), 46 Joy Street, see Museum of African American History

African Meeting House (Beacon Hill) 8 Smith Court, see Museum of African American History

Annunciation Greek Orthodox Cathedral of New England (Roxbury), 514 Parker Street, Divine Liturgy Sun 10am

Arlington Street Church (Back Bay), 351 Boylston Street, mid-May–Oct Mon–Sat 10am–3pm

Arnold Arboretum (Jamaica Plain), 125 Arborway, daily sunrise to sunset

Ars Libri (South End), 500 Harrison Avenue, Mon–Fri 9am–6pm, Sat (except Aug) 11am–5pm

Ayer Mansion (Back Bay), 395 Commonwealth Avenue, guided tours by appointment only one Sat and Wed each month except Aug www.ayermansion.org

Bakalar and Paine Galleries (Fenway–Kenmore), Massachusetts College of Art & Design Galleries (South Building), 621 Huntington Avenue, Mon–Sat 12am–6pm (Wed 8pm)

Barbara Krakow Gallery (Back Bay), 10 Newbury Street, Tue–Sat 10am–5.30pm

Barnes & Noble (Back Bay), 800 Boylston Street, Mon–Sat 9am–9pm, Sun 10am–8pm

Barnes & Noble (Fenway–Kenmore), 660 Beacon Street, Mon–Fri 9am–9pm, Sat 10am–6pm, Sun 12am–5pm

Bell in Hand (Downtown/Financial District), 45–55 Union Street, daily 11.30am–2am

Bikes not Bombs (Jamaica Plain), 18 Bartlett Square, Mon–Fri 11am–7pm, Sat 10am–6pm

Bleacher Bar (Fenway–Kenmore), 82a Lansdowne Street, daily 11am–2am

Bobby from Boston (South End), 19 Thayer Street, Tue–Sun 12am–6pm

Boston Athenæum (Beacon Hill), 10½ Beacon Street, Mon–Thu 9am–8pm, Fri 9am–5.30pm, Sat 9am–4pm, Sun 12am–4pm; guided tours Tue & Thu 3pm, Sun 1pm & Mon 5.30pm by appointment only www.bostonathenaeum.org

Boston Book Company (Jamaica Plain), 705 Centre Street, Mon–Sat 9am–5pm

Boston Center for the Arts (South End), 539 Tremont Street, Mon–Fri 9am–5pm

Boston Children's Museum (South Boston), 300 Congress Street, daily 10am–5pm (Fri 9pm)

Boston Common Visitor Center (Boston Common), 139 Tremont Street, Mon–Fri 8.30am–5pm, Sat & Sun 9am–5pm

Boston Fire Museum (South Boston), 344 Congress Street, Sat 11am–5pm

Boston Marathon Adidas RunBase (Back Bay), 855 Boylston Street, Mon–Wed & Fri 10am–7.30pm, Thu 10am–8pm, Sat & Sun 10am–6pm

Boston Marine Society (Charlestown), 100 1st Avenue, Mon–Fri 10am–3pm by appointment only www.bostonmarinesociety.org

Boston Planning & Development Agency Model Room (Downtown), Boston City Hall (9th floor), One City Hall, guided tours by appointment only Wed 10am & 11am www.bostonplans.org

Boston Public Library (Back Bay), 700 Boylston Street, Mon–Thu 9am–9pm, Fri & Sat 9am–5pm, Sun 1–5pm; guided art and architecture tours Mon 2.30pm, Tue & Thu 6pm, Wed, Fri & Sat 11am, Sun 2pm

Boston Public Market (Downtown), 100 Hanover Street, Mon–Sat 8am–8pm, Sun 10am–8pm; Farmer's Market May–Nov, Wed & Sat

Boston Sculptors Gallery (South End), 486 Harrison Avenue, Wed–Sun 12am–6pm

Boston Synagogue (West End), 55 Martha Road, for services www.bostonsynagogue.org

Boston Tea Party Ships and Museum (Downtown/Waterfront), 306 Congress Street, High Season daily 10am–5pm, Low Season daily 10am–4pm

Bova's (North End), 134 Salem Street, all hours

Brattle Book Shop (Downtown/Downtown Crossing), 9 West Street, Mon–Sat 9am–5.30pm

Brendan Behan (Jamaica Plain), 378 Centre Street, Mon–Sat 12am–1am, Sun 1pm–1am

Bromer Booksellers (Back Bay), 607 Boylston Street, Mon–Fri 9.30am–5.30pm

Bromfield Gallery (South End), 450 Harrison Avenue, Wed–Sun 12am–5pm

Bromfield Pen Shop (Downtown/Downtown Crossing), 5 Bromfield Street, Mon–Fri 8.30am–5.30pm, Sat 10am–5pm

Bryn Mawr Book Store (Cambridge), 373 Huron Avenue, Fri & Sat 12am–5pm, Sun–Tue & Thu 12am–7pm

BSA Space (Downtown/Waterfront), 290 Congress Street, Suite 200, Mon–Fri 10am–6pm, Sat & Sun 10am–5pm

Bunker Hill Monument & Museum (Charlestown), Monument Square, daily 9am–5pm (last Monument climb 4.30pm); Jul & Aug 9am–6pm (last Monument climb 5.30pm)

Caffé Vittoria (North End), 290 Hanover Street, daily 7am–12pm (Fri & Sat 12.30pm); Stanza dei Sigari daily 12am–1am

Cambridge Antique Market inc. Cambridge Used Bicycles (Cambridge), 201 Monsignor O'Brien Highway, Tue–Sun 11am–6pm

Cambridge Artists' Cooperative (Cambridge), 59 Church Street, Mon–Sat 10am–6pm (Thu & Fri 7pm), Sun 12am–6pm

Cambridge Center Roof Garden (Cambridge), 90 Broadway, daily sunrise–sunset

Cathedral of the Holy Cross (South End), 1400 Washington Street, daily 9am–6pm

Charles Street Supply Co. (Beacon Hill), 54 Charles Street, Mon & Thu 6am–7pm, Tue, Wed & Fri 8am–7pm, Sat 8.30am–6pm, Sun 12am–5pm

Charlie's Sandwich Shoppe (South End), 429 Columbus Avenue, Tue–Sun 7am–2am

Charlestown Navy Yard (Charlestown), Constitution Road, all hours; Visitor Centre Jan–Apr Thu–Sun 9am–5pm, May–Dec Tue–Sun 9am–5pm; USS *Constitution*, mid-Apr–early Jul Tue–Fri 2.30–6pm, Sat & Sun 10am–6pm, early Sep–early Nov Tue–Fri 2.30–5pm, Sat & Sun 10am–5pm, early Nov–mid-Apr Thu & Fri 2.30–4pm, Sat & Sun 10am–4pm (ID required); USS *Constitution* Museum, Apr–Oct daily 9am–6pm, Nov–Mar daily 10am–5pm; USS *Cassin Young* daily 10am–4.30pm

Cheapo Records (Cambridge), 538 Massachusetts Avenue, Mon–Wed & Sat 11am–7pm, Thu & Fri 11am–8pm, Sun 11am–6pm

China King (Chinatown–Leather District), 60 Beach Street, daily 11am–2am

Christ Church (Cambridge), Zero Garden Street Garden Street, Mass Sun 9am

Christian Science Center (Back Bay), Christian Science Plaza, junction of Massachusetts and Huntington Avenues, Mother Church and Extension Tue 12am–4pm, Wed 1–4pm, Thu–Sat 12am–5pm, Sun 11am–3pm (tours every half hour); Mary Baker Eddy Library Tue–Sun 10am–4pm (Mapparium guided tours every 20 minutes beginning at 10.20am)

Church of the Covenant (Back Bay), 67 Newbury Street, Summer Mon, Wed–Fri & Sat 11am–3pm, Sun 12.30am–4.30pm; Winter by appointment only www.cotcbos.org

Collection of Historical Scientific Instruments (Cambridge), Harvard University Science Center, Putnam Gallery, Harvard University Science Center 136, 1 Oxford Street, Mon–Fri & Sun 11am–4pm

Commonwealth Books (Downtown/Downtown Crossing), 9 Spring Lane, Mon–Sat 10am–7pm, Sun 11am–5pm

Congregational Library & Archives (Beacon Hill), 14 Beacon Street, Reading Room and Pratt Room Mon–Fri 9am–5pm; Archives by appointment only www.congregationallibrary.org

Copley Society of Art (Back Bay), 158 Newbury Street, Tue–Sat 11am–6pm, Sun 12am–5pm

Copp's Hill Burying Ground (North End), 21 Hull Street, daily 9am–5pm

Custom House Tower Observation Deck (Downtown/Financial District), 3 McKinley Square, 26th floor, Mon–Thu 2pm

De Luca's Market (Beacon Hill), 11 Charles Street, daily 7am–9pm (Fri 10pm)

Dorothy's Boutique (Back Bay), 190 Massachusetts Avenue, Mon–Sat 10am–7pm, Sun 12am–6pm

Druid (Cambridge) 1357 Cambridge Street, Mon–Fri 12am–2am, Sat & Sun 11am–2am

Durgin-Park (Downtown/Financial District), 340 North Market Street, Faneuil Hall Marketplace, daily 11.30am–10pm

Edward M. Kennedy Institute for the U.S. Senate (Dorchester), Columbia Point, 210 Morrissey Boulevard, Tue–Sun 10am–5pm

Eldo Cake House (Chinatown–Leather District), 36 Harrison Avenue, Mon–Fri 7am–7pm

Emmanuel Episcopal Church (Back Bay), 15 Newbury Street, Mass Sun 10am

Empire Garden (Chinatown–Leather District), 690 Washington Street, Dim Sum sold daily 8.30–11am, 2–3pm

Ether Dome (West End), Bulfinch Building, 55 Fruit Street (4th Floor), Massachusetts General Hospital campus, Mon–Fri 9am–5pm

Faneuil Hall (Downtown/Financial District), Congress Street, Visitor Centre daily 9am – 6pm, Great Hall daily 9am – 5pm; Marketplace Mon–Sat 10am–9pm, Sun 11am–7pm

Faneuil Hall Marketplace (Downtown/Financial District), see Faneuil Hall

Fenway Park (Fenway–Kenmore), 4 Yawkey Way, guided tours Apr–Oct daily 9am–5pm, Nov–Mar daily 10am–5pm (on game days last tour departs three hours beforehand)

First Baptist Church (Back Bay), 66 Marlborough Street, Mass Sun 11am

First Parish in Cambridge (Cambridge), 3 Church Street, Mass Sun 10.30am

Forest Hills Cemetery (Jamaica Plain), 95 Forest Hills Avenue, daily 7am until dusk; guided tours by appointment only www.foresthillscemetery.com

Fort Independence (South Boston), Castle Island, William J. Day Boulevard, guided tours only Sat & Sun from Memorial Day (last Mon in May) until Labor Day (first Mon in Sep) 12am–3.30pm

Fort Point Arts Community (South Boston), 300 Summer Street, Wed–Fri 10am–6pm

Franklin Park Zoo (Roxbury), 1 Franklin Park Road, Apr–Sep Mon–Fri 10am–5pm, Sat & Sun 10am–6pm, Oct–Mar daily 10am–4pm

Frederick Law Olmsted National Historic Site (Brookline), 99 Warren Street, Apr–mid-June Fri & Sat 9.30am–4pm, mid-Jun–end Summer Wed–Sun 9.30am–4pm

French Cultural Center (Back Bay), 53 Marlborough Street, Jul & Aug Mon–Thu 8.30am–9pm, Fri 8.30am–6pm (Library closed Aug), Sep–Jun Mon 5–9pm, Tue–Thu 9am–9pm, Fri & Sat 9am–6pm

Gallery NAGA (Back Bay), 67 Newbury Street, Sep–Jun Tue–Sat 10am–5pm, Jul 1–15 Tue–Fri 10am–5pm, Jul 16–Sep 5 by appointment only

Galley Diner (South End), 11 P Street, daily 7am–2am

Geekhouse Bikes (Charlestown), 50 Terminal Street, Building 1, Suite 700, visits by appointment only www.geekhousebikes.com

Gibson House Museum (Back Bay), 137 Beacon Street, guided tours only Wed–Sun 1pm, 2pm, 3pm

Grand Lodge of Massachusetts (Downtown/Theater District), 186 Tremont Street, guided tours Mon, Wed, Fri & Sat 10.30am–2pm

Grolier Poetry Bookshop (Cambridge), 6 Plympton Street, Tue & Wed 11am–7pm, Thu–Sat 11am–6pm

Guild of Boston Artists (Back Bay), 162 Newbury Street, Tue–Sat 10.30am–5.30pm

Happy Family Food Market (Chinatown–Leather District), 11 Hudson Street, daily 9am–8pm

Harpoon Brewery (South Boston), 306 Northern Avenue, Beer Hall Sun–Wed 11am–7pm, Thu–Sat 11am–11pm; guided tours Mon–Wed 12am–5pm, Thu & Fri 12am–6pm, Sat 11.20am–6pm, Sun 11.30am–5.30pm

Harriet Tubman Gallery (South End), 566 Columbus Avenue, Mon–Fri 8am–6pm

Harrison Gray Otis House (West End), 141 Cambridge Street, guided tours every half hour Wed–Sun 11am–4.30pm

Harvard Art Museums (Cambridge), 32 Quincy Street, daily 10am–5pm

Harvard Book Store (Cambridge), 1256 Massachusetts Avenue, Mon–Sat 9am–11pm, Sun 10am–10pm

Harvard College Observatory (Cambridge), 60 Garden Street, Harvard-Smithsonian Center for Astrophysics, Phillips Auditorium, every 3rd Thu (except Jun, Jul & Aug), 7.30pm

Harvard Coop Society (Cambridge), 1400 Massachusetts Avenue, Mon–Sat 9am–9pm, Sun 10am–7pm

Harvard Museum of Natural History (Cambridge), Harvard University, 26 Oxford Street, daily 9am–5pm

Harvard Semitic Museum (Cambridge), Harvard University, 6 Divinity Avenue, Mon–Fri & Sun 11am–4pm

Haymarket (Downtown), Blackstone & Hanover Streets, Fri & Sat 3am–close

Hing Shing Pastry (Chinatown–Leather District), 67 Beach Street, daily 8am–7pm

Holy Trinity Orthodox Cathedral (Fenway–Kenmore), 165 Park Drive, Divine Liturgy Sun 9.30am (doors open for an hour before and after)

Hooper-Lee-Nichols House (Cambridge), 159 Brattle Street, guided tours only last Sun in Jun, Jul, Aug & Sep 12am

Howard Gotlieb Archival Research Center (Fenway–Kenmore), Boston University, Mugar Memorial Library, 771 Commonwealth Avenue, Mon–Fri 9am–4.30pm

Howard Ulfelder Healing Garden (West End), Massachusetts General Hospital, Yawkey Center for Outpatient Care, 55 Fruit Street, Mon–Fri 9am–5pm

Independence Wharf (Downtown/Waterfront), 470 Atlantic Avenue (14th floor), Mon–Fri 10am–5pm

Institute of Contemporary Art (South Boston), 25 Harbor Shore Drive, Tue & Wed, Thu & Fri 10am–9pm, Sat & Sun 10am–5pm

Isabella Stewart Gardner Museum (Fenway–Kenmore), 25 Evans Way, Wed–Mon 11am–5pm (Thu 9pm)

J. J. Foley's (South End), 117 East Berkeley Street, Mon 11am–1pm, Tue–Thu 11am–11pm, Fri & Sat 11am–12.30pm, Sun 10.30am–10pm

J. Press (Cambridge), 82 Mount Auburn Street, Mon–Fri 9am–6pm, Sat 9am–5.30pm

Jacob Wirth (Chinatown–Leather District), 31–37 Stuart Street, Mon–Thu 11.30am–9pm, Fri & Sat 11.30am–12pm, Sun 11.30am–8pm

John Adams Courthouse (Downtown/Government Center), Pemberton Square, Mon–Fri 9am–5pm

John F. Kennedy Presidential Library and Museum (Dorchester), Columbia Point, daily 9am–5pm

John Fitzgerald Kennedy National Historic Site (Brookline), 83 Beals Street, mid-May–Oct 9.30am–5pm

John Joseph Moakley United States Courthouse (South Boston), One Courthouse Way, Mon–Fri 8am–6pm (ID required)

Judson B. Coit Observatory (Fenway–Kenmore), Boston University College of Arts and Sciences, 725 Commonwealth Avenue, Astronomy Department (5th Floor), Spring & Summer Wed 8.30pm, Autumn & Winter Wed 7.30pm, tickets www.bu-edu/astronomy/

Kaji Aso Studio (Fenway–Kenmore), 40 St. Stephen Street, Tue 7–9pm, Fri 1–5pm; Japanese Tea Ceremony Sun 4–6pm by appointment only www.kajiasostudio.com

Kelleher Rose Garden (Fenway–Kenmore), 73 Park Drive, mid-Apr–Oct daily sunrise to sunset

King's Chapel Burying Ground (Downtown/Finacial District), 58 Tremont Street, Mon–Sat 10am–4.30pm, Sun 1.30–12pm

Kingston Gallery (South End), 450 Harrison Avenue, Wed–Sun 12am–5pm

L. J. Peretti Co. (Downtown/Theater District), 2½ Park Square, Mon–Fri 8.30am–8pm, Sat 8.30am–7pm, Sun 12am–5pm

Larz Anderson Auto Museum (Brookline), 15 Newton Street, Tue–Sun 10am–4pm

Leavitt and Peirce (Cambridge), 1316 Massachusetts Avenue, Mon–Wed, Fri & Sat 9am–6pm, Thu 9am–8pm, Sun 12am–6pm

Lewis Wharf Hidden Garden (North End), off Commercial Street, daily sunrise–sunset

Longfellow House–Washington's Headquarters National Historic Site (Cambridge), 105 Brattle Street, end-May–Oct Wed–Sun 9.30am–5pm; gardens all year daily dawn to dusk

Lucy Parsons Center (Jamaica Plain), 358A Centre Street, Mon–Fri 6–9am, 12–6pm, Sat & Sun 1–7pm

Massachusetts Archives and Commonwealth Museum (Dorchester), Columbia Point, 220 Morrissey Boulevard, Mon–Fri 8.30am–4.30pm

Massachusetts Historical Society (Fenway–Kenmore), 1154 Boylston Street, permanent exhibition Mon–Sat 10am–4pm, library by registration Mon–Fri 9am–4.45pm, Sat 9am–4pm, building tours Sat by appointment www.masshist.org

Massachusetts State House (Beacon Hill), corner of Park and Beacon Streets, General Hooker entrance, Mon–Fri 8.45am–5pm (guided tours Mon–Fri 10am–3.30pm)

McGreevy's (Back Bay), 911 Boylston Street, Mon–Fri 11am–2am, Sat & Sun 10am–2am

Metropolitan Waterworks Museum (Brookline), 2450 Beacon Street, Dec–Mar, Wed–Sun 11am–4pm, Apr–Nov Wed 11am–9pm, Thu–Sun 11am–4pm

Mike's City Diner (South End), 1714 Washington Street, daily 6am–3am

Million Year Picnic (Cambridge), 99 Mount Auburn Street, Mon & Tue 11am–7pm, Wed 11am–10pm, Thu & Fri 10am–9pm, Sat & Sun 11am–9pm

MIT Department of Aeronautics & Astronautics (Cambridge), Guggenheim Aeronautical Laboratory (MIT Building 33), 125 Massachusetts Avenue, guided tours by appointment only Mon & Fri 1pm aeroastro-info@mit.edu

MIT List Visual Arts Center (Cambridge), 20 Ames Street, Tue–Sun 12am–6pm, (Thu 8pm)

MIT Museum (Cambridge), 265 Massachusetts Avenue, daily 10am–5pm (Jul & Aug 6pm); the museum will relocate to Kendall Square in 2020; Hart Nautical Gallery, 55 Massachusetts Avenue, daily 10am–5pm (Jul & Aug 6pm)

MIT Press Bookstore (Cambridge), 301 Massachusetts Avenue, Mon–Fri 9am–7pm, Sat & Sun 12am–6pm

More Than Words (South End), 242 East Berkeley Street, Tue–Fri 10.30am–7pm, Sat & Sun 10.30am–4pm

Mount Auburn Cemetery (Cambridge), 580 Mount Auburn Street, May–Sep daily 8am–8pm, Oct–Apr daily 8am–5pm; guided tours by appointment only www.mountauburn.org

Mul's Diner (South Boston), 80 West Broadway, daily 5am–2am

Murphy's Law (South Boston), 837 Summer Street, daily 11.30am–2am

Museum of African American History (Beacon Hill), 46 Joy Street, Mon–Sat 10am–4pm

Museum of Fine Arts (Fenway–Kenmore), 465 Huntington Avenue, Mon, Tue, Sat & Sun 10am–5pm, Wed–Fri 10am–10pm; Japanese Garden Apr–Oct

Museum of Science (West End), 1 Science Park, Sat–Thu 9am–5pm (Jul & Aug 9pm), Fri 9am–9pm; Gilliland Observatory Fri 8.30–10pm

Nam Bac Hong Chinese Herbs (Chinatown–Leather District), 75 Harrison Avenue, daily

Nantucket Lightship (East Boston), Boston Harbour Shipyard & Marina, 256 Marginal Street, www.nantucketlightshiplv-112.org

National Braille Press (Back Bay), 88 St. Stephen Street, guided tours by appointment only Mon–Fri 10.30am & 1pm www.nbp.org

Newbury Comics (Cambridge), 100 CambridgeSide Place, Mon–Sat 10am–9pm, Sun 12am–7pm

New Dongh Khanh (Chinatown–Leather District), 81 Harrison Avenue, daily 9am–10.30am

New England Aquarium (Downtown/Waterfront), 1 Central Wharf, Sep–Jun Mon–Fri 9am–5pm, Sat & Sun 9am–6pm, Jul & Aug Sun–Thu 9am–6pm, Fri & Sat 9am–7pm

New England Comics (Cambridge), 14A Eliot Street, Mon 12am–7pm, Tue & Sat 11am–7pm, Wed–Fri 11am–8pm, Sun 12am–6pm

New England Historic Genealogical Society (Back Bay), 99–101 Newbury Street, Tue–Sat 9am–5pm (Wed 9pm)

Nichols House (Beacon Hill), 55 Mount Vernon Street, guided tours only on the hour Apr–Oct, Tue–Sat 11am–4pm, Nov–Mar, Thu–Sat 11am–4pm

No Name Restaurant (South Boston), 15 1/2 Fish Pier East, Mon–Sat 11am–10pm, Sun 11am–9pm

New Old South Church (Back Bay), 645 Boylston Street, Mon–Fri 8am–7pm, Sat 10am–4pm, Sun 8.30am–7pm

Old Cambridge Burying Ground (Cambridge), junction of Massachusetts Avenue and Church Street, daily dawn to dusk

Old Granary Burying Ground (Beacon Hill), Tremont Street, daily 9am–5pm

Old North Church (North End), 193 Salem Street, Jan & Feb daily 10am–4pm, Mar, Apr & May daily 9am–5pm, Jun–Oct daily 9am–6pm, Nov & Dec daily 9am–5pm; Mass Sun 9am & 11am; Captain Jackson's Historic Chocolate Shop and Printing Office of Edes & Gill, mid-Feb–end-Feb Sat 11am–4pm, Mar–early Apr Sat & Sun 11am–5pm, mid-Apr–May daily 11am–5pm, Jun–Oct daily 11am–5.30pm, Nov Fri–Sun 11am–5pm, Dec Sat 11am–4pm

Old South Meeting House (Downtown/Financial District), 310 Washington Street, daily 9.30am–5pm

Old State House (Downtown/Financial District), 206 Washington Street, daily 9am–5pm

Oona's (Cambridge), 1210 Massachusetts Avenue, daily 11am–6pm

Original Tremont Tearoom (Downtown/Downton Crossing), 333 Washington Street, Jewelers Exchange Building, Suite 207b, Mon–Fri 11am–7pm, Sat 11am–6pm

Our Lady of Good Voyage (South Boston), 51 Seaport Boulevard, Mon–Fri 6.30am–6.30pm, Sat 9am–6pm, Sun 9am–8pm

Park Street Church (Beacon Hill), 1 Park Street, late Jun–Aug, Tue–Sat 9am–4pm

Paul Revere House (North End), 19 North Square, daily 9.30am–5.15pm

Paul S. Russell, MD Museum of Medical History and Innovation (West End), Massachusetts General Hospital, 2 North Grove Street, Mon–Fri 9am–5pm, Sat mid-Apr–mid-Oct 11am–5pm

Peabody Museum of Archaeology & Ethnology (Cambridge), Harvard University, 11 Divinity Avenue, daily 9am–5pm

Pizzeria Regina (North End), 11½ Thacher Street, Sun–Thu 11am–11.30pm, Fri & Sat 11am–12.30pm

Polcari's Coffee (North End), 105 Salem Street, Mon–Fri 10.30am–6.30pm, Sat 9am–6pm

Porter Square Books (Cambridge), 25 White Street, Mon–Fri 7am–9pm, Sat & Sun 8am–7pm

Public Garden (Back Bay), Boylston Street, daily 7am–9pm; Swan Boats Apr 15–Jun 20 daily 10am–4pm, Jun 21–Labor Day (first Mon in Sep) daily 10am–5pm, after Labor Day–Sep 17 Mon–Fri 12am–4pm, Sat & Sun 10am–4pm

Raven Used Books (Cambridge), 23 Church Street, Mon–Sat 10am–9pm, Sun 11am–8pm.

RH Boston (Back Bay), 234 Berkeley Street, Mon–Sat 10am–7pm, Sun 12am–6pm

Robert Klein Gallery (Back Bay), 38 Newbury Street (Suite 402), Tue–Fri 10am–5.30pm, Sat 11am–5pm

Sacred Heart Church (North End), 12 North Square, Mass Sun 9am

Samuel Adams Brewery (Jamaica **Plain), 30 Germania Street, Mon–Thu & Sat 10am–3pm, Fri 10am–5.30pm**

Santarpio's Pizza (East Boston), 111 Chelsea Street, daily 11.30am–11.30pm

Shreve, Crump and Low (Back Bay), 39 Newbury Street, Mon–Wed, Fri & Sat 10am–6pm, Thu 10am–7pm

Sevens Ale House (Beacon Hill), 77 Charles Street, Mon–Sat 11.30am–1am, Sun 12am–1am

Skywalk Observatory (Back Bay), Prudential Tower (50th Floor), 800 Boylston Street, Winter daily 10am–8pm, Summer daily 10am–10pm (last admission 9.30pm) (ID required); Top of the Hub restaurant, Mon–Sat 11.30am–1am, Sun 11am–1am

Society of Arts and Crafts (South Boston), 100 Pier 4 Boulevard (Suite 200), Tue–Sat 10am–6pm (Thu 9pm)

Society of St. John the Evangelist Episcopal Monastery (Cambridge), 980 Memorial Drive, visits and stays by appointment only www.ssje.org

South Boston Candlepin (South Boston), 543 E Broadway, Mon–Fri 3–10pm, Sat 12–11pm, Sun 12–8pm

South Street Diner (Chinatown-Leather District), 178 Kneeland Street, open 24 hours

SoWa Artists Guild (South End), 450 Harrison Avenue, First Fridays each month 5–9pm; SoWa Open Markets May–Oct Sat & Sun 10am–4pm; SoWa Vintage Market Sun 10am–4pm, Sat 11am–4pm (May–Oct only)

Sports Museum of New England (West End), 100 Legends Way, Mon–Fri 10am–4pm, Sat & Sun 11am–4pm; guided tours on the hour, Behind the Scenes tours from end of Playoffs until weekend of Labor Day (first Mon in Sep)

St. George Cathedral (South Boston), 523 East Broadway, Divine Liturgy Sun 10am

St. John the Baptist Hellenic Orthodox Church (South End), 15 Union Park Street, Divine Liturgy Sun 9.30am

St. Leonard's Church (North End), 320 Hanover Street, Mass Sun 10.30am (Italian), 12am (English)

St. Stephen's Church (North End), 401 Hanover Street, daily 8am–5pm, Mass Sun 11am

Sts. Constantine and Helen Greek Orthodox Church (Cambridge), 14 Magazine Street, Divine Liturgy www.stsconstantineandhelen-cambridge.org

Sullivan's (South Boston), William J. Day Boulevard, last weekend Feb to last weekend Nov, daily 8.30am–9pm

Sunken Garden (Cambridge), Radcliffe Yard, Appian Way, daily sunrise–sunset

Temple Ohabei Shalom (Brookline), 1187 Beacon Street, services Fri 6pm, Sat 10.30am

Temple Ohabei Shalom Cemetery (East Boston), 147 Wordsworth Street, guided tours by appointment only www.ohabei.org

Trident Booksellers & Café (Back Bay), 338 Newbury Street, daily 8am–12pm

Trinity Church (Back Bay), 206 Clarendon Street, Copley Square, Wed–Sat 10am–4.30pm, Sun 12.15am–4.30pm; free tours Winter Sun 12.15am, Summer 11am

Union Oyster House (Downtown/Financial District), 41 Union Street, Sun–Thu 11am–9.30am, Fri & Sat 11am–10pm; Union Bar daily until midnight

USS *Constitution* & USS *Cassin Young* (Charlestown), see Charlestown Navy Yard

V. Cirace & Sons (North End), 173 North Street, Mon–Thu 10am–7pm, Fri & Sat 10am–8pm

Van's Fabrics (Chinatown-Leather District), 14 Beach Street, Thu–Tue 11am–6pm

Vilna Shul (Beacon Hill), 18 Phillips Street, Wed–Fri 11am–5pm (guided tours at 1 & 3pm); also Sun May–Sep 1–5pm (guided tours at 2 & 4pm)

Wally's Café Jazz Club (South End), 427 Massachusetts Avenue, daily 11am–1.30am

Ward Maps (Cambridge), 1735 Massachusetts Avenue, Tue, Wed & Fri 10am–6pm, Thu 10am–7pm, Sat & Sun 12am–5pm

Warren Anatomical Museum (Fenway-Kenmore), Harvard Medical School Francis A. Countway Library of Medicine (5th floor), 10 Shattuck Street, Mon–Fri 9am–5pm

Warren Tavern (Charlestown), 2 Pleasant Street, Mon–Fri 11am–1am, Sat & Sun 10am–1am

West End Museum (West End), 150 Staniford Street (Suite 7), Tue–Fri 12am–5pm, Sat 11am–4pm

William Hickling Prescott House (Beacon Hill), 55 Beacon Street, Oct Sat 12am–4pm

Wings Live Poultry (Chinatown-Leather District), 48 Beach Street, daily 8am–4pm

Yankee Lobster (South Boston), 300 Northern Avenue, Mon–Wed & Thu–Sat 10am–9pm, Sun 11am–6pm

Bibliography

GUIDEBOOKS

The Complete Guide to Boston's Freedom Trail (Charles Bahne), Newtowne Publishing, 2013

Walking Boston (Robert Todd Felton), Wilderness Press, 2013

Historic Walks in Old Boston (John Harris), Globe Pequot, 2000

Off the Beaten Path: Boston (Patricia Harris & David Lyon), Globe Pequot, 2004

Rough Guide to Boston (Sarah Hull), Rough Guides, 2011

Boston Women's Heritage Trail: Seven Self-Guided Walks through Four Centuries of Boston History (Polly Welts Kaufman et al), Applewood Books, 2012

Frommer's EasyGuide Boston (Marie Morris & Laura M. Reckford), Frommer Media, 2014

Boston A to Z (Thomas H. O'Connor), Harvard University Press, 2000

DK Eyewitness Travel Boston (Various), Dorling Kindersley, 2015

Insight Guides: Explore Boston (Various), Insight Guides, 2014

Wallpaper City Guide Boston* (Various), Phaidon Press, 2012

Fodor's Boston (Various), Fodor's, 2016

Lonely Planet Boston (Mara Vorhees), Lonely Planet, 2015

SECRET AND UNUSUAL BOSTON

Hidden Gardens of Beacon Hill (Beacon Hill Garden Club), Regent Publishing Services Ltd., 2013

Boston Curiosities: Quirky Characters, Roadside Oddities, and Other Offbeat Stuff (Bruce Gellerman), Rowman & Littlefield, 2010

What They Never Told You About Boston (Walt Kelley), Down East Books, 1993

Peaceful Places Boston: 121 Tranquil Sites in the City and Beyond (Lynn Schweikart), Menasha Ridge Press Inc., 2011

Not for Tourists Guide to Boston (Various), Sky Pony Press, 2016

ART AND ARCHITECTURE

Old Boston in Early Photographs 1850–1918 (Philip Bergen), Dover Publications, 1990

Inventing the Charles River (Charles Haglund), MIT Press, 2002

Lost Boston (Jane Holtz Kay), Houghton Mifflin, 1980

Boston Then and Now (Patrick L. Kennedy), Pavilion Books, 2016

Mapping Boston (Ed. Alex Krieger et al), MIT Press, 2001

Back Bay: A Living Portrait (Barbara Moore & Gail Weesner), Centry Hill Press, 1995

Heroic: Concrete Architecture and the New Boston (Mark Pasnik, Michael Kubo & Chris Grimley), The Monacelli Press, 2015

AIA Guide to Boston: Contemporary Landmarks, Urban Design, Parks, Historic Buildings and Neighborhoods (Susan & Michael Southworth), Globe Pequot, 2008

Boston: A Topographical History (Walter Muir Whitehill), Belknap Press, 2000

SHOPS, RESTAURANTS AND BARS

The Historic Shops and Restaurants Of Boston: A Guide to Century-Old Establishments in the City and Surrounding Towns (Phyllis Meras), Little Bookroom, 2007

Historic Taverns of Boston (Gavin Nathan), iUniverse, 2006

Dining Out in Boston: A Culinary History (James O'Connell), UPNE, 2016

Discovering Vintage Boston: A Guide to the City's Timeless Shops, Bars, Restaurants (Maria Olia), Globe Pequot Press, 2015

HISTORY

A Short History of Boston (Robert Allison), Commonwealth Editions, 2004

The Proper Bostonians (Cleveland Amory), Parnassus Imprints, 1984

Paul Revere's Ride (David Hackett Fisher), Oxford University Press, 1995

The North End: A Brief History of Boston's Oldest Neighborhood (Alex R. Goldfeld), History Press, 2009

Common Ground: A Turbulent Decade in the Lives of Three American Families (J. Anthony Lukas), Vintage, 1986

All Souls: A Family Story from Southie (Michael Patrick MacDonald), Beacon Press, 2007

Behind the Frontier: Indians in Eighteenth-Century Eastern Massachusetts (Daniel R. Mandell), University of Nebraska Press, 2000

Boston Miscellany: An Essential History of the Hub (William Marchione), The History Press, 2008

Boston Firsts: 40 Feats of Innovation and Invention That Happened First in Boston and Helped Make America Great (Linda Morgenroth), Beacon Press, 2016

Gaining Ground: A History of Landmaking in Boston (Nancy Seasholes), MIT Press, 2003

The Curse of the Bambino (Dan Shaughnessy), Penguin, 2004

The Boston Massacre (Hiller B. Zobel), W. W. Norton, 1996

ILLUSTRATED BOOKS

Boston: A Visual History (Jonathan Beagle), Imagine, 2013

Cityscapes of Boston: An American City Through Time (Robert Campbell & Peter Vanderwarker), Houghton Mifflin, 2000

Boston: A Keepsake (Arthur P. Richmond), Schiffer, 2016

Boston Rediscovered (Ulrike Welsch), Commonwealth Editions, 2002

FICTION

The Handmaid's Tale (Margaret Atwood), Anchor Books, 1998

The City Below (James Carroll), Houghton Mifflin, 1994

The Scarlet Letter (Nathaniel Hawthorne), Signet Classic, 1999

The Bostonians (Henry James), Cambridge World Classics, 2011

Darkness Take My Hand (Dennis Lehane), Avon Books, 2007

Folly (Susan Minot), Washington Square Press, 1992

Love Story (Erich Segal), Avon Books, 2012

Boston Adventure (Jean Stafford), Harcourt Brace, 1984

TOUR COMPANIES

Boston by Foot *(www.bostonbyfoot.org)*

Boston National Historical Park's Freedom Trail *(www.nps.gov/bost)*

Beantown Trolley History Tours *(www.beantowntrolley.com)*

Old Town Trolley Tours *(www.trolleytours.com)*

Boston TV and Movie Sites Tours *(www.onlocationtours.com/boston-tours/)*

Tours of Harvard *(www.trademarktours.com/tours-of-harvard/harvard-art-museums/)*

Urban AdvenTours (cycling) *(www.urbanadventours.com)*

WEBSITES

www.boston.com (Boston Globe news, listings & reviews)

www.bostonusa.com (Boston Convention & Visitors Bureau)

www.bostonblogs.com (Boston's blog network)

www.museumsofboston.org (Boston's museums at a glance)

www.nps.gov/bost (Boston National Historical Park)

www.freedomtrail.org (Freedom Trail Foundation)

www.bostonhistory.org (Bostonian Historical Society)

www.bwht.org (Boston Women's Heritage Trail)

www.mysecretboston.com (Insiders' Boston travel blog)

www.universalhub.com (Boston news, gifts and Boston English dictionary)

www.bostonpedicab.com (Green three-wheeled tours)

www.thephoenix.com (Arts listings and restaurant reviews)

www.mbta.com (Massachusetts Bay Transportation Authority)

www.massvacation.com (Massachusetts Office of Travel and Tourism)

View from Castle Island, South Boston (see no. 58)

Acknowledgements

For kind permission to take photographs, as well as for arranging access and the provision of information, the following people are most gratefully acknowledged:

Father Robert Arida and Inga Leonova (Holy Trinity Orthodox Cathedral), Amelia Benstead (Boston African American National Historic Site), Sabina Beauchard and Anne Bentley (Massachusetts Historical Society), Ken Baughman (The Christian Science Publishing Society), Patrick Boyce (National Park Service), Brattle Book Shop, Sam Brewer (Boston Symphony Orchestra), Barbara Callahan (Gibson House Museum), Michelle Chapman (Boch Center Wang Theatre), Margaret Connors, Dan Crowley (Boston Marathon Adidas RunBase), Carolyn Cruthirds (Museum of Fine Arts, Boston), Martha Davis (MIT Museum), Isabella Donadio (Harvard Art Museums), Bob Andrews, Matt Ellis and Bruce Guarino (West End Museum), Lauren Elmore (The McGraw Agency), Sara Frankel and Maureen Ton (Collection of Historical Scientific Instruments), Gabriel Antonio Francisco-Garcia, Romayne Gayton, Hannah Gersten (Boston Athenæum), Brittany Gravely (Harvard Film Archive), Dominic Hall (Warren Anatomical Museum), Wes Hagan & Dan Col (Union Oyster House), Jillian Jennett & Jessica Steytler (Congregational Library & Archives), Rich Kaszeta, Peggy Kelly (Murphy's Law), Barnet Wolf Kessel (Vilna Shul), Anne Kilguss, Robin LaPlante (Boston Center for the Arts), Donna La Rue, Marilynn Stein Langley, Katherine Leahy (Boston Center for the Arts), Ewald Lichtenberger and Roswitha Kirchsteiger-Lichtenberger, Bill Litant and Marie Stuppard (MIT AeroAstro), Stephanie Loeber (Boston Tea Party Ships & Museum), Madison Lougheed and Deborah Wakefield (CityPASS), Cynthia Mackey (Peabody Museum of Archaeology and Ethnology), Mary Blue Magruder (Harvard Museum of Natural History), Ashley Mancini, Michelle Marcella (Massachusetts General Hospital Ether Dome), Bob Marino, Sean McGann (Leavitt and Peirce), Taryn McNichol, Dorothy Rivera and Bert Hogan (Mary Baker Eddy Library), Ed Methelis, Whitney Mooney and Jaclyn Sheridan (National Braille Press), Marilyn and Joe Nucci, Dan O'Neill (Boston Fire Museum), Rebecca Ostriker (Boston Globe), Mark Owen, Teofilo Paolucci (Polcari's Coffee), Jeanne Pelletier (Ayer Mansion), Christoph Pereira and Lorrie Butler (General Electric), Doug Perkins, Iris Perrin, Eden Piacitelli (Collection of Historical Scientific Instruments), Elena Francesca du Plessis (SoWa Art Studio), Polly Latham Asian Art, Steve Prentis (Grand Lodge of Massachusetts), Lauren Prescott (South End Historical Society), Rosemary Previte (Hooper-Lee-Nichols House), Marek Pryjomko, Rachel (Charlie's Sandwich Shop), RH Boston (The Gallery at the Historic Museum of Natural History), Christopher D. Rooney (Grand Lodge of Massachusetts), Jonte Samuel, Kathy Sharpless and Sarah Whitling (Isabella Stewart Gardner Museum), Mary Smith, Mary Smoyer (Boston Women's Heritage Trail), Society of St. James, Sheldon Steele (Larz Anderson Auto Museum), Quinn Sykes (Judson B. Coit Observatory), Kimberly Tavares (John Joseph Moakley United States Courthouse), Karen Taylor (Beacon Hill Garden Club), Ryan Thomas (Museum of Science), Pierre-Antoine Tibéri (French Cultural Center), Toby True, Rodger Vine and Gaby Whitehouse (Arlington Street Church), Bertie and Andy Walker, and Catherine T. Wood (Norman B. Leventhal Map Center).

Special thanks to Rose Blackadder for undertaking several research trips on my behalf and Philip Adsetts for a most enjoyable day exploring Boston together. To both I am especially indebted.

Also to Ekke Wolf (www.typic.at) for his design excellence in creating the layout and editing the photos, Carolyn S. Bennett at the Boston Planning & Development Agency and Kyrill Schrayber at VectorMaps for the maps, and Thomas Klemas for the accommodation in Cambridge.

Thanks also to my mother Mary and great cousin James Dickinson for bringing interesting news items to my attention, and to Richard Tinkler for managing my websites.

Finally, special thanks to Roswitha Reisinger for her tireless support of my work, and to my late father Trevor for inspiring me to track down things unique, hidden and unusual in the first place.

1st Edition published by The Urban Explorer, 2018
A division of Duncan J. D. Smith
contact@duncanjdsmith.com
www.onlyinguides.com
www.duncanjdsmith.com

Graphic design: Stefan Fuhrer
Typesetting, picture editing and cover design: Ekke Wolf (www.typic.at)
Maps: street map original base map created by The Office of Digital Cartography and GIS, Boston Planning & Development Agency; subway map created by Vector Maps www.vectormaps.info
Printed and bound by GraphyCems, Spain

ISBN 978-3-9504218-1-1